TT Mixture

David Wright

David Wright

TT MIXTURE

Copyright ; David Wright 2003

ISBN 1 901508 07 2

Published by Amulree Publications
Lossan y Twoaie
Glen Road
Laxey
Isle of Man
Tel: 01624 862238
Email: amulree@mcb.net

****

BY THE SAME AUTHOR

Vincents, HRDs and the Isle of Man

Travelling Marshals at the Isle of Man TT and MGP Races

Vincent - The Complete Story

'TT Mixture'

CONTENTS

INTRODUCTION

The Isle of Man Tourist Trophy races are famous the world over. For almost 100 years successive generations of racing motorcyclists have tested their skills against the incredible TT Mountain Course. Through towns and villages, across moorland and mountain, the 37 ³/₄ miles of ordinary roads that comprise a lap of the TT Course offers a unique racing experience.

Riders have always seen the Mountain Course as the ultimate challenge and many great names have made their reputation with winning rides. Anyone who participates in a TT knows that it will subject them to a roller-coaster of emotions ranging through anticipation, excitement, fear, frustration, triumph, disappointment, elation and joy.

Manufacturers regard the Mountain Course as the ultimate proving ground for their motorcycles and the mighty Honda concern stand as testimony to that fact. Showing considerable courage, Soichiro Honda opened his bid to get Honda products known in the Western world by entering the Isle of Man TT in 1959. Although found wanting on their debut, Honda nevertheless returned and over the next few years won all the solo classes at the TT, so achieving immense world-wide publicity and opening-up huge new export markets in the West.

For spectators the TT takes the form of an annual pilgrimage carried out amongst many thousands of their own kind. For two weeks of the year the 'TT Festival' provides them with biking entertainment of almost every type, and it all takes place in an atmosphere fuelled by the high-octane action of the TT races.

'TT Mixture' traces the history of the Tourist Trophy races since their inception in 1907. It looks at the pioneer men and machines, mechanical developments, rising speeds, ever more powerful racing bikes, triumphs and tragedies, the fluctuating fortunes of the event, famous riders down the years, and the status of the TT in the 21st century. All the above is presented in a well-illustrated and easy-to-read style with enough facts and figures to give a proper understanding of the TTs development. Recounting all major events in the TT's history, every opportunity has been taken to tell many of the associated stories and anecdotes that the event has generated.

Even today one must admire the organisers for running the Tourist Trophy races over the 37 ³/₄ mile laps of the Manx roads, but the audacity and vision shown nearly 100 years ago in sending single-speed, belt-driven, pioneer motorcycles over the narrow, twisty and unsurfaced Manx roads was quite extraordinary - and so is the story of the TT.

ACKNOWLEDGEMENTS

I have been fortunate to have my own memories augmented, and in some cases corrected, by others with extensive general and specialised knowledge of the Tourist Trophy races, and my thanks go to Paul Bradford, Pete Busby, Geoff Cannell, David Crawford, Ralph Crellin, Des Evans, Bill Snelling and Paul Wright.

Photographs have come from Bill Dale, Bobby Dobson, FoTTofinders, Sean Loder, Manx Racing Photography, Mortons Motorcycle Media Archive, John Watterson and from private archives. Cover design was by Vic Bates and the book was typeset and printed by Premier Print, Isle of Man.

Chapter 1
EARLY DAYS

The expression TT is often used as a general way of describing the motorcycle races held on the Isle of Man in June each year, but it should be made clear that TT is really an abbreviation for Tourist Trophy. The original Tourist Trophy is a magnificent silver statuette of Mercury poised on a winged wheel that was provided by the Marquis de Mouzilly St Mars. It is still awarded each year to the winner of the premier race, known as the Senior TT, and amongst the names engraved on its plinth are those of the world's greatest motorcycle road-racers. The Marquis was undoubtedly a man of foresight who must be looked upon as one of the founders of the TT races, yet he and his fellow organisers could hardly have imagined that the event they created in 1907 would become the most important road race in motorcycle history and would still be flourishing almost 100 years later.

More than 90 years after it was first awarded, and with its base covered in the names of the world's great road racers, the Senior Tourist Trophy is held aloft by 2000 winner David Jefferies.

The First TT

The first motorcycle race for the Tourist Trophy was held on the Isle of Man on 28th May 1907. With only 75 motor vehicles registered for the Manx roads at the time (about 25 being motorcycles), it is difficult to see where the enthusiasm to give the Island's roads over to motorcycle racing came from. Perhaps it was because the Island's Lieutenant Governor of the time was himself a pioneer motorist and had given encouragement to some earlier car racing. Whatever the reason, it was fortunate for the TT that the Manx Government was prepared to close its roads, for the rest of Britain had refused to do so.

*

Organised by the Auto-Cycle Club, forerunners of the Auto-Cycle Union (ACU), the first TT race used a triangular course in the west of the Island that was just over 15$\frac{1}{2}$ miles long. This narrow, undulating and poorly-surfaced circuit had to be ridden ten times, giving a total race distance of 158$\frac{1}{2}$ miles.

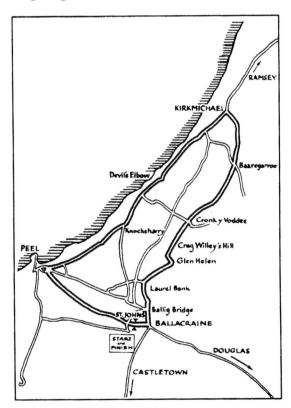

The first TT course for motorcycles. Originally known as the St John's Circuit, it is nowadays remembered as the Short Course.

Start and finish point was the historic Tynwald Hill at St Johns, a place where the proclamation of Manx laws has taken place annually for over 1,000 years. A rudimentary arrangement of Pits and Scoreboards served the 25 riders gathered to compete for the Tourist Trophy. Regulations for the first race specified that machines had to be in road trim, and riders were required to make a compulsory 10 minute refuelling stop at half-distance. Fuel was supplied by the organisers, although competitors had to pay for it at 1/3 (6p) per gallon and they were restricted as to the amount they could use. Entry fees were 5 guineas (£5.25) for trade entries and 3 guineas (£3.15) for private entrants.

*

Most of the machines ridden in the early races were belt-driven with only a single speed. This offered the rider a compromise gearing best suited for riding on mainly flat roads and slight hills. The ups and downs of the first TT course meant that in places the bikes were over-geared and some riders had to dismount and run alongside their machines on the up-hill stretch after Glen Helen. A few were able to provide themselves with a little additional propulsive power by use of the pedals that were still fitted to their bicycle-derived machines. The right-angled corner of Ballacraine soon after the start, (which riders approached from the opposite direction to today's racers), had a deepish drainage channel on the outside that acted like a magnet as riders tried to corner without losing speed.

Two riders negotiate the difficult left-hand turn at Ballacraine in a pre-1911 TT race.

The organisers later provided a wooden ramp on the outside of the bend that covered the drainage channel. Their aim was to assist riders to maintain corner-speed and so help with the ascent to Ballaspur that followed, but it proved to be a mixed blessing. In 1910 H Bowen (BAT) led the race in the latter stages but crashed out on the Ballacraine ramp and lost his chance of TT glory.

*

The excitement generated at Ballacraine by the early TT races was too much for one Manxman. The 'Peel City Guardian' reported that *'Most probably as an outcome of the motorcycle race practising, the death occurred on Friday evening of Mr.John Crellin, dyer of Ballacraine, aged 73. He was lying against a hedge, where he had full view of the riders in their difficult task of rounding Ballacraine corner. Suddenly he collapsed and fell. Quickly lifted up, in a few seconds he was found to be dead'.*

*

The first TT comprised two races. One was for single-cylinder and the other for multi-cylinder machines, although both races were run as one event. The Tourist Trophy went to the rider of the winning single-cylinder machine, of which 17 were entered. There were 8 entries for the multi-cylinder race, although all 8 were twins. Those pioneers of motorcycle racing rode machines from early makers like Triumph, Norton, Matchless, Rex, Vindec, NSU, with their engines rated in horsepower (ranging from 3½ - 5hp) rather than cubic capacity.

*

Part of the official pre-race preparations included the weighing of each machine and rider at the nearby St John's Railway Station. Lightest machines were the single-cylinder Triumphs at 140 lbs (63.5 kg) and heaviest was the Roc at 237 lbs (107.5 kg). Riders varied in weight from 126 lbs (57 kg) to 183 lbs (83 kg).

*

The official start-time of the first TT was 10.00 a.m., and under grey skies riders were despatched in pairs at minute intervals, with Jack Marshal and Fred Hulbert being the first away. However, as the local paper reported that *'the starting of a motorcycle is a very awkward and uncertain business'*, it sounds as though not all riders made a smooth get-away.

*

Despatching the riders in pairs with one minute between them (as opposed to a massed start), gave the TT races the interval starting system that endures to this day. It is a characteristic of the races which means that riders are competing against the clock, as well as against fellow competitors on the Course. It is a feature that is liked by most TT fans, but for those brought up on short circuit racing it can make following the progress of the race a little difficult.

*

As he dismounted after the end of five laps for his compulsory stop, Oliver Godfrey's bike burst into flames. A report of the time said *'There was difficulty in putting out the blaze until a stalwart Manx policeman extinguished it with his coat'*. It is known that Godfrey's machine was too badly damaged for him to continue but the state of the stalwart policeman's coat was not recorded!

*

Winner of that very first motorcycle TT was Charlie Collier. Averaging a speed of 38.22 mph for the race and consuming petrol at the miserly rate of 94.5 mpg, he took the Tourist Trophy on his single-cylinder Matchless after racing for over four hours. The multi-

that had the advanced feature of mechanically operated overhead valves. But reports of the time told that Rem Fowler on his side-valve Peugeot-engined Norton had problems, for he fell off twice, had to repair a front-wheel puncture (taking 22 minutes), change sparking-plugs several times, tighten his drive belt twice and fix a loose mudguard.

*

Rem Fowler recalled in later years that he was physically run-down before the race and how *'twenty minutes before the start a friend of mine fetched me a glassful of neat brandy tempered with a little milk. This had the desired effect and I set off full of hope and Dutch courage'*.

*

Second man on a single in 1907 was Jack Marshal on a Triumph that delivered an incredible 114 mpg.

Rem Fowler with his winning twin-cylinder Peugeot-engined Norton at the 1907 TT.

cylinder race went to Rem Fowler on his twin-cylinder Norton at 36.22 mph, and he set the fastest lap of the race at 42.91 mph whilst averaging 87 mpg. Twelve of the twenty-five starters finished the race.

Charlie Collier had a relatively trouble-free run for his 1907 TT win on his JAP-engined Matchless

Showing that even from its earliest days the racing game was full of 'what ifs', Triumph's post-race advertising claimed *'The Triumph made faster time than any machine in the race after deducting time lost for repairing punctures'*.

*

Each 1907 winner received £25 in prize money, with £15 going to the second placemen and £10 to the third. Most machines were 'works' models supplied by manufacturers, and a smaller prize of £5 went to the first private owner on single and twin-cylinder models. There were sundry other awards.

*

Norton mounted Rem Fowler may well have been the first TT rider to receive a pit signal, for part way through the race 'Pa' Norton held out a board bearing the word 'OIL'. It was a reminder to Rem to keep his engine well supplied with lubricant, for it was before the days of automatic oil-pumps. He provided his engine with oil by way of an occasional push on a plunger operated pump mounted on the side of the petrol tank, and that delivered a metered supply to the engine on the 'total loss' principle. There were other controls mounted on the side of the petrol tank, and it was often a perilous job for the rider to take a hand off the handlebars at speed to make adjustments.

The tank-mounted plunger used to supply oil to the engine of Rem Fowler's Norton.

It was soon after their TT success of 1907 that Norton began to use the word 'Unapproachable' in their advertising. It went on to become one of the company's favourite slogans for more than 50 years.

"THE UNAPPROACHABLE" NORTON
Motorcycle through 1911.

Unapproachable' was the claim by Norton in their advertising.

*

Present at the first TT were Dunlop Tyres. Still a young company, it distributed red and yellow balloons to the local children and constructed a triumphal finishing arch over which was draped a Dunlop banner. It was the start of a long association with the races.

*

After the 1907 TT the Auto-Cycle Club (later ACU) made an ex-gratia payment of £250 to the Manx Highway Board for use of the Manx roads. Today it is the Isle of Man authorities who pay the ACU several hundred thousand pounds to run the races over the Manx roads.

*

The road surfaces of the time were unsealed and the dust clouds created by passing vehicles were a major nuisance. Before the 1907 race the roads of the course were treated with a special dust laying preparation called Akonia. Its efficiency is not known, but other products were tried in later years to reduce the problem from dust, including one that was hastily dropped when it attacked riders' clothing, causing holes to appear.

Roadsters not Racers

The early TT regulations were framed to encourage the mechanical development of motorcycles that were fit for road use, and the organisers regarded the TT races more as long-distance speed trials, with the restrictions on the amount of fuel that could be used serving to emphasise that point. It was a deliberate attempt to counter the trend in those early days of building freak racing machines just for out-and-out speed. For 1908 the regulations were tightened and pedalling gear was banned, proper mudguards were required, silencers had to work and each machine had to carry a minimum of 5 lbs of tools. There were also tighter restrictions on the amount of fuel that a competitor could use, with single-cylinder machines allowed one gallon for every 100 miles of race distance and multis required to cover 80 miles to a gallon (the allowances in 1907 had been 90 and 75), so emphasising the need to balance speed with economy.

*

The number of entries increased from 25 to 36 in 1908, with twins proving more popular than singles. (There was also an entry from a four-cylinder, shaft-drive F.N.) The race was held in September in good weather. The 1907 winners were given the honour of being first men away but it was Jack Marshal who took his Triumph single to victory. His success helped boost sales of Triumph motorcycles to 3,000 the following year.

*

Captain Sir R.K. Arbuthnot, Bt. took his Triumph to third place in the single-cylinder class of the 1908 TT.

*

Although riders paid an entry fee to race, the organisers paid most of that out in prize money. In an attempt to raise funds the ACU appealed to motorcyclists of the day with *'Motorcyclists who feel disposed to assist the ACU in awarding some cash prizes to the successful competitors in the Tourist Trophy Race, should forward a postal order for one-shilling or twelve stamps to the secretary of the Auto-Cycle Union'*. Results of the appeal were not reported.

*

Practising for the race was only loosely controlled and at a meeting of the Peel Commissioners just before the 1908 race, a Mr Rhead moved *'That the Town Commissioners object to motorcyclists practising at racing speed through the streets of Peel after 8 o'clock in the morning, and should this request be disregarded will prosecute any offender'*.

*

Restrictions on the amount of fuel that could be used were abandoned in 1909 and engine capacity limits were defined as 500cc for singles and 750cc for multis. Both singles and multis were eligible to win the Tourist Trophy from 1909 and first prize was increased to £40. Because of concerns over the speeds being attained, maximum engine size for multis was reduced to 670cc the following year, but H H Bowen on a BAT set the fastest lap of the race at 53.15 mph, that being 10 mph faster than Rem Fowler's fastest lap in the first TT a mere three years before. Entries also increased, going up to 83 with an almost equal split of singles and multis.

Mountain Course

The early TT events proved successful in contributing to the general development of motorcycles and, in an attempt to accelerate the introduction of multiple gears and clutches, the races were moved to the longer, hillier, and much more testing Mountain Course in 1911 (see map inside front cover). Rising to the challenge, which included the long eight-mile Mountain climb from Ramsey to Brandywell, 104 riders submitted entries for the 1911 race, for which the entry fees were: Trade entries 10 guineas (£10.50), private entries 7 guineas (£7.35).

*

Even today one can not help but admire the audacity of the current TT organisers in running a race with a 37³/₄ mile lap, but back in 1911 it must have required extraordinary vision to set those early motorcycles against 5 laps (188³/₄ miles) of competition with each other and against the primitive Manx roads.

*

The Mountain Course used from 1911-1914 was almost the same as today's except that towards the end of the lap riders turned right at Cronk ny Mona and cut across to the top of Bray Hill, so missing out the present stretch to Signpost Corner, Governor's Bridge and the Glencrutchery Road.

The route taken by the 1911 course from Cronk ny Mona to St Ninian's at the top of Bray Hill is shown as a dotted line.

The starting point in 1911 was on the flat a little way above Quarter Bridge. Soon after came a useful downhill stretch for those who experienced difficulty with the tricky job of push-starting cold engines. Pre-race warming of engines was not allowed.

Senior and Junior Races

Two separate races were run in those early years on the Mountain Course and they were called the Senior and Junior events. The Junior race was for singles up to 300cc and twins of up to 340cc. Run over 4 laps, for a race distance of almost 150 miles, the 1911 race win went to Percy Evans (Humber) at 41.45 mph. The Senior event took place a few days later and catered for 500cc singles and up to 585cc multis, and was run over 5 laps totalling over 180 miles. Victory in the Senior race went to Oliver Godfrey on his twin-cylinder Indian fitted with a two-speed countershaft gearbox and all chain drive. Although only possessing two speeds, Godfrey's ability to vary the ratios on his Indian was essential on the ups and downs of the Mountain Course. He recorded a race average speed of 47.63 mph to head an Indian 1-2-3 in a gruelling event for machines and riders. Even the winner took almost 4 hours to complete his race, and many lesser competitors were racing for nearer five hours. Veteran Pa Applebee (whose son Frank went on to win the 1912 Senior race at record speed on a Scott) was quoted as saying *'a rider was considered amazingly fresh if he could stand at the end of a race'*.

*

Spills were plentiful on the loose-surfaced roads and when Hart Davis came off his Triumph it was reported that *'he split his racing waistcoat and knickerbockers'*. A more serious fate befell Victor Surridge, for while practising on his Rudge for the Senior TT of 1911 he crashed soon after Glen Helen and became the first Island racing fatality. This not only brought the seriousness of racing home to riders and organisers but also to the Manx people, for this was the first 'motoring' fatality on their roads. The Rudge team withdrew from the race as a mark of respect.

*

A small but vocal element of the Manx population opposed the races for *'desecrating the peace of Mona with these dangerous nuisances'*, but the majority supported them. One early newspaper report told that *'The Island indulged itself in a National Holiday'* on race-day and, recognising the inevitable, the Manx authorities eventually declared the day of the Senior TT race to be a Bank Holiday - as it is today.

*

The shaping of road-traffic legislation was still in its infancy and motorcyclists needed to be aware of quirks in the system. Few machines were properly equipped to carry pillion passengers but that did not stop some riders from doing so, usually by seating the passenger on a cushion strapped to the rear carrier. However, anyone visiting the Isle of Man for a two-up holiday at the TT would have received a nasty shock, for carrying a pillion passenger on Mona's Isle attracted a penalty of up to £50 in fines and three months' imprisonment.

*

In 1913 the race format changed. The Junior event was over 6 laps with 2 of those laps being run on the morning of Wednesday 4th June. The Senior event was over 7 laps, 3 of which were run on the Wednesday afternoon. Machines were then impounded by the organisers and all finishers from the record 147 entries who rode in Wednesday's events, were eligible for the 'Final' two days later when 500s and 350s were sent off alternately to complete their remaining laps. Both Senior and Junior winners were declared at the end (Hugh Mason and Tim Wood) and to differentiate between the classes, riders wore coloured waistcoats: red for Seniors and blue for Juniors.

*

Boris Kremlev came all the way from Russia to ride in 1913. Going well on his belt-driven Rudge, he crashed at Hillberry on his last lap, a mere 2 miles from the finish. In the same year, a Manufacturers'

A picture from 1914 showing Norman Norris (Dunkeley Precision) dressed to race. His helmet has the obligatory cut-outs around the ears.

Team Award was presented for the first time and was won by Rover.

Crash Helmets

Riding gear was very basic in the early days, though many riders did recognise the advantage of wearing leather. Crash helmets were hardly known, but 'Ebby' Ebblewhite, Timekeeper for the TT races, Tom Loughborough, Secretary of the ACU and Dr Gardner who was the medical officer at Brooklands, got together and produced an ACU approved design of helmet that was made compulsory wear for TT competitors in 1914. Whatever form of headgear was worn in those pioneering days, the race regulations required that riders' head coverings had cut-outs around the ears that allowed them to hear overtaking riders.

*

When the first TT was held in 1907 there were 34,664 motorcycles registered for the road in the United Kingdom. By 1914 there were 123,678 and the number of motorcycles on the roads was slightly greater than the number of cars. Seemingly, most motorcyclists of the day bought the magazines 'The

Motor Cycle' and 'Motor Cycling' both of which covered the TT races in detail. Indeed, many probably bought both, for the former was estimated to sell 90,000 copies a week, with the latter not far behind.

Day Trips

The TT races quickly established their popularity with spectators, but for those who could not get to the Island to watch, 'The Motor Cycle' arranged for cablegrams to be sent to prominent UK motorcycle dealers with up-to-the-minute race positions and results. The dealers then posted the information in their showroom windows. 'Motor Cycling' was equally determined to involve its readers in the TT scene and organised day-trips to the 1914 Senior TT by rail and boat from several parts of Britain. Telling its readers that: *'Men who have watched every kind of sporting event have often said that nothing in the world is so thrilling to watch as this hotly-contested struggle for the blue ribbon of the motor cycling world'*, the all-up cost in 1914 was 22/6 (£1.12^1/$_2$) from London, including meals, and 12/- (60p) from Birmingham. Such trips ran for over 50 years and became a traditional method of seeing the Senior race for the many enthusiasts who could not manage a week's holiday at TT time.

*

In 1914 the starting point for the races was moved to the top of Bray Hill, on the Quarter Bridge side of St Ninian's crossroads. The Junior and Senior events reverted to the more familiar format of individual races run on separate days.

*

The outbreak of the First World War put a stop to racing on the Island, although the 1914 TT did take place. The Senior race had a healthy 97 starters and victory went to Cyril Pullin on his Rudge at a race average speed of 49.49 mph. It turned out to be the last TT to be run for six years and the last-ever TT victory for a belt-driven machine.

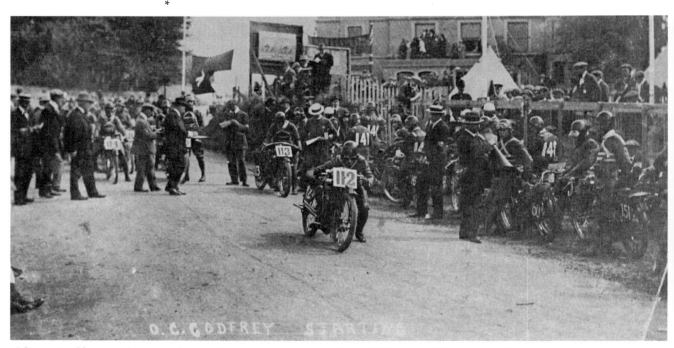

Oliver Godfrey push-starts his Indian from the top of Bray Hill in the 1914 Senior TT.

Chapter 2
SPEEDS INCREASE

When the TT races returned to the Mountain Course in 1920, it was to the same 37 ³/₄ miles of ordinary Manx roads that are used today. (There was a minor detour in Ramsey to overcome a private road problem but that was resolved by 1922.) The 1920 route was almost the same as the one used in 1911 when riders first took on the challenge of the Mountain Course, the exception was a change in the last few miles that saw them travel via Signpost Corner and Governor's Bridge, (rather than turning right at Cronk ny Mona). The reason for the change was to take advantage of the far better Start/Finish and Pits facilities offered by the open spaces of Nobles Park off the Glencrutchery Road.

*

Very little of the Mountain Course had a sealed tarmacadam finish in 1920. Most of the 37 ³/₄ miles were - in broad terms - of rolled macadam without any tar-binding. This gave a riding surface that was loose and dusty when dry, muddy and slippery when wet, and one that tended to develop ruts and potholes. The Mountain Road received less maintenance than other parts and the joke among riders was that if you got in a rut leaving Ramsey, you had to stay in it until you were almost at Douglas. Whilst probably not quite as bad as that, there is little doubt that the rutted roads added spice to the already dangerous job of overtaking another rider through a cloud of dust.

*

Stanley Woods told how the road surface improved slightly as riders came down the Mountain and approached Creg ny Baa in the early 1920s, but he still considered that 'it resembled a gravelled drive more than a road'. A party of Scottish TT goers were regular watchers at the Creg, and they used to arrive with brushes and sweep several hundred yards of the approach to the corner. Of the 1923 Junior race 'The Motor Cycle' reported: 'The sliding wheels of Woods Cotton threw up a bow-wave of dirt and stones', and that was at the high-speed Hillberry right-hand curve, close to the outskirts of Douglas.

*

The poor roads all added to the excitement of racing unsprung, spindly-tyred motorcycles that slipped and slithered over the loose surfaces as riders juggled with the variety of control levers at their disposal. These many levers gave less than precise operation of throttle, ignition, air, oil-pump, exhaust-valve lifter, clutch, gearchange and brakes. There were other hazards to riding, amongst them being the many horseshoe nails that littered the Course and punctured tyres, for most vehicles on the Manx roads were still horsedrawn. As well as losing nails from their shoes, the many horses trudging the Course were responsible for leaving other substantial deposits on the racing line!

*

The John Bull Rubber Company issued a promotional booklet each year called 'Advice to Tourist Trophy Visitors' and in the early 1920s it warned: 'the corners, humps, rough surfaces and gradients of the Mountain Road have to be seen to be believed'. Many competitors made use of John Bull products, and some still carried a couple of their butt-ended inner tubes wound round their waists. In the early 1920s there was a move away from studded front tyres to the use of a ribbed pattern.

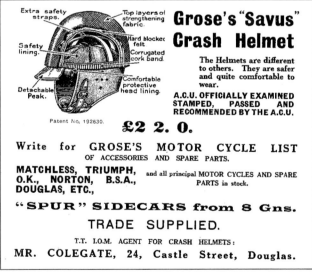

The type of ACU approved crash helmet used in the early 1920s and available to TT riders from the manufacturer's Agent in Douglas.

Riders still carried tools, usually using a small leather tool-box retained by straps to the rear mudguard stays.

Sad Sunday
The very busy Sunday before the races that everyone

now calls 'Mad Sunday' was, around 1920, known as 'Sad Sunday'. (Some called it 'Dead Sunday'.) This was because in their efforts to get the Course in the 'best' condition for racing, the authorities prohibited ordinary users from travelling on it for the day. This restriction was abolished for 1922.

*

There was talk of removing the 500cc machines from the 1920 races because of worries over their increasing speed. However, the ACU decided to retain them and they extended the programme to cater for three classes: Senior 500cc, Junior 350cc and 250cc. TT machines no longer had to be roadster based and this encouraged a gradual move to the use of out-and-out racers.

*

Winner of the 6 lap Senior race of 1920 was Tommy De La Hay on a Sunbeam, and he took 4 hours 22 minutes and 23 seconds to cover the 226 1/2 mile race distance at a record average race speed of 51.48 mph. Victory in the 5 lap Junior 350cc class went to Cyril Williams (AJS) at 40.74 mph, with R.O. Clark (Levis) the best 250cc at 38.30 mph. Clark's victory was achieved despite him badly bending his bike in an incident at Keppel Gate.

*

The First World War was responsible for rapid development of the internal combustion engine for aviation purposes, but motorcycle design stagnated. The result was that there were few technical advances in racing motorcycles in the period 1914-1920. One racing milestone passed in 1920 was Norman Black (Norton) being the last man to ride a belt-driven machine in a TT. Norton continued to sell belt-driven models for road use for another two years.

AJS was one of the motorcycle companies that had been heavily involved in war-time aero-engine work and they were one of the few firms who produced a new engine in 1920. Fitted to their Junior machines the ohv unit with valves set at an angle of 90 degrees gave an output of 10 bhp at 6,000 rpm and also enjoyed the advantage of four-speeds (achieved by way of two primary drives that could be coupled to the gearbox by a sliding dog on the engine shaft). The new AJS should have swept aside the outdated opposition, but the AJS team riders got involved in personal scraps and although way ahead of the field, they suffered mechanical failure and crashes. Only surviving rider for AJS, Cyril Williams, saved the day for them by pushing and coasting from Keppel Gate to take first place - and he still finished 10 minutes ahead of the runner-up. Whilst the race confirmed the performance superiority of the AJS machines, it also showed the need for controlled riding to secure a TT victory - or even a finish.

TT Replicas

It's perhaps worth repeating that only one rider in a race can win a Tourist Trophy, although to cater for the growth in the number of races run during TT week, copies of the Tourist Trophy were made to award to the winners of each race. In the early days those finishing within half an hour of the winner were awarded gold medals. From 1922, miniature silver and bronze replicas of the Tourist Trophy have been awarded in each race to riders who finish within a specified fraction (or percentage) of the winner's time - although initially silver replicas only went to those finishing in the first six.

*

For many years the Tourist Trophies were displayed above the Grandstand scoreboards on race-days. Also, when a winner received one at the post-race presentation he would take it away with him and it would be shown at various functions throughout the winter. A TT win brought much prestige and, as a minimum, there would be celebratory dinners and sometimes a Civic Reception back in a rider's home town. Amazingly the Trophies survived such treatment but their value is such that, nowadays, they only come out of secure storage for presentation ceremonies and other special events.

The Tourist Trophies were displayed above the Leader Board on race-days.

*

The first of only three Manxmen to have won a solo TT race was Tom Sheard. He rode his AJS to victory in the 1922 Junior event and also took the 1923 Senior on a Douglas.

*

The Senior TT of 1922 was the last to be won by a side-valve machine, when Alec Bennett brought his Sunbeam home in first place. Alec had considerable experience of dirt-track riding from his youth and was quite capable of sliding his bike round some of the loosely surfaced bends of the TT Course. A man with a reputation for 'riding with his head', he took another four TT wins during the 1920s. Third place in the 1922 Senior race went to Freddie Dixon on an Indian that was fitted with an extremely small front brake. Some machines of the time ran without any front brake and others still used the pedal-cycle-derived stirrup type. In 1923 Dixon was again Indian mounted but he had discarded his front-brake, whilst most runners were moving towards using the internal-expanding drum type on each wheel.

*

Later to achieve fame at the Isle of Man races and beyond, Walter Handley, Jimmy Simpson and Stanley Woods all had their first TT rides in 1922. Those three young men were part of the early twenties explosion of interest in motorcycles that saw annual registrations in the UK leap from 114,700 in 1919 to 278,600 in 1920 and 373,200 in 1921. That increase in demand resulted in the arrival of many more motorcycle manufacturers on the scene and there were estimated to be well over 200 in Britain in the early 1920s. Despite calling themselves manufacturers, many were merely assemblers of a collection of proprietary products such as Villiers or

The massed start of the three-lap Ultra-Lightweight race of 1924 which was won by J A Porter on his New Gerrard at an average speed of 51.20 mph. From the projecting time-keeper's box on the left, basic information on the progress of the race was conveyed to nearby spectators via the swivelling megaphone. There was also a man with a 'roving megaphone' who walked around and passed information to more distant parts of the Grandstand and Paddock.

JAP engines, Burman gearboxes, Druid forks, etc. However, there was no shortage of ambition amongst those small companies and quite a few regarded entry in the TT races as an ideal way in which to publicise their new models. By the middle of the decade the Senior TT attracted entries from 20 different manufacturers.

*

Not all TT entries brought successful publicity to their makers. BSA, one of the largest manufacturers, entered six machines with a new design of engine in the 1921 Senior race. It had shown promise by producing 16 bhp @ 4,000 rpm under test and it lapped Brooklands at 73 mph. But perhaps BSA underestimated the demands of a TT event on any machine, new or established. Whatever the reason, all six of their entries retired from the race due to mechanical failure, resulting in public humiliation for the BSA motorcycle empire.

*

By 1922 there had been some worthwhile advances on the mechanical side of motorcycles produced for racing. In his book 'Racing Round The Island', Bob Holliday describes how *'Nortons had produced their*

first ohv model; Rudges introduced their four-speed gearboxes; Barr and Stroud sleeve-valve engines appeared; the new big port AJS made much use of aluminium and aluminium-bronze. And the most exciting innovation was a two-port overhead camshaft 350cc JAP engine, designed by Val Page, in Bert le Vack's New Imperial. It was the first ohc unit seen in the TT'.

*

An Ultra-Lightweight race was introduced in 1922 for machines up to 175cc. It was one that, for the first time, featured a mass start of the 17 riders entered, but it was dropped from the programme after 1925.

Disc Brakes

By 1923 machines were required to be fitted with two independent brakes and they were usually of the internal expanding-shoe type. At the 1923 TT the Douglas factory experimented with a disc brake on the front wheel of its race bikes, where a v-section friction shoe was pressed radially against a bevelled hub flange. New Imperial runner Bert Kershaw had what is believed to be the first steering damper fitted to his machine.

Winner of the 1923 Senior TT, Manxman Tom Sheard poses with his disc-braked Douglas.

Sidecars

A three-lap sidecar race was introduced in 1923 and although there were only 14 entries they yielded plenty of excitement, with winner Freddie Dixon (passengered by Walter Perry) averaging 53.15 mph. Sidecar manufacturers were not particularly supportive of the race, feeling that it gave the wrong image to their family-transport orientated products. The sidecar race ran for only three years, but one side effect of its introduction was that a third race day had

Graham Walker tackles Ramsey Hairpin on the Norton outfit that he rode into second place behind Freddie Dixon (Douglas) in 1923.

to be provided to accommodate the total of 170 entries in solo and sidecar classes.

Clarrie Wood pitted the strength of his Scott sidecar outfit against a Foden Steam Wagon during a collision in practice. The Scott came off second best and Clarrie's passenger decided he had had enough of sidecar racing and left the Island on the first available boat. Clarrie contented himself with riding in the solo events.

*

The first double TT win in a week occurred in 1925 when Wal Handley won the Junior and Ultra-Lightweight (175cc) events.

*

Race speeds accelerated rapidly through the 1920s. The 1920 Senior race was won at an average speed of 51.48 mph and when winning the 1922 Senior, Alec Bennett missed the first 60 mph lap by a whisker when he circulated in 37 minutes 46 seconds for a lap speed of 59.99 mph. By 1929 the average race speed of the winner had increased to 72.05 mph. Responsible for a 5 mph jump in race-winning speeds in the middle of the decade was Howard Davies on his HRD.

*

** HOWARD DAVIES **

Howard Davies was a particularly remarkable man amongst the generally remarkable breed of men who raced in the Isle of Man TT races. Born in 1895, he went into the Midlands' motorcycle trade straight from school and competed in his first TT in 1914 where he finished second on his Sunbeam. That was a fine first-time performance, but it was an unusual one because Davies tied for second place with 1911 winner O.C. Godfrey. There have been very few such ties for TT podium places.

War service in the Royal Flying Corps saw him reported in the motorcycling magazines as having being shot-down and killed, but Howard Davies returned to the post-war TT scene and won the 1921 Senior race on an AJS. That Senior win was sufficient in itself to guarantee his place in motorcycle history for it was achieved on a Junior (350cc) machine, the only time such a feat has been achieved at the TT. But that was not the end of his history-making TT rides for, dissatisfied with the motorcycles offered to him to race, in 1924 he set about producing his own road and racing motorcycles. Bringing the results of his early efforts to the 1925 races he staggered the motorcycling world by taking second place in the Junior race and then going on to win the Senior TT at an average race speed that was 5 mph faster than the previous record. It was the last time a manufacturer ever raced his own machine to victory, and when Howard Davies took the chequered flag on the machine that bore his initials of HRD (Howard Raymond Davies) he left the best racing motorcycles from established names like Norton, AJS, and Scott, to trail in behind and take the lesser places.

HRD was amongst the first to use the stylish saddle-tank and low seat that gave its bikes such attractive lines. But although modern styling and racing success brought welcome publicity and orders for the HRD marque, they were not sufficient to keep a small motorcycle manufacturing business running in the depressed economic conditions of the late 1920s. The HRD concern did take another TT win with Freddie Dixon riding their Wolverhampton-made product to victory in the 1927 Junior race, but at the end of that year the business foundered after having produced just over 800 motorcycles. It was taken over by Philip Vincent and he went on to produce the Vincent HRD motorcycles that later earned their own share of TT success.

*

In this photograph taken during practice for the races, Howard Davies sits astride the HRD that he used to win the 1925 Senior TT.

Practice

In the caption to the photograph above of Howard Davies it is mentioned that it was taken during practice for the races. This is apparent because for many years riders were only required to carry front racing numbers during practice, adding side numbers just for the race. Also, at the time the photograph was taken, the front number plate used in practice had to be circular with white digits on a black background, whilst for the race a square front plate was used with black digits on a white background. The photograph also shows that his race machine was registered for the road. The reason for this is straightforward - if alarming! Until

1928 the roads of the TT Course were not closed to ordinary traffic during practice sessions for the races. Although the racers could only practice during defined early morning periods when the roads were least busy (between 4.15 and 8.00 a.m.), they still had to share the Manx highways with ordinary traffic, and thus their machines had to be registered, insured and silenced for road use. (Not necessarily Manx registered as the HRD was.)

*

The race regulations for 1925 specified that every rider had to complete at least 5 practice laps and, to be allowed to race, at least one of those laps had to better the qualifying time laid down for each class

SPEEDS

The speeds achieved on the closed roads of the TT Course during races have always held a fascination for motorcyclists, for the racers invariably travelled faster than ordinary riders could ever hope to do on open roads.

*

During the first TT races on the St John's Course (1907-1910), Rem Fowler estimated that he reached just over 60 mph.

*

When the TT resumed in 1920 after the first World War, Norton claimed that its bikes were reaching 76 mph down the Mountain. The braking on those factory Nortons consisted of an early cycle-type stirrup brake at the front and a single block operating on a dummy belt-rim at the rear. It took brave men to travel downhill at 76 mph over loose-surfaced roads with such primitive stopping equipment.

*

The rapid increase in speeds in the 1920s saw many riders struggling in the braking department. The right-hander at Quarter Bridge followed a downhill approach and has always been a stern test of a bike's brakes. In 1925 it was told how *'C.W.Johnson (348 Cotton) came down the hill practically all out, relying on his brakes to pull him up for the corner, but with both brakes hard on he found himself sliding forward in a straight-line at almost undiminished speed. The machine hit a refreshment stall at the bottom. Johnson was thrown over the counter and bruised his ribs and sides besides grazing his knees'.* Made of stern stuff, 'Paddy' Johnson got underway again but retired from the race with mechanical trouble. He had his first TT race in 1922 and his last in 1951, taking a win and several second places on the Cottons that he favoured.

*

At the 1927 TT, Stanley Woods and Joe Craig both averaged 93.7 mph over a one mile stretch of the Sulby Straight on their 500cc Nortons. By this time all machines were fitted with drum brakes to front and rear.

*

---

of: Senior 45 minutes, Junior 50 minutes, and Lightweight 55 minutes. They had been substantially reduced from the previous year and were demanding targets over the TT Course of 80 years ago.

*

In the early years of the TT, official practice was spread over two whole weeks and manufacturers would sometimes arrive with their latest machines in virtually un-tested condition. They would then spend the entire practice period in getting them raceworthy. Two weeks of such high-speed activity on open roads amongst ordinary traffic was a recipe for disaster. After many scrapes and near misses, tragedy struck just outside Kirk Michael during practice for the 1927 TT, when Archie Birkin was in collision with a fish cart on the Course and was killed. The bend now bears his name.

Every TT race requires the public issue of a Road Closing Order that defines exactly which roads are closed to the public and for what period of time. After the Archie Birkin tragedy, additional Road Closing Orders were sought and the roads of the TT

Course were no longer open to ordinary traffic during the official practice periods for the races. They were all early morning sessions at that time.

*

For 1926 the race regulations changed and competitors were not permitted to use the alcohol fuel that had contributed to the increase in speeds in the early 1920s. They were restricted to using commercially available petrol-benzole mixes. This affected some makes more than others and the bigger JAP engines seemed to particularly miss the cooling effects of alcohol (and perhaps the tuning expertise of Bert Le Vack who had moved from JAP to New Hudson). The change of fuel did not slow the AJS machines and Jimmy Simpson set the first 70 mph lap during the Senior race.

*

'Weighing-in' was a formal pre-race procedure where machines were physically weighed and where the rider declared the makes of components he used, name of company supplying his petrol, etc. In a particularly strict interpretation of the race regulations, Italian rider Pietro Ghersi was stripped of a podium place in the 1926 Lightweight race when it was discovered at the finish that his Moto Guzzi was fitted with an Italian Fert sparking-plug, rather than the Lodge plug specified at the pre-race weigh-in. Strangely, he was officially credited with the lap record that he set in the race. Perhaps this was because, in official language, he was *'excluded from the awards'*, rather than being disqualified from the race.

*

In 1926 the pattern of TT races settled into one which was to be maintained for many years. After their experiments with Sidecars and Ultra-Lightweights in the few years previously, the organisers decided that their revised solos-only race programme would see the Junior event held on the Monday of race-week, the Lightweight on Wednesday and the Senior on Friday. Each race would be over 7 laps, a distance of 264 miles.

The Island Square
As winner of the 1925 Senior TT, Howard Davies was awarded riding number 1 for the 1926 Senior race, with the remaining numbers being subject to ballot. It was James Sheldon who wrote about riders *'facing*

Howard Davies stands on the 'Island Square' prior to the start of the Senior TT race of 1926.

the moment of truth' as they stood on the white-painted starting area known as the Island Square. He went on: *'At the drop of a flag they are away, alone and unpaced. There was no one to follow, but every known type of bend and gradient ahead. If they could ride, the motor cycling world was there to hail them. It was as much their ability as the manufacturer's genius which was under test'*.

*

A permanent Grandstand was under construction near the Start and Finish line in 1926. When finished, entry to enclosed areas was 10/6 (52$\frac{1}{2}$p), with reserved seats available at extra cost ranging from 5/- (25p) to 7/6 (37$\frac{1}{2}$p). Entrance to the Paddock was 1/- (5p).

*

Spectators were encouraged to come to the Island and help fill the Grandstand. One persuasive advert said: *'there is no difficulty whatsoever in getting the motorcycle aboard at Liverpool, and plenty of porters are available should no pals be present to assist up the gangway at high tide. It is less easy to get it ashore at Douglas, but here again there are porters in plenty, though it is wise to fix a fee with them before giving the order'*.

*

Organised betting on the outcome of TT races was permitted during the 1920s and several bookmakers used to set up their stalls behind the Grandstand on race-days.

*

Similarities with horse racing (the natural home of bookmakers) could also be found in other aspects of the TT race organisation. Prize money was paid to the entrant rather than the rider, race-cards were sold for each event listing the riders, the conduct of the meeting was controlled by a set of Stewards, there was a 'weigh-in' procedure, and manufacturers could send their riders out to race in their own colours, like jockeys. In 1921 Douglas racing colours were blue and white with white sleeves, James were brown and gold with gold sleeves, and Sunbeam were black and gold.

Winnings
Good riders made far more money from a TT win than their entrants did from the prize money (£125 for first place in the mid 1920s). They did so by way of bonus payments received from the 'Trade'. The advertising potential of TT success increased considerably when the glamour of average race speeds of over 60 mph could be linked to a company's products. Members of the 'Trade' included motorcycle manufacturers, component suppliers (sparking plugs, chains, carburettors, etc) plus the petrol, oil and tyre companies, and they all wanted to be associated with the high-speed image of TT success. So profitable was the bonus system that 'The Motor Cycle' claimed that a canny rider could earn himself £3,000-5,000 from a TT win in the mid 1920s. That figure can be multiplied by a factor of about 40 to give an indication of its value in today's money!

*

One man who always had an eye towards bonus payments was Freddie Dixon, winner of the 1923 Sidecar and the 1927 Junior TTs. 'Customising' his machines with footboards, flyscreen, backrest to the saddle, foot-controlled clutch and an unusual arrangement of handlebar controls, Freddie also had some rather distinctive habits. He generally rode without goggles or gloves and at his pit-stop during his 1927 winning ride it was reported *'a swallow of champagne and Fred is off . . . .'*.

No gloves or goggles for a race of 264 miles during which he averaged 67.13 mph - 1927 Junior TT winner Freddie Dixon speeds through Parliament Square Ramsey on his HRD.

Dixon's 1927 HRD was fitted with a JAP engine, Burman gearbox, Coventry chains, Webb forks and brakes, Lycett saddle, Binks carburettor, Bosch magneto, KLG sparking plug, Hutchinson tyres, Andre steering damper, Fibrax brake linings and Pilgrim oil-pump. Fuel and oil were supplied by BP Spirit and Wakefield Castrol, with Tecalemit providing grease. No doubt Freddie invited all of the above to recognise his TT win with appropriate bonus payments.

The 'Trade'
The 'Trade' was the name given to the commercial firms who, by providing essential services and supplies for riders and tuners during the practice and race periods, made extremely important contributions to the success of the TT races. Dunlop was one of the largest companies involved in the late 1920s, bringing hundreds of tyres, plus rims, saddles and accessories. To deal with these they would have three tyre-fitters, one wheel-builder and one saddle-fitter on duty.

KLG advertised the success of their product at the 1927 TT.

Motorcycle manufacturers and riders looked to the specialist representatives of Trade companies to solve problems relating to lubrication, carburation, ignition, etc. The TT was a busy time for all concerned and as the manufacturers were often trying new developments on their TT machines, they had to rely on the Trade reps to keep their secrets. For their part, the Trade reps knew that racing was the most exacting form of product testing that their companies could employ, and that the TT was the most demanding of all races in which to test them.

*

The inevitable effect of the increased commercial value to be gained from a TT win was to see manufacturers like Norton and Velocette create racing departments to develop specialised ohc engines purely for racing use, (Norton probably more so than Velo'). It was Joe Craig of Norton who said *'the ideal racing engine has power designed into it'*. This was all bad news for the many small manufacturers and privateers who approached their racing from the opposite direction - that of tuning roadster engines to generate more power. It had the gradual effect of squeezing the smaller concerns out of racing. To help guarantee their TT successes, the firms with specialised race departments also hired the best riders, for they knew that the TT races had grown to be the most important and prestigious in the world.

*

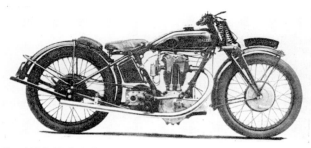

In 1928 Raleigh contested the Senior race with this 500cc model, but small manufacturers found it increasingly difficult to compete against the specialised race machines used by the big concerns.

The Norton factory supported racing from its earliest days, and Gilbert Smith, who spent over 40 years with the company, part of the time as Managing Director, explained that: *'The name and quality of Norton motorcycles has been built up very largely by successful participation in racing. As the years have gone by, so the efforts have been more serious. Detailed and properly organised effort is essential, with a good team. Races are mostly won or lost before the machines leave the works, provided the right jockeys have been signed up'.* He was certainly aware of the benefits of a TT win, saying: *'Undoubtedly an Isle of Man win means that the winning make of machine is publicised in every important newspaper in the world; this is valuable publicity and would normally cost more than any motorcycle manufacturer could spend'.*

*

A smiling Alec Bennett after his win on a Velocette in the 1928 Junior TT.

Velocette made use of their new positive-stop foot-change mechanisms on the gearboxes of their 1928 TT machines, and Alec Bennett rewarded them with a record-breaking win in the 350 race that saw him become the first rider on a Junior (350cc) machine to lap at over 70 mph. Similarly mounted Harold Willis finished second. The other winners in 1928 were Frank Longman (OK Supreme) in the Lightweight and Charlie Dodson (Sunbeam) in the Senior.

*

Any challenge that AJS might have presented in the 1928 Junior was nullified by the company's unwise decision to change the make of valve-springs used on its 350 engines between the end of practice and the race. Five of its six machines retired from the race with broken valve-springs, and the sixth broke its big-end.

'The TT Special'

A publication called 'The TT Special' had made its first appearance in 1927 under the editorship of Geoff Davison and it was back again in 1928. Initially an 8 page newspaper that contained reports on the three TT races and was published at the end of race week, it grew to three editions to give individual coverage of each race. Further expansion came when it decided to produce editions covering each practice session. This all involved hectic work for its temporary staff. (It over-reached itself on one occasion when it produced a mid-race issue. Although this was rushed out to popular spectating spots like Hillberry and Quarterbridge - that had no public-address commentary - hardly anyone bought it because they could not believe that it contained up-to-date race information). Generally available on the Island shortly after the completion of each practice and race, 'The TT Special' was also sent to subscribers off the Island. Containing information on all race entries, riders' performances, race forecasts and detailed results, it also featured gossip, rider interviews, photographs, adverts, etc. For those who received it on the Island it was an interesting source of 'inside' information and for those off the Island (and it went around the world), reading 'The TT Special' was the next best thing to being at the races.

Extending its reporting activities to cover the MGP as well as the TT, Geoff Davison published 'The TT Special' until his death in 1966. Fred Hanks took over the same year and although the number of issues was reduced from its 'glory' years, he continued to publish it until 1985. It was a valuable chronicle of TT history for nearly 60 years.

*

Pietro Ghersi's performance on his Italian built Moto Guzzi in 1926 (when he lost a podium place on a technicality), made British manufacturers aware that there were continental firms who could challenge their hold on the TT races. This was confirmed when Archangeli (who had ridden in 1926 on a Bianchi) took a Moto Guzzi to second place in the 1927 Lightweight race and thus increased concerns among British makers.

The TT organisers would sometimes accept reserve entries and manufacturers would use these to try new machines or components. A slight ripple of concern went round the Paddock when one year in the late 1920s a reserve rider was listed as Ferodo Vaselini. Putting in some swift laps on several different makes of machine that included New Imperial, Sunbeam and Scott, Signor Vaselini would always slip away after practice and rumours began to circulate about this mystery 'Italian' who was beginning to look a strong prospect for a race win. Only when the final race entries were announced did Geoff Davison announce that he was the mysterious Ferodo Vaselini and that making a reserve entry under Ferodo's name allowed him to carry out practical tests of various models and report on them in 'The TT Special'. Geoff was a past TT winner who took a Levis into first place in the 1922 Lightweight race.

Chapter 3
BIRTH OF THE
MANX GRAND PRIX

The Manx Grand Prix races are held at the end of August over the TT Mountain Course. Intended to be for amateurs, they have always provided a flow of talented riders to the TT races. They were first called The Manx International Amateur Motor Cycle Road Race Championship, a cumbersome title that was soon abbreviated to the Amateur Races. Created to provide races over the Mountain Course for those not receiving Trade support and thus, in theory, offering competition that was unsullied by commercialism, the Amateur races unfortunately failed to live up to their high ideals in that direction.

*

The first Amateur race was run by the Manx Motor Cycle Club in 1923 over 5 laps, a distance of almost 190 miles. It was a race for 500s, with a subsidiary award going to the best 350cc. Out of 35 entries there were 31 starters and 18 finishers. Several riders held the lead during the race but at the finish it was Les Randles on his side-valve Sunbeam who took the win, with Ken Twemlow (New Imperial) as best 350 (and second-placed man overall).

*

Many of the competitors in the early Amateur races were true amateurs. A practice report of the 1925 event told that *'Mr Purslow wore Oxford bags this morning, and as he went past they were flapping in the wind very badly, thus retarding his speed'*. Another competitor in 1925 was Donald MacLennan on an HRD. He called at the company's works in Wolverhampton en-route to the Island to have his bike checked over for the race. On discovering that MacLennan did not possess any racing leathers, HRD boss and 1925 TT winner Howard Davies lent him his own set.

*

In 1926 the race distance was increased to six laps and in 1928 the 350s were separated from the 500s and given their own race on the Tuesday of race-week. The 500s ran on the Thursday and the two races adopted the titles used in the TT of Senior (500cc) and Junior (350cc). The combined entry totalled 77, made up of 28 Junior and 49 Senior machines.

*

It soon became apparent that the organisers' attempts to run their races on a strictly amateur basis

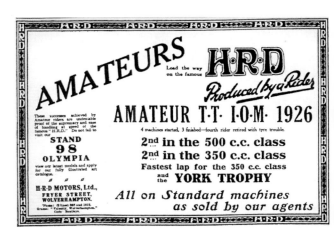

HRD were just one of the firms who considered it worthwhile advertising the success of riders using their machines in the Amateur races.

involved the setting of standards that were impossible to maintain. In their attempts to avoid the taint of commercialism they even avoided reference to the makes of machine ridden, and riders were warned that they could be asked to produce receipts for all purchases connected with their racing - even down to a new sparking plug. From the outset there was talk of 'shamateurism', with claims that likely winners were given Trade support by companies who recognised that useful publicity could be gained from an Amateur win. By 1929 there had been so many identified infringements of the Amateur rule that British motorcycling's governing body, the ACU, considered that the issue threatened to bring the sport into disrepute and indicated that they would refuse to issue permits for future events.

Manx Grand Prix
Not wanting to lose the races which they had worked so hard to establish, the organising Manx Motor Cycle Club changed their format and in 1930 the Amateur races were replaced by an event known as the Manx Grand Prix - usually abbreviated to MGP. Its simplified rules stated that entries would only be accepted from riders who, at the time of race entry and for 5 years previously, were domiciled in the British Isles and Eire who, since 1920, had not competed in an international race and who were not world's motorcycle record breakers.

The first Manx Grand Prix meeting in 1930

comprised Senior and Junior races, each over 6 laps and, unlike the TT, the use of alcohol fuels was permitted. Ralph Merrill on a Rudge won the Senior, whilst Doug Pirie took the Junior on his new KTT Velocette. The next seven places were also filled by the products of Veloce Ltd, who had produced the KTT to provide private owners with the nearest possible to a 'works' machine, all for £80.

*

Manxman Wilf Harding almost provided a local victory in the Junior race of 1930 when he took the lead on the fourth lap, but Doug Pirie pulled back some 50 seconds in the closing stages to take victory by almost half a minute. Later to lose an arm in a car crash, Wilf went on to become a guide and mentor to many young MGP riders, some of whom stayed at his 'Albion' guest-house in Douglas where full-board was provided in the 1930s for 49 shillings (£2.45) a week.

*

There were advantages in staying with other riders in somewhere like Wilf Harding's establishment, particularly for newcomers. As they set about a substantial Manx breakfast after morning practice, riders would swap experiences and there was always something to be learnt. Wilf also knew all the local workshops that would undertake a bit of urgent welding or turning to help a competitor with mechanical problems. He also knew the officials of the meeting, the whereabouts of the Trade depots, and who to speak to and get a little priority in sorting problems.

*

The annual MGP meeting has always been watched with keen interest by manufacturers and sponsors, for it is an event in which the competitors are usually the principal players rather than their machines, and where the races could be guaranteed to reveal riders of promise. This was shown in the Amateur race days (even before the event became the MGP). Charlie Dodson made two appearances in the Amateur races (1924 & 1925), then in 1928 & 1929 he won the Senior TT. Progressing in similar manner, winner of the 1928 Senior Amateur race, Tim Hunt, moved up to the TT the following year and took wins in the Senior and Junior races of 1931. He was the

Ken Bills receives congratulations on his Senior MGP win in 1938. On the far left is former rider Wilf Harding.

first ever Senior/Junior double TT winner. Tim was also the only rider in an Amateur or MGP race (1928) to break the absolute Course record.

*

Convincing winner of the 1931 Senior MGP by a margin of 10 minutes was J. Muir. However, his moment of triumph was spoilt when he slammed on the brakes after passing the finishing line and took an embarrassing tumble in front of the Grandstand crowds.

*

A Lightweight class was introduced to the 1933 MGP and the 250cc machines ran concurrently with the 350s, although there were only 4 entries in the smaller class. In 1934 the Lightweights had their own race for their 15 entries, still running with the 350s. Several riders who were later to enjoy TT successes finished on the leaderboard or set fastest lap in the 1933 and 1934 MGP races. Among them were Harold Daniell, Freddie Frith, Bob Foster and John 'Crasher' White.

*

There were many other riders who later went on to star at the TT who used the MGP for their competitive introduction to the Mountain Course. During the second half of the 1930s Maurice Cann, Johnny Lockett, Tommy McEwan and 1938 double-winner Ken Bills made their names at the MGP, before moving on to the June events.

*

One MGP winner who did not go on to the TT was J. Kelly Swanston. He rode from 1931-35, improving his placings year on year and finally winning the Senior race of 1935 from the highly-rated Freddie Frith. His win was achieved despite losing much time over a plug change at the end of the first lap. Having by 1935 qualified as Doctor Swanston, he decided that his career should take precedence over racing, and so he retired from the sport. Dr Swanston

was one of many fine riders who contributed to making the MGP a major meeting and to lifting the race average speed of the Senior MGP from 70 to 85 mph during the 1930s.

*

The Manx Grand Prix

Emblem of the Manx Motor Cycle Club Ltd.

Even today the Manx MCC pride themselves on running a race-meeting that keeps red tape to a minimum. Renowned for looking after their competitors, the mature members of the Manx MCC always knew they offered young motorcyclists of the day the opportunity of a great adventure in their races. However, it was one time Club President the Rev. Bertie Reid who wrote: *'Everything humanly possible is done to ensure their safety and comfort. When they make their first appearance they will be assisted, guided, warned, encouraged and controlled in such an easy, friendly way that they will unconsciously find themselves being smoothly absorbed into a great sporting fraternity'.*

Chapter 4
THE 1930s

The TT races by now ran to an established time-table that saw Junior, Lightweight and Senior events run on the Monday, Wednesday and Friday of race-week, but there were changes made to the practice period in 1930. Instead of two complete weeks of practice as before, the new arrangements were spread over ten days and comprised nine early morning sessions that started on a Thursday and finished on the Saturday before race week.

*

The majority of riders started their practice laps from opposite the official Timekeepers' box at the Grandstand but they could, with official approval, also start from Ballacraine or Ramsey. Whilst Douglas was the preferred place for most riders to stay, in earlier years the Levis and Douglas teams usually lodged in Peel, and the Scott team favoured Ramsey. Wherever riders started their practice, they would only be timed from Douglas.

Foreign Riders

The organisers provided financial assistance to encourage foreign riders to the TT in 1930 and this resulted in an entry by Kenzo Tada from Japan. He finished thirteenth in the Junior race on a Velocette. There were also riders from Austria, Belgium, Egypt, Hungary, Iraq, Jamaica, South Africa, Sweden, Australia and South Africa. Prize money was increased to £200 for the winning entrant of each race.

*

Racing motorcycles of the early 1930s were almost exclusively single-cylinder models. There had been little progress in the area of suspension, with girder forks at the front and rigid rear-ends being the norm. Bigger section tyres and the use of steering dampers helped to improve the ride but many competitors wore body belts to counter the jarring they received at speed over the bumpy Manx roads.

*

The Rudge concern had made only a moderate impression with previous TT entries, but in 1930 they all but swept the board in the Junior and Senior classes. Bringing a new and relatively untried model with a fully radial four-valve head operated by pushrods and complex transverse rockers, they took the first three places in the Junior race. In the Senior, using an earlier design of engine, they had to be

satisfied with just the first two places and with their race-winner, Wal Handley, setting the first under 30 minute lap (29 minutes 41 seconds, an average speed of 76.28 mph). Wal's Senior win made him the only man to have won all four solo classes (Senior, Junior, Lightweight and Ultra-Lightweight, the latter race run only in 1924 & 25).

Wal Handley rounds Creg ny Baa on his way to victory on his Rudge in the 1930 Senior TT.

Despite their success, all members of the Rudge team had experienced problems during practice for the Junior race with pistons cracking around the gudgeon pin. New pistons were fitted and designer George Hack calculated that they would last 8 laps before they failed. However, as each rider had to do one steady pre-race running-in lap of the new pistons and the race itself was over 7 laps, confidence was not particularly high in the Rudge camp before the race.

The Rudge radial four-valve head with transverse rockers operated by pushrods.

Although the Rudge engines were a sensation in 1930, they provided the last Senior and Junior TT victories to be taken by push-rod engines, thereafter the wins went to overhead camshaft models.

*

Second place in the Senior and third in the Junior of 1930 went to Graham Walker. Although some may think that his greatest claim to fame is to have been the father of race-commentator Murray Walker, he was justly famous in his own right. With a TT race career spanning 1920-1934, he won the 1931 Lightweight TT for Rudge. Then, for many years he held the influential position of Editor of the magazine 'Motor Cycling'.

transmissions and his race reports went around the world. When combined with the extensive reports that appeared in the specialist and popular press, it meant that the TT races were very much in the public eye, as were the riders and manufacturers who took part.

*

Rudge had further TT wins in the Lightweight race in the 1930s, including that of Jimmy Simpson in 1934. Jimmy was a top-class rider, but one with an unusual record. He rode in 26 TTs and set 8 fastest laps but he only finished in 11 races. The 1934 Lightweight was the only race he won. During his career he gained a reputation as a bike-breaker

Graham Walker (Rudge) at the end of one of his TT rides, with son Murray.

Whilst the many readers of his magazine became familiar with Graham's written words, they, and millions of others, also became familiar with his voice via his TT race commentaries that were broadcast by the BBC. Those commentaries started in the late 1920s with the voice of 'Ixion' of 'The Motor Cycle'. Graham Walker took over in 1935 and eventually the BBC's

(something he denied), but he earned his true place in TT history by being the first rider to lap at 60, 70 and 80 mph during a race. Fittingly, his name is still remembered by the annual award of The Jimmy Simpson Trophy to the rider setting the fastest lap at each year's TT.

*

A group of race competitors at Cunningham's Camp in 1933.

Whilst top riders spent their TT fortnight in hotels and others made use of smaller guest houses, there were some who camped and that included the ones who made use of the organised facilities of 'The Cunningham Young Mens Holiday Camp' above Douglas.

At this men only establishment the weekly charge was 2 guineas (£2.10), which included breakfast, dinner, tea and supper. Riders could make use of garage buildings and the Camp had its own Grandstand at Governor's Bridge. A few regulations applied to those staying there, amongst them: *'Only youths and men of good moral character are eligible for admission to the Holiday Camp, and should anyone unfortunately prove, by word or deed, to be otherwise, he will be liable to instant expulsion. It is scarcely necessary to say that the use of intoxicants, gambling and improper language are strictly prohibited. Persons who are not already pledged abstainers are understood by their attending Camp thereby to promise to totally abstain from all intoxicants, in and out of Camp, during their stay. Orderlies are employed to patrol the Camp throughout the night and it will be their duty to report any Campers who by talking, laughing or singing, or in any other way, disturb their fellow Campers between 11.45pm and 7am. The orderlies will also report any Campers who are not in their tents with lights out before 11.45pm weekdays and 11.30pm Sundays. Applications to be out after 11.45pm*

cannot under any circumstances be considered'.

*

A Sidecar race was planned for the 1933 TT, but as only 14 entries were received it was deleted from the programme. Quite how they would have coped with passing each other on the Mountain stretch is not known, for it was still only a single car width and a first-time visitor in 1934 wrote: *'the grass verge had to be used for overtaking'*. Sidecar races had been run for a few years in the mid-1920s and, presumably, they made full use of the grass verges!

Norton Dominance

It was Norton who took command of the Senior and Junior TT classes through most of the 1930s. Indeed the dominance they achieved with their Walter Moore/Arthur Carroll designed ohc racing engine was considered by some to be detrimental to the sport, for racing was an expensive pursuit and without success to advertise and boost sales, other manufacturers became discouraged by Norton's superiority. With former TT racer Joe Craig in charge of the factory's race efforts, Bracebridge Street machinery took the Senior TTs of 1932-34 and 1936-38, and the Junior from 1932-37. For good measure they were also victorious at the MGP meeting, taking the Senior from 1931-38 and the Junior in 1934-35 and 1937-38.

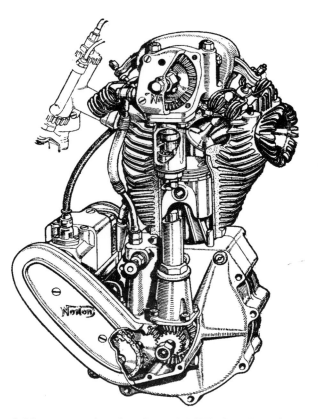

The Norton race team's gradual development of their superb single-cylinder racing engine saw them raise Senior TT winning speeds by 17 mph during the 1930s. With revised bore and stroke on both 350 and 500 models for 1938, Harold Daniell set a pre-war lap record of 91.00 mph when winning that year's Senior race.

*

The Norton racer may have offered top riders the chance to win a TT, but it did not provide them with an easy ride. Girder-forked and without any form of springing at the rear until 1936 when a primitive plunger suspension system was added, the bumps of the TT Course and the vibration from the highly stressed engine could be very wearing. Works rider Harold Daniell told of how he once took his left hand off the handlebar to adjust his goggles whilst flat out down Sulby Straight. Such was the blur of vibration that, in his words, *'when I went to put my hand back on the bars, I couldn't tell which one I should take hold of'*. That was nothing to do with the fact that he wore glasses, although problems with his eyesight were later to see this 1938 Senior TT winner rejected for war service.

*

Not only did Norton produce the best in racing machinery during the 1930s, they also employed the finest riders of the day in men like Jimmy Guthrie, 'Crasher' White, Vic Brittain, Freddie Frith, Harold Daniell and Stanley Woods.

A Norton engine for the 1934 TT showing the new hairpin valve springs. It also had an aluminium cylinder barrel around its steel liner and the cylinder head was of a bronze shell with aluminium surround.

** STANLEY WOODS **

One of the greatest of TT riders, Stanley Woods recorded 10 TT wins in an Island racing career that spanned the years 1922-1939. Just 18 years of age when he made his TT debut, Stanley used slightly devious means to gain his first Island ride. Writing to several manufacturers of 500cc machines, he told them that he had a 350 ride arranged and could they help him out with a 500. Also writing to several 350 makers, he told them he had a 500 arranged and could they help him with a 350. Only one manufacturer rose to the bait and that was the relatively new firm of Cotton from Gloucester. They offered him a 350 and a contribution to his expenses, subject to the receipt of satisfactory references. Stanley gave the writing of those references his personal attention, and the deal was done.

Taking a highly creditable 5th place in his first race on the borrowed Cotton in 1922 (despite managing to set fire to his leathers during his refuelling-stop), Stanley came back in 1923 and won the Junior TT - again on a Cotton. Thereafter he took 5 wins for Norton, 2 for Velocette and 2 for Moto Guzzi.

Clearly blessed with natural ability as a motorcycle racer (he was an all-rounder on road, dirt and even ice) he still had to work hard for his success. A firm believer in keeping fit, he was also capable of shrewd and original thinking. In the early 1930s he devised his own signalling system. It was designed to provide him with race information half-way round the TT Course. This was in addition to receiving a conventional pit signal at the Grandstand like other riders. Stanley knew that those conventional pit signals were of limited value, because, with a near 40 mile lap, much of the information that could be passed to a rider at

Stanley Woods in the winner's enclosure on his Norton after his success in the 1933 Junior TT.

the pits was often a lap old. In addition, the frightening flat-out descent of Bray Hill that followed the Pits was not the best place for a rider to attempt to mentally juggle information on how far he was behind the rider in front and how close his challengers were behind.

For his personal signalling system Stanley stationed an assistant in a public telephone box on the Sulby Straight, enlisted the help of a friendly householder with a telephone close to the Start and, in his words, *'blarnied the telephonists in the local exchange to give the calls priority'* (it was before the days of direct dialling, all calls went via an operator). Not only did his system allow him to outwit the opposition, but on a couple of occasions when Norton wanted his fellow teamsters to win races, Stanley, by using the information gained from his private signalling station, realised that Norton's pit signal for him to slow the pace was not because he had an enormous lead, but because they wanted someone else to make up enough time to win the race. Stanley kept his head down!

Although they were good friends, Stanley classed Jimmy Guthrie as one of his keenest rivals and the 1935 Senior TT showed the lengths that Mr Woods would go to for a win. Moto Guzzi had signed him on a 'name your own fee' basis to ride for them in both the Lightweight and Senior events, and he duly delivered them their first TT win on the 250 horizontal single-cylinder machine (that suffered serious failure in the valve-gear as it crossed the finishing line). However, Stanley's biggest concern was at the opposition offered by the Norton of Guthrie in the Senior. During practice he made no attempt to counter the rumour that his new twin-cylinder Guzzi was heavy on fuel and that he would have to stop twice during the race to refill. What he did not publicise was the fact that he had an enlarged petrol tank available just for the race. As the riders approached the last lap of that 1935 Senior TT, Jimmy Guthrie held a healthy lead of 26 seconds.

Jimmy (riding number 1) was well ahead of Stanley (riding number 30) on the road and when the Norton personnel saw Stanley's pit-attendant making early preparations for his expected last lap fuel stop, they told their rider to hold his pace. Imagine their horror when a little later Stanley came past the pits flat on the tank in pursuit of Guthrie, without stopping for fuel. Unable to warn their rider, Norton could only wait in suspense whilst Stanley, who knew what he had to do, revved the Guzzi well beyond agreed limits, set a new lap record of 86.53 mph and snatched race victory by four seconds. It was a triumph of strategy for Stanley and Moto Guzzi but a bitter disappointment for Jimmy Guthrie. He had received the chequered flag and been hailed as the winner. A multitude of photographs were taken, congratulations proffered and the press were already writing their stories of his win, when canny Stanley's last lap dash turned the race result on its head.

Stanley Woods moved on to Velocettes after 1935 and in the book 'Always in the Picture - Velocette' by Bob Burgess and Jeff Clew, reference is made to *'the great assistance that he was able to render Velocette in "navigational" matters'* - in other words, his experienced input considerably improved the handling of Velocette race machines. He went on to take three second places in the Senior TT on Velos and two victories in the Junior.

Stanley's tenth and last TT win was the 1939 Junior. Resisting the temptation to make a post-war comeback, he remained involved in the sport as an entrant. When invited to 'parade' a Moto Guzzi at the TT's fiftieth anniversary celebrations in 1957, he lapped at well over 80 mph. Thereafter, he participated in occasional parades and was often present at the races, for he retained his enthusiasm for the TT until he died in 1993.

Although the Norton concern was highly successful in the field of racing during the 1930s, it did not take success for granted, particularly at the Isle of Man races. To maintain its superiority it always kept a close watch on the opposition to see that they did not gain an advantage. Dennis Mansell of Norton told of how after secretly timing their own riders and the best of the opposition during practice for the 1931 Senior race, they found that the Nortons were some 12 seconds quicker on the stretch from Kates Cottage to Hillberry. Convinced that they were genuine times and that the opposition were not 'foxing', Norton decided to lower the compression ratio of their racers to aid reliability. They still took the first three places in the Senior race.

*

Soon after Stanley Woods introduced his personal signalling system the Norton factory team realised the importance of providing their riders with information at two spots on the Course (Pits and Ramsey) and so it arranged for the provision of temporary telephones with connection between those two points.

*

Whilst serious racing firms like Norton and Velocette were regulars at the TT, many smaller concerns also made entries. British firms like Royal Enfield, Dunelt, Excelsior, New Imperial, AJS and Scott all tried for glory in the early 1930s. In 1934 Vincent HRD made their first TT appearance with three machines in the Senior. It was still a young company and, like many small concerns, used JAP engines in its spring frame road machines. But although its TT entries for 1934 were powered by JAP's newest 500cc race engine, they proved to be at least 10 mph slower than the best Nortons and far less reliable.

The JAP powered Vincent HRD that contested the 1934 Senior TT.

New the JAP motors at the 1934 TT may have been, but they did not live up to the pre-race promises made by their manufacturer J.A. Prestwich & Co of Tottenham. This resulted in all three Vincent HRDs retiring from the race with engine trouble. The failure of those JAP engines spurred Vincent HRD into designing its own 500cc road-going engine. Returning to the TT in 1935 with tuned versions of its new roadster engine, it achieved creditable finishes in the Senior race in competition against many other makes.

*

For a small company like Vincent HRD, taking part in the TT meant disruptions to normal production on the run-up to the event and round-the-clock working on the Island for all involved in the race effort. At the 1936 event their Chief Engineer, Phil Irving, claimed that he only got to bed six times in eleven days over the practice period. Race mechanics from the Norton team would also be busy, but there were usually enough of them to avoid 'all-nighters'. Also, whilst Norton 'works' riders would fill their non-racing time with rounds of golf and socialising, Vincent HRD riders like Arthur Tyler and Jack Williams returned to the team's garage at the Falcon Cliff Hotel after practice and helped to get the bikes ready for the next session. Small teams could not afford 'prima donnas', they needed riders who were prepared to get their hands dirty. Of his dealings with the top riders, Norton's Joe Craig said: *'in some cases and in certain circumstances, the riders can be as temperamental as the machines usually are'*. One

manufacturer of the time tried to persuade its riders to get themselves into proper shape for the demands of TT racing, because *'they realised that it was little use spending a lot of money to prepare racing machines unless the jockeys were really fit and so encouraged their riders to live an ascetic life for some time prior to practice'*. How successful they were with such encouragement was not revealed!

*

It was just prior to the 1934 TT that the gate across the Mountain road at Keppel Gate was removed. Prior to that date, it always had to be opened before a race or practice. Although the gates were removed because the Mountain Road had been fenced to contain grazing sheep, a few refused to be contained and wandering sheep were a recognised hazard to racers.

Bending the Rules
Whilst the organisers considered that the TT

Gunnar Kalen sits astride his 500cc v-twin Husqvarna at the 1934 TT. Husqvarna also entered Ernie Nott and Stanley Woods in the same race. Stanley held second place until he ran out of fuel on the last lap, but Ernie and Gunnar retired with mechanical problems.

31

regulations existed in order to be applied to the letter, racers usually had a far more free and easy approach to the matter. Manliff Barrington told that at his first TT in 1934, where he had a Lightweight entry, he suffered major problems with his Rudge 250 in practice. Being a newcomer and wanting to take advantage of every practice session, he borrowed a friend's 500 Rudge, put his own number plates on it, and went off and did several more laps while his own bike was being repaired. No one was more surprised than Manliff when his name later appeared on the practice leader-board for the Lightweight class. It did not take the organisers long to find out what he had been up to, and his practice times were scrubbed; but Manliff was not the first (or last) to change numbers and machine in an attempt to qualify.

*

Late arriving for practice at the 1934 TT were the Swedish Husqvarna firm because when a lorry loaded with their 350 and 500 cc v-twin racers was being loaded onto a ship at Gothenburg, a cable snapped and the lorry fell to the dockside, finishing upside down. That was no way to treat a batch of 'works' racing bikes and they had to go back to the factory for repairs.

*

As each TT approached, the motorcycling press tried to raise their readers interest with facts and speculation about the races, and 1935 was no exception. As well as expected entries of the fast Italian, 120 degree, twin-cylinder Moto Guzzis in the Senior event they wrote of the exciting prospect of Rondine bringing their new four-cylinder, water-cooled, supercharged 500 that had beaten the Guzzi on the Continent. Unfortunately the pre-race build-up was to no avail, as the Rondine failed to appear.

*

Despite the many technical developments of the time, some riders preferred tried and tested features. Cecil Barrow, who first competed in 1925, still rode with a lever throttle on his Royal Enfield that he brought home to eighth place in the Senior. It was Cecil's last TT and, surely, the last time a lever throttle was used in an Island race.

*

The start of the 1935 TT period just caught the end of a General Strike on the Island. Conditions were still chaotic in Douglas and as porters and taxi-drivers were amongst those on strike, passengers had to carry their own baggage from the boats. It brought home to many just how hilly Douglas was away from the Promenade.

Postponed

The 1935 TT saw the introduction of Travelling Marshals on race-days. A closer look is taken at these essential members of the race organisation later in this book, but during their first year of duty they were witness to the first ever postponement of a TT race, indeed their weather reports from around the course helped the Clerk of the Course and Race Stewards make the difficult decision to postpone. With the weather considered unfit for them to race on the traditional Friday, runners in the Senior TT had to wait until the Saturday to race.

Postponement of the 1935 Senior race caused considerable chaos, for the Island had no experience or contingency plans to cope with such a happening. The result was that cafes and pubs filled with damp spectators seeking to dry out and consider their transport and accommodation arrangements. As well as the many thousands of spectators who were over for the whole of race-week, the Isle of Man Steam Packet Company had landed an additional 11,000 race fans on the Island before 7.30 a.m. on Friday, specifically to see the Senior race. As there were only 4 telephone lines from the Island to the UK, they were swamped by people trying to make new arrangements.

Although postponement of the 1935 Senior race was bad news for many people, some race fans from England (who had not been able to get the Friday off work) took Friday night boats over to the Island and were able to watch the rearranged race on the Saturday.

*

An important introduction in 1935 was to allow riders to warm-up their engines before the start of each race. This took away some of the start-line worries that arose from the customary flat-out blind down Bray Hill with cold engines. Of course, with engines being required to be stopped some 15 minutes before the actual start, and with interval starting, the last man away had probably sat for an engine-cooling half an hour before getting under way.

*

The warming-up of engines before the start was achieved by competitors riding their machines up and down a stretch of the Glencrutchery Road defined by dustbins down the middle. The noise of unsilenced engines and the heady smell of castor-based oils all helped to build the race atmosphere in front of the crowds in the Grandstand. To enhance the pageantry, 1935 saw the introduction of Boy

Scouts parading the national flags of competing riders before the start. Riders walked with their machines behind their national flags to take their places on the grid.

'No Limit'

Whilst most people were concerned with the serious business of racing at the 1935 TT, George Formby and Florence Desmond were on the Island filming the classic TT based comedy 'No Limit'. They made use of the presence of the riders, machines and Grandstand crowds to give atmosphere to the film that featured the legendary 'Shuttleworth Snap'.

*

By the mid-1930s the TT races were very well-established and the Manx people had also embraced the use of the internal combustion engine. There were 1,000 motorcycles registered for use on the Manx roads, plus 2,918 motor cars, 87 lorries, 374 hackney cars and, still, 1,700 horse drawn vehicles.

*

Since their inception in 1907 the TT races had been organised by the London based ACU. They relied on a veritable army of Manx volunteers to help carry out official duties and to marshal the Course but the ACU's attitude sometimes suggested that they were not entirely happy with the location of the races. As far back as 1912 they considered transferring them to France or Ireland and they also had thoughts of running the 1922 event in Belgium. The principal reason was because the Isle of Man Government refused to offer financial support. It eventually did so from 1930, allocating £1,500 to the ACU for the prize fund and £3,500 to subsidise the expenses of competitors from overseas. Its contribution has increased ever since.

Mist on the Mountain

The growth of race speeds created increased concern for the safety of riders and in the mid-1930s the race organisers arranged for the painting of a broken yellow line down the middle of the road on the Mountain section. The idea was that riders would have something to follow when there was 'mist on the mountain'. For several years around the mid-1930s races were badly affected by thick cloud and rain (known in TT parlance as 'mist on the mountain'), and such adverse conditions for the racing of motorcycles eventually resulted in the first ever postponement of a race (the previously mentioned 1935 Senior TT). This, and the prospect of future cancellations, brought into question the suitability of the Mountain Course for racing. One report of the time said: *'The TT races are too important an International event to be postponed, and if the nature of the course is such that postponement is unavoidable, clearly the course must be altered'*. Easier said than done! Alternative courses on the Island that avoided the Mountain were proposed, but nothing came of them. However, the problem did not go away and the 1936 TT Programme noted that *'although considerable controversy arose following the 1935 races, the ACU, for various reasons, has decided for this year at least, to utilise again the course that has been used for every post-war Race - known throughout the world as the Mountain Course'*. After the 1936 races the ACU appointed a sub-committee to consider the topic of the Course. After several meetings it recommended that the ACU *'should carefully explore the possibilities of a new course for 1937'*. As we now know, nothing came of the wish to change, but as TT spectators are only too aware, 'mist on the mountain' has not gone away!

*

SPEEDS

'The TT Special' knew that the topic of top-speed was a popular one with its readers and often carried out unofficial timing of the racers. The results were then published with their TT reports. One favourite stretch for timing was the Sulby Straight. It was no coincidence that the best riders set the fastest speeds there, for the time taken to cover the one-mile timed section of the Sulby Straight depended upon the speed of exit from the preceding Quarry Bends and how early/late a rider applied the brakes for Sulby Bridge. Because speeds were taken here on a regular basis it is possible to see the way they increased. Here are a few examples of the fastest 500cc runners:

1934 TT, Jimmy Simpson (Norton) was timed at 106.5 mph.
1935 TT, Stanley Woods (Moto Guzzi) 112.5 mph.
1937 TT, Stanley Woods (Velocette) 122.49 mph
1938 TT, Jock West (BMW) 130.4 mph.

Most of those speed increases during the 1930s arose from the increased power outputs and marginally improved handling of the race bikes, for the Course was still over narrow roads that had the customary lumps and bumps that arose from their day-to-day use by ordinary traffic.

*

Nowadays, the nature of the TT Course allows riders to take full advantage of their top speed, for there are plenty of stretches where full throttle can be maintained for comparatively long distances. This is in contrast to most short circuits where top speed is rarely achieved and where acceleration can sometimes be a more important factor.

*

Each year the speeds of the top works runners of the 1930s were usually within 5 mph of each other, with the best privateers about 10 mph off the fastest man's pace.

*

In a long race like the TT, speed was of no use without reliability that would permit the completion of the 264 mile race distance. Although the name of Norton featured only once amongst the fastest speeds quoted above, they won three out of those four Senior TTs.

Spectators have never been charged to watch the TT races (unless they chose to use a Grandstand or private enclosed area), but from the 1920s through to the 1960s owners of visiting vehicles were obliged to pay Manx road-tax for the duration of their stay. The vigour with which this was enforced varied down the years, as did the amount - from 2/6, (12½p) to 5/-, (25p), and the documentation issued was called an Exemption Registration Certificate. A temporary Manx driving licence was also required, costing 1/-, (5p).

Another piece of Manx legislation that was only occasionally enforced in the 1930s was a requirement to sound a vehicle's horn at crossroads. One man to fall-foul of a zealous policeman on this particular point was TT winner Jimmy Guthrie. Summoned to appear before the Island's High Bailiff the following day, it was clear that the Court's sympathies lay with the famous TT rider. Fined 10/- (50p), there was laughter in Court when Jimmy was asked if he needed time to pay. Another year, Jimmy and several fellow riders were fined for riding unsilenced machines up to the start of morning practice. They again received a sympathetic hearing. Clearly the occasional Manx policeman was not in tune with the TT, even though most recognised that it provided them with sufficient overtime to give them their biggest pay-packets of the year.

Rear Suspension

One technical feature of the 1935 TT that had not gone un-noticed was that Stanley Woods' Senior winning Moto Guzzi was fitted with rear suspension. Although Stanley had the suspension tightened so hard that there was only restricted movement, the handling of his bike (and that of the

In the mid-1930s Norton moved from the use of a straight-through exhaust of uniform diameter to one that finished with a 'megaphone'. This 1937 model is fitted with an auxiliary silencer to satisfy the Manx constabulary when the machine was being ridden to and from practice.

Vincent HRDs that also had rear suspension) made other firms take heed. Rear suspension had been fitted on occasional road-going motorcycles over many years, but although it may have improved comfort it did not always improve handling. Attitudes were changing however and 'Motor Cycling' wrote in its editorial in March 1936 that *'every manufacturer who supports road racing has been thinking about spring frames since the success of the Guzzi spring frame in the last TT'.* It saw such developments in road racing benefiting all motorcyclists and *'held the view unswervingly that eventually the spring frame will come'.* In 1936 the Norton racers appeared at the TT with a basic form of plunger rear suspension and Velocettes were fitted with what they called oleomatic units at the rear that used air as the springing medium assisted by oil.

*

The plunger form of rear suspension first fitted to the Norton racers in 1936.

Prior to its flattening in the mid-1930s, Ballig Bridge had been the 'humpiest' point on the Course. Fast riders were air-borne for long distances and Stanley Woods spoke of riding the bridge diagonally, left to right, maintaining that *'one's right-hand handlebar would have been over the parapet of the bridge if you were travelling at the maximum speed and on the best line'.* He omitted to mention that you also had to be well and truly airborne to get your handlebar over the parapet!

*

AJS brought two of their exciting air-cooled V-fours to the 1936 Senior but riders George Rowley and Harold Daniell retired both machines.

*

By the end of the nine early morning practice sessions only three competitors had failed to qualify. Although riders could appeal to the Clerk of the Course to be allowed to ride, failure to meet the qualifying standards usually meant that they were not allowed to race in the events that they had entered.

*

Bob Foster's victory in the 1936 Lightweight TT on his New Imperial was the last time the 250 event was won by a push-rod engine. Unusually for a British machine of the time, Bob's New Imperial had its engine and gearbox constructed in a single unit (unit construction) and primary drive was by gear, rather than the chain used on machines with the customary separate engine and gearbox.

*

A winner of several earlier TT races, Wal Handley caused something of a stir when he advocated that the TT should be for production machines rather than out-and-out racers. Another unusual point in 1936 was that the Lightweight race had the biggest entry, although that was only 34 riders. The Senior race had the smallest ever entry for what was supposed to be the 'Blue Riband' event. Only 20 entries, but it was an exciting race between Jimmy Guthrie (Norton) and Stanley Woods (Velocette), with victory going to Jimmy.

*

Few racing bikes of the 1930s were fitted with rev counters. Riders judged the revs by ear and changed gear accordingly.

Early Morning Practice
Early morning practice sessions had been a feature of the TT since 1907, and although not universally popular (by the mid-1930s there were nine sessions at the TT and MGP) they were accepted as a fact of IOM racing life. One hotel even advertised *'guaranteed practice calls at 3.45 am, with refreshments'.* A report of an early morning practice of 1936 wrote of Jack (CJ) Williams being first in the queue of starters at 4.15 am with his Vincent HRD. When the course inspection car arrived back at the start he was told *'good visibility, lots of wind and millions of rabbits'.* First man away - and unpaid rabbit scarer - he was despatched at 4.33 am.

*

For many years Cadbury's (and sometimes Dunlop) provided a welcome hospitality tent at the rear of the Grandstand during the early morning practice periods. There they supplied hot cocoa to riders and officials chilled by the early morning Manx air. It was a place where riders, mechanics, factory executives, trade representatives and sponsors all rubbed shoulders. In the damp, cigarette-smoke-filled early morning air they exchanged information, hatched riding and sponsorship deals and settled arguments regarding machine performance, racing lines, etc. In the words of well-known competitor, Phil Heath:

'Practising, especially, was great fun. There was nothing to beat the excitement of a couple of laps in good weather with the bike running well and the prospect of a chinwag and hot cup of cocoa at the end'.

Evening Practice

The year of 1937 was the one in which an evening practice session (Thursday) was first introduced at the TT. Carburation troubles had become increasingly prevalent due to competitors setting-up their machines to suit the cool air experienced during early morning sessions. This led to difficulties on race days when these increasingly sophisticated engines were asked to deliver maximum output under the differing atmospheric conditions of morning and afternoon running, and at altitudes ranging from sea-level to 1400 feet above. The organisers listened and acted on the riders requests, and in the years that followed the number of evening practice sessions were increased and the number of morning ones reduced.

*

The first evening practice brought many more locals out to watch than the morning ones did. It also suited Jimmy Guthrie, for he took his Norton round in record-breaking time. Unfortunately, only speeds set during an actual race can count as official lap records.

*

The TT period had always seen much carburettor testing and tuning, much of it done at times other than during official practice sessions. During the 1920s the Ballamodha Straight between Foxdale and Castletown was the scene of much such activity. The Mountain Mile was also popular, particularly after the arrival of megaphone exhausts in the mid-1930s made it sensible to run machines as far away from human habitation as possible. For many years, carburettor manufacturers considered that the TT

Much of the testing of Norton race engines was done at the factory and this scene shows (from left) Frank Sharratt, Joe Craig, Henry Laird, Gilbert Smith and Graham Walker casting their eyes over a race engine prepared for test.

races offered the ultimate practical testing conditions for their products. Nowadays, most testing outside practice is done in done in slightly more official form at Jurby Airfield.

*

Reflecting the increased speed and improved handling of the race machines plus the benefits of Course improvements, Freddie Frith set the first 90 mph lap in 1937 while winning the Senior TT on his Norton. Freddie won by 15 seconds from Stanley Woods whose Velocette had a frame that truly cradled the narrow crankcase that was topped with a new square finned cylinder head and barrel.

Italian Victory

Omobono Tenni's victory on a Moto Guzzi in the 1937 Lightweight race was the first by an all-Italian partnership of rider and machine. He set a new lap record for the Lightweight class of 74.72 mph as he sped to victory over British Excelsiors and what were perhaps the noisiest ever racing motorcycles, the potent split-single, two-stroke DKWs from Germany. DKW, who had a huge racing department, had a convincing victory in the 1938 Lightweight TT.

*

Omobono Tenni at Quarter Bridge on his 250 Moto Guzzi in 1937.

Excelsiors put up excellent performances in the 1937 Lightweight, for as well as taking second place with 'Ginger' Wood riding, the marque had several more leader-board places. Although the company sought to capitalise on its TT successes by naming its road-going sports models 'Manxman', their racing models soon became outclassed by faster foreign lightweights.

Several other TT participating manufacturers offered 'TT Specials' that, for a premium, were usually tuned versions of their standard sports models.

*

Bowing to rider superstition, the TT organisers did not allocate rider number 13 from 1937 onwards.

*

Most riders attempt to make as much use of the practice sessions as possible, but the first three sessions at the 1938 TT took place in atrocious weather and resulted in all-time low figures for rider turnout. In the first session there were only 4 riders and in the third session there were 8. Marshals had to be at their posts whatever the weather and one was heard to comment in 1938 that the most exciting thing they had seen in Parliament Square was a fight between two cats!

*

Late arriving for practice in 1938 was American stunt-rider Putt Mossman. Conspicuous by his white leathers (and his use of a uni-cycle in the Paddock), it was his second TT visit and he drew further attention to himself by taking wrong turnings on the Course, falling off, and retiring his Excelsior from the

Harold Daniell on his Norton after his winning ride in the 1938 Senior TT. On the left is 'works' mechanic Bill Mewis and on the right Frank Sharratt who also worked at Norton.

Lightweight race. He had also entered the Senior on an Indian and the Junior on a Harley Davidson but those machines did not materialise.

*

Mossman was not the first to wear coloured leathers at the TT. Back in 1910 Frank Phillipp turned out with his leathers dyed Scott purple and other Scott riders followed his example in later years. In 1922 those of the Rudge team were vivid green. Wal Handley is also believed to have made an appearance in white leathers in 1930.

*

There were technical and speed advances in all classes during the TT races of the 1930s, but Norton generally managed to keep their finely honed single-cylinder engine ahead of the rest of the field in the 500cc category. In one of the greatest TT battles ever seen, Harold Daniell had to push his Norton to a new lap record of 91.00 mph when winning the 1938 Senior race from Stanley Woods and Freddie Frith.

*

The TT races of the 1930s yielded great days for Norton Motors Ltd but racing was an expensive business. The enjoyment and success experienced by a rider who won a TT was quite understandable but, as well as the difficulty in quantifying commercial returns, did the hard-headed businessmen of the motorcycle trade gain satisfaction from their TT participation? Gilbert Smith of Nortons was always good for a quote and he indicated that *'If one could reveal the truth, the whole truth and all of it, the TT is the manifestation of every human emotion . . . of victory . . . of triumph . . . but sometimes of tragedy and pathos. Here one learns some of the basic truths of human experience - of human struggle and rivalry - of exultancy and despondency. Here one learns the incredible facts of human nature . . . of grit and ambition . . . of subtlety and cunning . . . of wisdom and folly, jealousy, duplicity and bargaining, and all the flames of human passion. It is here one discovers men whose word is their bond, where character shines under disappointment and disillusionment. Here one sees the lonehand earnestly pursuing the road to fame - the diehards, too, seeking for honours still. Here one sees big business at work with all its might . . . '.* He made it sound a heady and irresistible mixture.

*

Spectator interest remained high for the TT races. The 1930s were still the comparatively early days of motorcycling and the spectacle of speed, noise and the show of daring by riders lapping close to 90 mph was a huge attraction. Everyone wanted to see the TT

Norton were proud of their TT achievements.

races, but not everyone could afford to be there for a week or fortnight. To help meet demands, 'Motor Cycling' still offered their one-day excursions by rail and boat to see the Senior race.

*

Despite the high level of spectator interest, the TT had relatively low entries in the late 1930s. The Senior race of 1937 had only 29 runners, in 1938 it was 32.

*

The Regulations for the 1939 event were published in February of the year and were little changed from 1938. Entry fee for individual events was £10, total prize money was £1,800 and evening practice sessions had grown to three. There were still six early morning sessions.

*

38

The magazine 'Motor Cycling' ran excursions to see the Senior TT and a young Geoff Duke travelled on their 1939 trip in his first visit to the Isle of Man.

Norton did not come to the 1939 TT with official works machines (they supplied 1938 bikes), claiming that they were too busy fulfilling contracts for the Government. BMW did come, bringing their supercharged, double ohc, flat-twins for Georg Meir, Karl Gall and Jock West to ride in the Senior. Gall was killed in a practice accident at Ballaugh (where he is remembered by a small wall-mounted memorial) and Georg Meir was a convincing winner of the Senior, with Jock West second. Meir just broke the race record, averaging 89.38 mph, but he did not break Harold Daniell's 1938 lap record. Perhaps he didn't need to.

*

AJS brought their supercharged and water-cooled Vee-4 to the 1939 TT but, although the four had been around for several years and was said to develop 55 bhp, it still weighed-in at a hefty 405 lbs (184 kgs) compared to the winning BMW's claimed 305 lbs (138 kgs). The 'Ajay' required 2% oil added to its petrol to lubricate the Zoller supercharger that passed fuel to the cylinders at a pressure of about 5 pounds to the square inch.

*

Walter Rusk sits astride his watercooled and supercharged AJS Vee-4 before going out to practice for the 1939 Senior TT.

Velocette also brought the new and untested, supercharged, shaft-driven, ohc, vertical twin 'Roarer' with its contra-rotating crankshafts; but they only used it in practice and their riders used single-cylinder engines in the Junior and Senior races, with Stanley Woods bringing the 350 home to victory in the Junior.

*

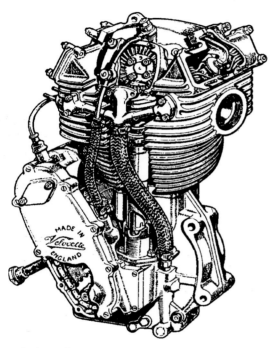

The single-cylinder engine used by Velocette at the 1939 TT.

Going down Bray Hill on lap two of the 1939 Lightweight race, Chris Tattersall had a narrow escape when a gas main burst and hurled a metal grating in his direction. In that same Lightweight race, Ted Mellors rode a Benelli to victory in the company's first TT appearance. It was a strong hint of things to come in the field of Lightweight racing.

*

At a meeting soon after the 1939 TT the ACU considered proposals for a 'Stock-Machine' race, but they rejected them due mainly to the difficulty of determining and policing exactly what was a 'Stock-Machine'. However, they were amenable to the idea of what they called a 'Roadster-Machine' race. They envisaged *'machines on standard lines which might be altered from the regular specification in certain respects'*.

*

To publicise the MGP and boost entries, it was the custom of the Manx MCC to offer free entries to their races to winners of nominated Clubman's events in the UK. In the summer of 1939 two club officials, Doug Hanson and Norman Brown, attended such a Clubman's meeting at Donington and offered free entries to Lesley Parsons and Stanley Barnett. Neither was in a position to accept at the time but, as will be seen later, they did not forget the offer.

*

Although everything was in hand to run the MGP in September 1939 (even the programmes were printed), the outbreak of the Second World War meant that the event was cancelled on the day before practising was due to start. It was to be seven years before any further racing took place on the Isle of Man.

Chapter 5
RACING RETURNS

With the arrival of peace it was not the world-famous TT races that were first to run again on the unchanged and enduring 37 ¾ mile Mountain Course, it was the Manx Grand Prix of 1946. Barely a year after the war had ended, food, clothes and petrol were still rationed and a general air of austerity prevailed. Nevertheless, the Grandstand was patched-up, the Scoreboards repainted, flags and bunting were rigged, and a few other strings must have been pulled to ensure the availability of fuel for the September races.

*

Among the 194 entries for the first post-war event were Messrs Parsons and Barnett. They were the two Clubman winners from the pre-war Donington meeting who had each received the offer of a free entry to the 1939 MGP. Both wrote to ask if the Manx MCC offer still held good and, perhaps admiring their cheek, the Club said yes.

*

After the build-up and preparation, the first post-war practice session eventually got under way and a reporter who was present wrote: *'the last seven years rolled away like the mist off Snaefell this morning and brought us back the scene we've waited for so long'*.

Late Starters

The seven year halt to racing had taken a major slice out of many racing careers and made other riders late starters. One man who found his racing ambitions thwarted by the war was Nigel Seymour Smith. He had managed just one pre-war ride in a Clubman's meeting at Donington in May 1939 so, when he arrived at the MGP in 1946 on a 1936 Vincent HRD Series A 'TT Replica', it was in riding kit that he described as: *'a Cromwell helmet, bought in 1939 for thirty shillings from Lewis's of Carburton Street, racing leather jacket and breeches from Marble Arch Supplies, price two pounds ten shillings, and army despatch rider lace-up boots'*. The entry fee for the 1946 race was £6, so that exceeded the cost of Nigel's riding gear!

*

Nigel Seymour Smith with his 1936 Vincent HRD Series A 'TT Replica' in front of the Pits before the start of the 1946 Senior MGP.

Refuelling during both TT and MGP races was done from standard containers supplied by the petrol companies, that were mounted on a concrete post at each Pit. As can be seen in the above photograph, that was one facility that was not available at the 1946 MGP and riders had to use their own cans for refuelling.

For the first few years after the war the petrol available for road and race use was of a lowly 72 octane and known as 'Pool'. It was of variable quality and riders were forced to reduce compression ratios from their pre-war levels of about 10.5:1 down to just over 7.0:1. The adverse effect this had on machine performance contributed to keeping lap speeds down below those of the pre-war races for several years.

*

The 1946 MGP was the first to use an afternoon practice session and it was held on the Thursday of practice week. The session was not popular with schools around the Course and the authorities complained of disruption to lessons caused by the noise. No doubt their pupils saw (and heard) things differently! The afternoon practice did become popular with riders, as it still is. One of its biggest advantages was that it offered a much longer period on the Course in conditions more akin to race-days. Most riders saw it as a race rehearsal and used it to build up their speeds. Entering fully into the spirit of things at that first afternoon practice, local Travelling Marshal Harry Craine came into Sulby Bridge far too quickly and 'came a beautiful box of tacks'. Fortunately he suffered nothing more than dented pride and scratched motorcycle.

*

In pre-war years Norton ran two garages at the TT. Both were in Douglas, with the one servicing private owners located in Victoria Road and the other at the Castle Mona Hotel kept for the bikes of the factory appointed riders. Although they had given only partial 'works' support to the 1939 TT, Norton had taken masses of spares over and left them at the Castle Mona ready for use at the 1939 MGP. That event was cancelled at the last minute and the cache of spares remained intact throughout the war. The availability of those spares in the immediate post-war period contributed to the construction of several new Norton racing bikes in 1946.

*

The weather was atrocious during the 1946 Senior MGP, and the man who led the field and eventually took the win was the brave and talented Ernie Lyons. He was riding an early version of the Triumph 'Grand Prix' and, after an excursion into a roadside ditch, it finished the race with a broken frame. When asked if he knew when the frame broke, he is said to have replied: 'I think it must have been when the bicycle began to steer much better'! Second place in the Senior went to pre-war MGP winner Ken Bills. (It was still the time when a MGP winner could come back for another try.) Ken had won the Junior earlier in the week.

*

Ken Bills was one of those interesting characters that the Isle of Man races tend to turn up. He was an optician by profession, but after the early death of his brother he also ran his Estate Agency. It was an unusual combination, but one that funded a healthy competition career that started in grass-track racing and off-road events. His first MGP ride was in 1934 and he progressed to a 3rd place in 1936, 2nd place in both 1937 races, a double victory in 1938 and a Junior win in 1946. He was a man who rode to his own personal limits (not allowing himself to be pushed by others) and who rarely stressed a bike to its maximum, preferring to ride with revs in hand to ensure a finish. It was a policy that paid dividends in IOM races. Ken also used his skills as an optician to produce goggles with prescription lenses for those riders who needed a bit of help in seeing their way around the Course.

*

Vision

Seeing the way around the Mountain Course properly has always been an important task for riders. In most cases this is usually linked to the weather and the related 'Mist on the Mountain', but in other instances it can be due to eyesight problems and mention has already been made that 1938 Senior TT winner Harold Daniell was turned down for military service due to his eyesight.

*

Tommy McEwan had a successful TT & MGP career through the 1930s and 40s, but on one occasion complained to Francis Beart and others that he 'suffered from poor vision whilst cornering'. It was a problem that had everyone baffled for a while, but Francis solved the mystery when he examined Tommy's goggles and found that they were fitted with correcting optical lenses, something that Tommy did not need.

*

Manxman Bertie Rowell was another successful pre-war MGP rider and in the early post-war period he served as a Travelling Marshal.

Bertie Rowell, Ariel Square Four mounted for post-war Travelling Marshal duty.

Although he did not wear glasses, Bertie had a small vision problem when riding. He always wore a helmet with a peak and, so the story is told, by having the peak set slightly off-square at the front he found that this largely overcame the difficulty.

*

A very common problem for the racers was dealing with the insects that plastered their goggles during practice and race sessions. Twice a TT winner in the 1920s, Freddie Dixon had his own way of dealing with the situation, he just dispensed with goggles and raced without any form of eye-protection.

*

It eventually became the custom for riders to fix a mesh flyscreen on the top of the forklegs to intercept winged insects, but this was only effective when riders were flat on the tank, and many got through to splatter against goggles and seriously interfere with vision.

*

The front of Harold Daniell's 1938 Senior TT winning Norton showing that its fly-screen did its job.

Graham Walker had his own way of dealing with dirty goggles and wrote: '*a sucked glove finger quickly applied (to the goggles) on a fine day will remove squashed flies before they congeal*'. Each finger was to be used just once one assumes, although how, in the heat of a race, a rider remembered which finger to suck is best glossed over.

*

After fairings came into use many of the flies were intercepted or deflected by their perspex screens although, inevitably, some still got through as riders sat up to brake or corner. For a while it was fashionable to fix a tennis ball with the top sliced off in a position behind the screen. The tennis ball served as a container for a damp piece of sponge that could be used to clean goggles and then returned to its place for further use.

*

Although riders now use visors with their full-face helmets rather than goggles, the problem of squashed flies, particularly on warm June evenings, persists. Some helmets can be fitted with tear-off strips of clear plastic. These form the outer layer of the visor and when peeled-off and discarded by the rider, have the effect of providing a fresh clear visor through which to see. It is also increasingly common practice for riders to change visors at their pit-stops, with some even changing helmets.

Jim Moodie is a modern rider who likes to change his helmet and visor at pit-stops but he also uses 'tear-off' strips over his visor. What look like ears on his helmet are the ends of those tear-off strips that he grasps to pull them off.

1947 TT

With the MGP having shown the way, the first post-war TT was run in 1947. As the 1939 Senior TT was won by Georg Meir on his BMW, the original Tourist Trophy had gone to Germany with him. The organisers were extremely pleased to find that it had been in safe-keeping, and Arthur Simcock (one of the first Travelling Marshals) played a part in seeing that it was back on the Island for the 1947 event. Similarly, the 250 Tourist Trophy had gone to Italy in 1939 with winners, Benelli. Bill Lomas tells how that one was buried for safe-keeping and, come 1947, it was also returned. The Isle of Man was keen to have the racers back and the Manx Parliament (Tynwald) approved a grant of £6,000 to the TT to help with the running costs. The Senior and Junior MGP winners from 1946, Lyons and Bills, were promoted to the Norton 'works' team and, despite petrol-rationing, thousands of TT-starved spectators made it across the Irish Sea for the races held on 9th, 11th and 13th June. There were more cars and motorcycles at the 1947 TT than in pre-war years and with the strict petrol-rationing that was still in force, one can but speculate on the means spectators adopted to obtain sufficient fuel for their journeys. Account had to be taken of the fact that to meet the regulations of the Isle of Man Steam Packet Company, motorcycle tanks would be pumped

TT fans queue at Liverpool Docks for a boat to take them to the Isle of Man.

virtually dry before they were allowed on to the boats. That was a practice carried out for many years - much to the disgust of TT fans. Rumbles of discontent could often be heard as motorcyclists queued on the dockside to have their tanks emptied, and many were the rumours as to what actually happened to all the precious petrol 'stolen' from their machines.

*

Most of the bikes being raced in 1947 were of pre-war manufacture and one writer later described it as *'the greatest Vintage meeting of all time',* but the FIM's decision in late 1946 to ban supercharging meant that some of the more exotic pre-war models were missing. Other pre-war models had been subject to redesign, whilst planned 250cc supercharged four-cylinder models from Benelli and Gilera were shelved. Amongst the new sights was the AJS parallel flat-twin Porcupine with spikey cooling fins covering its gear-driven double overhead camshaft engine. Unfortunately, the initial design of the Porcupine took place during the war and was for a supercharged model. Although it went on to perform very well in post-war years, it never really seemed to meet its design potential. Meanwhile, Norton introduced improved telescopic front-forks, but Velocette still ran with girders.

Clubman's Race

As well as the traditional Senior, Junior and Lightweight races that attracted 105 entries, an introduction at the 1947 TT was a Clubman's race of National status for riders of road-based sports machines. This was probably a development of the proposal for a 'Roadster-Machine' race that the ACU considered just after the 1939 TT. The Clubman's race regulations varied over the years but riders were generally allowed to use racing tyres and straight-through exhausts, although megaphones were banned. For some of the races, lights and stands had to be removed and footrest and control positions could be modified. One particularly testing requirement was that riders had to kick-start their machines at the start of the race and after their compulsory pit-stop. The intention behind the introduction of the Clubman's event was to encourage race participation by more manufacturers of sports machines.

Each rider in the Clubman's races was entered by

Les Graham offers a good view of the 1949 version of the twin-cylinder AJS Porcupine as he rounds Quarter Bridge.

A few of the many sporting dealers who advertised in the motorcycling magazines at TT time.

his local motorcycle club, and as new motorcycles were in very short supply (most going for export to earn foreign currency), the clubs usually had to prevail upon their local sporting motorcycle dealer to ensure that their rider was mounted on a current model. It was often a condition of supply that the bike went back to the dealer after the race, so that he could sell it on. Whilst he could hardly claim that it had had *'one careful owner'*, the fact that it had been raced on the Island would usually be an attraction to buyers.

*

Opening practice for the 1947 TT took place on the morning of Monday 29th May. First man away in the just breaking dawn was privateer Les Higgins on a Velocette. It was a nostalgic moment for Les and for many of those watching, for he had been first away at the start of 1939 TT practice, eight years earlier.

*

Although the race organisers always tried to make the maximum amount of time available for practice, it was rarely enough for everyone. In 1947 the Clubman's classes were given only 4 sessions, and that was hardly sufficient for newcomers to learn the demanding Mountain Course. Come race time and the three Clubman's classes were run concurrently, Seniors and Juniors did 4 laps and Lightweights did 3.

*

Prize money was reported as being £250 for first place in each International TT race in 1947 (although in later years it was £200), and £50 for a class win in the National Clubman's race.

*

It was not a happy return to TT racing for top runner Freddie Frith. Out in practice on his very rapid Moto Guzzi 500 twin, he had the front brake lock on the approach to Ballacraine. His subsequent lengthy flight through the air and impact with a roadside curb served to break his shoulder and ruin most of his racing season.

*

Race victories at the 1947 TT went to established pre-war runners. Harold Daniell (Norton) took the Senior, Bob Foster (Velocette) the Junior, and Manliff Barrington (Moto Guzzi) the Lightweight. Each may have had 8 years taken out of their racing careers, but they were good enough to come back and win. In the Clubman's classes the winners were Senior, Eric Briggs (Norton), Junior, Denis Parkinson (Norton) and Lightweight, Bill McVeigh (Triumph).

*

Seasoned MGP competitor Jack Cannell (father of current TT commentator Geoff Cannell) was amongst the fancied runners in the Senior Clubman's class at the 1947 TT and, noticing his good performances during practice, Triumph factory personnel offered to look over his Grand Prix model prior to the race. Jack did not ask what they had done to the bike, but he soon found out what they had not done when the carburettor fell off at Ballacraine on the first lap. Jack completed the race by lashing the carb back into place with his bootlaces, but Triumph's error robbed him of a possible win.

Advice for Newcomers

Conscious perhaps that the early post-war period would see many newcomers entering the Island races, the weekly magazine 'Motor Cycling' published a booklet: 'If I Were You . . .'. It was written by its TT-winning Editor, Graham Walker. In the booklet he took newcomers through mental attitude to the races, machine preparation, learning the Course, pit-stop procedures and many other items useful to first timers. He advised: *'Regard yourself in your first year as serving an apprenticeship . . . don't be drawn into time and attention-wasting scraps (during practice) . . . it is better to enter a corner slow and leave it fast than vice versa'.* He warned that: *'odd things happen in the Island with cambers . . . apt to lose ground clearance with remarkable rapidity',* and, at racetime: *'crowds of spectators at, and on, the approach to corners can change its appearance and may mask previously learnt braking points',* also: *'towards the end of a race the nearside of the rear tyre will be covered in oil thrown off by the chain'.*
After recommending that: *'the drinking of beer or stout in moderation will do more good than harm - but lay off the spirits',* he went on to give his own tried and tested pre-race breakfast recipe: *'two eggs beaten up in a pint of milk and laced with a double brandy, the delightful concoction being taken precisely two hours before starting time'.*

*

To the Manx people it must have seemed that their Island had become a permanent race-track in the early summer of 1948. The week before the TT period was 'Motor Car Racing Week' (using a round-the-houses circuit in Douglas and Onchan), then there was the TT proper taking just over two weeks and this was followed by 'Cycle Racing Week'. All involved road closures of one sort or another. The Manx press explained the locals' acceptance of the inconvenience with: *'Manxmen have TT racing in their blood, and many of us look forward eagerly to those annual meetings with old acquaintances who come here year after year, some on business, some just because away back along the years they were bitten by the TT bug and have simply got to come to the Island at this time'.*

*

With racing re-established, the days before practice started saw every boat to the Island bring a cargo of racing bikes. After making the sea crossing on deck, the bikes were swung ashore in batches by the busy harbour cranes while worried owners and riders watched with bated breath and crossed fingers.

*

In the early post-war era very few riders possessed vans. Many would bring their bikes by rail to Liverpool and then wheel them onto the boat. Luggage would often be sent 'in advance'. The few that did own vans rarely brought them to the Island. Most left them at garages in Liverpool, a favourite being the premises of former TT rider and motorcycle dealer Victor Horsman.
Lack of their own four-wheeled transport even extended to some of the motorcycle factories. Norton brought 63 cases of spares and equipment to the Island to support the 1948 TT. Although the 'works' lorry probably took them from the factory to Birmingham Station, thereafter they would have been moved by porters and dockers.

*

The 1948 Senior Clubman's TT had an excellent entry and included machines from many British makers.

Phil Heath took second place in the 1948 Senior Clubman's TT on his Vincent HRD. Supplied by Harold Avery Ltd it was carefully prepared and was fast and handled well. Phil didn't worry too much about its tendency to ground its primary chaincase cover on bumpy left-handers and thoroughly enjoyed his ride. New machines were in very short supply in 1948 and immediately after the TT it went to Ross Motors of Hinckley to be sold. The photograph shows Phil about to deliver it to Hinckley.

Ten Vincent HRD riders decided to pit their 1000cc machines against the Mountain Course in the Clubman's and nine finished the race (the other threw it away at Hillberry), thus giving a useful demonstration of both reliability and speed. The Stevenage Twins took the overall win and several high places. Some of the opposition, who pre-race had ridiculed the big-twins as too heavy and cumbersome for the TT Course, were afterwards heard protesting that it was unfair to use 1000cc against their 500s.

*

An early post-war tale told by Cyril Quantrill (Editor of several motorcycle magazines down the years) concerned an early Series 'B' Vincent Rapide that Charlie Markham of 'Motor Cycling' had with him on the Island for test. Many well-known names from the world of motorcycling were over for the TT and several took the opportunity to try the new model, particularly those staying at the Castle Mona Hotel. All were impressed by the power, handling and braking, and the TT Course was the ideal place for them to put the Twin through its paces.

The Island drew big-name variety acts during the summer season and staying at the Castle Mona was George Formby. He had a genuine enthusiasm for motorcycles, owning an Ariel Red Hunter and Norton International among other machines. Of course, he was shown the Vincent and was clearly taken with it as he listened to accounts of its performance. George was a star entertainer of the day with a high income and his associates (one hesitates to say "minders") made it clear that trying the Vincent was not on. One can imagine that the "minders" and the motorcyclists at the Castle Mona were like oil and water, and it is pretty certain that the motorcyclists considered it unfair on George that he was prevented from having a ride on the Vincent. The situation offered something of a challenge, and a plan was devised with George to spirit him from his hotel room just before daybreak. This was achieved and they joined a group of co-conspirators outside the Castle Mona. From there they went up to the Mountain Mile and, in the just breaking dawn, George Formby, in borrowed Stormcoat and hat, had his sought after ride on the Rapide. After a couple of wind-swept but satisfying blasts up and down the Mountain, a delighted George was, according to Quantrill, successfully returned to Douglas and his room at the Castle Mona. He later bought a Vincent twin!

Testing the Winners

It was customary for racing firms like Norton and Velocette to make their race-winning machinery available for appraisal by the two best known magazines of the day, 'The Motor Cycle' and 'Motor Cycling'. This usually occurred early on the morning after a race, somewhere on the Mountain section of the Course. There a trusted representative of each magazine would take the previous day's TT winning machine for a blast and report his findings to the ordinary motorcyclists who purchased the magazine and who could only dream of such an experience. One TT rider who went on to become a journalist was Vic Willoughby. His race experience stood him in good stead when it fell to him to carry out the enviable job of testing TT winning machines and reporting the results in the pages of 'The Motor Cycle'.

*

Ultra keen to ride in the 1948 TT was Australian, Eric 'Mouse' McPherson, who travelled 13,000 miles for the pleasure. Spending 4 weeks on a steamer to reach Marseilles, he then travelled overland to the Island, arriving almost a week before practice started in order to familiarise himself with the course. Going out in the first official practice, 'Mouse' completed a lap in 32 minutes but on his second lap he took a simple fall at Governor's Bridge, damaged his pelvis, and put himself out of the race. Although his long-cherished dream of a TT ride remained unfulfilled in 1948, he returned in 1949 & 1950 to record creditable performances in both Senior and Junior races. In those days before regular air-travel, a rider like 'Mouse' had to commit three months of the year for the round trip from down-under to the Island to ride in the TT - that's enthusiasm!

*

The Lightweight TT of 1948 saw its 26 competitors despatched on a massed start, and victory went to Maurice Cann (Moto Guzzi). Maurice's privately tuned Guzzis were often faster than the factory's race machines and, importantly, they held together. There were only 6 finishers in this race.

*

AJS brought their new 350cc 7R model to the Junior race. Distinctive with its relatively simple single-cylinder, chain-driven ohc engine finished in a gold-coloured corrosion-inhibiting paint, it shared the same bore and stroke as Velocette's Mk VIII (74x81mm), made use of heavily ribbed magnesium alloy crankcases and hubs, had a modified Porcupine-style swinging-arm frame and weighed

Maurice Cann with his privately-owned AJS 7R at the 1948 TT. His was the first 7R home when he finished 5th in the Junior race. He also won the Lightweight 250 race on his Moto Guzzi.

just under 300 lbs (135 kg). There were 25 of the new 7R models entered in the 1948 Junior TT but it was out-performed by the established Norton and Velocette marques.

One performance of great merit that did take place on an AJS 7R in 1948 was that of Geoff Murdoch. On that 350cc machine he took 4th place in the Senior race against the 500cc opposition. It was the nearest that anyone had come to emulating Howard Davies Senior race win on a 350 AJS in 1921. Geoff Murdoch later went on to become competitions Manager for Esso, a post in which he exercised considerable influence on the careers of many riders through the sponsorship deals and contracts he negotiated on behalf of Esso at the TT and elsewhere.

*

'Trade' support was still of vital importance to individual riders and to the race organisation. Dunlop was a major supplier of racing tyres in the 1940s and their Competions Manager, Dickie Davies, had an eight-man team to service the TT. Bringing their own benches, wheel-building equipment, cylinders of compressed air and publicity banners, they also brought sufficient tyres to cope with hundreds of racing motorcycles across the various classes. But there were no special wet weather tyres, variations in compound, or changing tyres mid-race in those days. In Dickie's words of the time: *'a rider uses one pair of tyres for practising and another pair for the*

race', but it was still a mammoth operation that also required Dunlop to provide tubes for the tyres, plus rim-tapes, security-bolts, balance-weights, etc. Although alloy rims had been used for racing pre-war, they came into more general use in the late 1940s and Dunlop was the main supplier to British riders.

Dunlop always had a man on duty when riders collected their bikes before a race, and he would check tyre-pressures and top-up where necessary. Another of the Company's services was to dispense large numbers of stout rubber bands (made of inner tube rubber), and on the start-line they could usually answer last-minute requests from competitors for french chalk to apply to their handlebar grips.

*

Another vital area of trade support came from suppliers of sparking plugs such as KLG. Riders required different plugs for warming-up the engine and for the race, and the variety of machines created a wide variation in demands which could also be affected by the weather. Today's plugs tend to be multi-purpose, and the procedure of warming-up with soft plugs and then, when the order comes for all competitors to stop engines, changing to harder plugs for the race, is less common than it used to be. One writer described such a pre-TT moment after the signal had been given to cut engines with: *'the silence was such that one could hear a hundred plug spanners clink, as racing plugs were fitted'.*

'Plug Chop'
Much can be discovered about an engine's operating condition from the expert 'reading' of a sparking plug when extracted immediately after a high speed 'plug-chop'. The variable petrol of the early post-war years made it doubly important to have the right sparking plug and carburettor settings. To assist riders with plug readings, a representative of KLG would sometimes position himself at the end of Sulby Straight during practice. Riders could then cut their engines at high-speed ('plug-chop'), pull in at the end of the Straight remove the plug and get an expert opinion.

Motorcycle manufacturers who tackle the TT races go to great pains to stress the technical excellence of their products, but the very nature of racing, where machines are stressed to their limits, means that failures are not uncommon. Understandably reluctant to admit to their own failings, it is not unknown for motorcycle makers to point the finger of blame at some subsidiary component like sparking plugs, brakes or ignition;

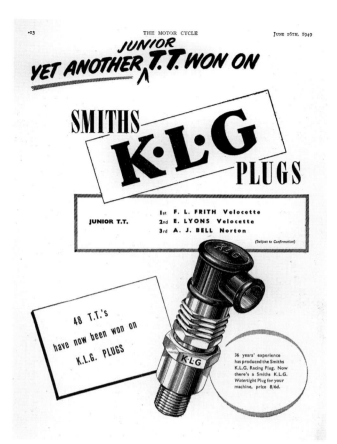

How KLG advertised their sparking-plugs at the 1949 TT.

much to the chagrin of the firms who supply the (allegedly) faulty parts.

*

Competitors seemingly had concerns about the reliability of the sparking plugs available in the 1930s and 40s and it was common practice for a rider to carry a spare plug in the pocket of his leathers and a plug-spanner tucked into the top of his boot.

The TT Course was still very bumpy and it was not unknown for the plug-spanner to be missing from the rider's boot at the end of the race. Some preferred to carry the spanner taped to a frame rail but this was outlawed in 1951 and spanners had to be carried in a container.

*

Treading the narrow line of delivering maximum performance from their engines, allied to reliability, was always an exciting and precarious business for manufacturers, particularly in the long and demanding TT races. Velocette came back to race with success in the early post-war years and Development Engineer for Veloce Ltd, Charles Udall,

A steady approach to Quarter Bridge for this Norton rider. Note the precautionary plug-spanner tucked in the top of his boot.

said: *'One of the most fascinating occupations in the motorcycle industry is that of obtaining the maximum power output, consistent with the necessary degree of reliability, from a given swept volume'.*

Former TT winner Henry Tyrell Smith worked on the development of Triumphs in post-war years and he considered: *'that a run of 5 hours at full throttle, at the revs at which maximum bhp is attained, will prove an engine to be capable of finishing the TT without trouble'.*

*

The 1948 MGP saw the introduction of 'round the course' commentaries via loudspeakers at eight locations. Prior to this, the race commentary could only be heard by those in the vicinity of the Grandstand.

*

On the approach to the 1949 TT, Tynwald (the Isle of Man's Parliament) considered the introduction of a tax on the temporary grandstands erected by private owners at popular vantage points. The aim was to recover some of the £10,000 that the Manx Government contributed to the cost of the races each year. The tax was not implemented.

*

Despite the fact that petrol was still in short supply for the ordinary motorcyclist, the number of visitors to the TT continued to grow.

Copies of 'The Motor Cycle' and 'Motor Cycling' were flown to the Island at TT time, so ensuring that TT visitors had their magazines at least a day before anyone else. The covers of such copies were usually over-printed *'Special Edition By Air'* by 'The Motor Cycle', with 'Motor Cycling' doing a similar thing

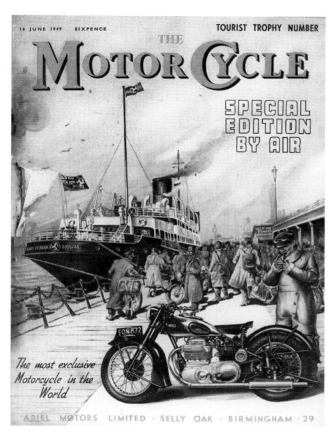

How the front cover of 'The Motor Cycle' represented the quay-side as the 'Lady of Mann' prepared to receive another load of early post-war TT-bound motorcyclists.

and adding *'Air Edition'* to the front of their Island-bound TT issues.

*

A newcomer to the BBC's race commentary at the 1949 TT was Murray Walker. It is perhaps not generally known that Murray competed with some distinction in off-road motorcycle sport at about the time he started his career as a commentator.

*

Although they retained the custom of allowing the previous year's race winner to start on his own at number 1, in 1949 the organisers decided to despatch the remainder in pairs at 20 second intervals. Also new for 1949 was the creation of a 1000cc Clubman's class to augment the original Senior (500cc) and Junior (350cc) Clubman's classes. Although very popular with competitors, the Clubman's races failed to grip spectators in the way that the out-and-out racing machines did.

*

The Junior TT had 100 entries but only 3 different makes of machine: 38 AJS, 27 Norton and 35 Velocette. It was a thrilling race in which AJS held the lead in the early stages and threatened to overturn the long-established supremacy of Norton and Velocette. Unfortunately, AJS star riders Les Graham and Bill Doran struck trouble and this let 40 year old Freddie Frith through for a win on his Velocette with its improved but ageing dohc engine.

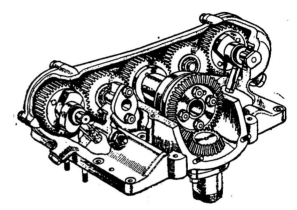

Valve-gear of Freddie Frith's 1949 Junior TT winning Velocette.

World Champions

Les Graham, along with the other AJS 'works' riders was forced to add the AJS logo to the front of his helmet for the 1949 races. Les initially refused, for it was a topic about which he was superstitious. However, when orders came from 'on high' he complied with the Company's wish. The result was that not only did he retire from the Junior race when highly placed, he was also forced out of the lead in the Senior when the magneto shaft sheared just a few miles from the finish when he had a ninety second lead. Les pushed in to finish tenth, but AJS had lost the chance of a long-hoped for TT victory with their Porcupine model. After the TT he removed the logo and went on to take the inaugural World 500cc Championship.

*

Velocette still had a small 'works' racing team but they relied on a single-cylinder engine whose design could be traced back to 1924, and their competitive days were numbered. Freddie Frith won the first 350 World Championship for them in 1949 but said later: *'The TT was the Blue Riband of racing then, worth more than a World Championship to people in the sport'.* The 1949 Junior was Freddie's fifth win on the Island (TT and MGP) and he retired at the end of the season. Wins in the other classes continued to go to established pre-war names like Harold Daniell

(Senior) who gave Norton their twenty-second TT win, and Manliff Barrington (Lightweight) on a highly-tuned Moto Guzzi that was reckoned not to come on the 'megga' until 6,000 rpm. The theme of established riders taking the highest places was repeated for all podium-men, their average age being 36, but the Senior Clubman's class saw a win for a relatively new name on the road-racing scene, 26 year old Geoff Duke.

*

** GEOFF DUKE **

Most people regard Geoff Duke's win in the 1949 Senior Clubman's as his first Isle of Man competition success, but that ignores the fact that before (and to some extent during) his road-racing career he was a top-flight off-road rider, competing on 'works' machinery in Trials and Scrambles for Norton, Ariel and Royal Enfield. He actually made his Isle of Man competition debut at the time of the 1948 TT in an off-road event, taking a fine second place in the Peveril MCC's TT Scramble held in front of thousands of spectators on a track near Windy Corner. (He had entered for the 1948 Senior Clubman's TT but was rejected for lack of road-race experience.)

Although he had a successful off-road competition career, Geoff Duke became a public personality and a household name in Britain through his road-racing exploits. Gaining an entry on a 350 for the 1948 MGP he failed to finish after leading the race, but his efforts on the Island in 1949 and 1950 saw him rocket to the top of the road-racing tree. After winning the Senior Clubman's of 1949 he returned to the MGP to win the Senior and take second in the Junior. Moving on to the 1950 TT he again took a record-breaking Senior win on the new featherbed Norton (with Artie Bell second) and second place in the Junior (behind Bell).

A pioneer of one-piece racing leathers, Geoff was a stylish rider who rode in a further 9 TT races, winning 4 of them, coming 2nd and 4th, and retiring 3 times. It was a tremendous achievement and, to add to his TT successes, he also took four 500cc and two 350cc World Championships with Norton and Gilera.

Geoff's racing career can best be summed-up by use of the title of his autobiography 'In Pursuit of Perfection'. He later moved to the Isle of Man and developed many business interests.

Geoff Duke (Norton) at Parliament Square, Ramsey, on his way to winning the 1951 Junior TT.

A man whose racing career ran alongside that of Geoff Duke for a few years and who also eventually 'retired' to live on the Isle of Man was Robin Sherry. His motorcycling started in the armed forces (again similar to Duke's) and his first Clubman's was also in 1949 where he finished *somewhere about 8th* on a Triumph. Going on to race the Triumph in the 1949 MGP, Robin told in 'Classic Legends' how: *a conrod broke and cut the engine in half. It happened on those fast bends after Handley's - no warning, bang! All the crankcase was chopped off, bits were swinging in the wind against my legs. It was a horrible sight, all the metal embedded in the road'*. In 1951 he won the Junior MGP with a non-stop ride on an AJS 7R and brought the prototype G45 Matchless twin into 4th place in the Senior. He helped with riding development of the G45 and the Porcupine, rode Nortons in 1952 and broke world records with Vincents at Montlhery the same year. Although he achieved 'works' status with AJS and probably could have gone on to greater things, Robin did not take kindly to being told what to do within a team and, setting up his own garage business, he soon turned his back on the sport and the opportunities that many less talented racers could only dream of. In later years he spent 10 years as a respected Travelling Marshal at the TT and MGP.

*

Most people accept that racing is an expensive business, but in 1949 'The Motor Cycle' reported that *'It is more expensive than outsiders fancy. For example, a suit of leathers is apt to cost anything up to £25'*.

*

Although the Race Control Tower at the Start and Finish area had been enlarged when the main Grandstand was refurbished after the war, in the late 1940s the ACU pressed the Manx authorities for an enlarged (and roofed) Grandstand, together with additional pit space and permanent buildings for the race organisation. It was to be a further 40 years before even part of their demands were met.

*

Seven makes of machine contested the 1950 Senior TT race. Norton dominated with 41 entries, then there were 11 AJS, 9 Triumphs, 7 Velocettes, 5 Vincents, 1 Moto Guzzi and 1 BSA.

*

The first practice was on a Thursday morning, and it was said that after the completion of their laps: *'early arrivals complained of bitter cold on the Mountain, and there was much finger-warming on dismounting in the enclosure'*. A quick rider who got out early at morning practice could put in three laps - if he could stand the

cold! Riders will confirm what early-morning spectators soon discover, that, perhaps surprisingly, June (TT) practice mornings are generally colder than August/September (MGP) ones.

An early morning practice shot at Creg ny Baa with G.P. Clark on his 1000cc Clubman's TT Vincent. Spectators obviously decided to stay in bed. This bike was already 5 years old when it took part in the Clubman's and belonged to the rider's brother who used it for travelling to work. Not only was owner Bill Clark glad to get it back in one piece, he was also still riding it over forty years later.

Helmet Inspection
During practice it was reported of a notorious ACU scrutineer: *'Vic Anstice looked like a street balloon-vendor when he returned to the Peveril Hotel on Saturday evening loaded with fifteen to twenty condemned crash-hats in all colours of the rainbow'*. Perhaps it was Anstice who in Vic Willoughby's words: *'put my "pudding basin" under his arm and, with an almighty tug, ripped out the inner harness. I protested that no prang could produce such a result but he insisted I should get another helmet. On a phoney pretext I persuaded him to release the damaged lid and took it to a cobbler who restitched the harness right through the shell. To camouflage the large stitches showing on the outside, I painted the whole thing black. Vic's helmet was accepted when next presented for inspection.* Checking of crash-helmets has always been part of the pre-race scrutineering process. As far back as 1925 it was written: *'the inspection yielded three helmets, all of which were in perfectly disgraceful condition, and would not even keep the rain out'*.

*

SPEEDS

When racing restarted after the Second World War speeds were noticeably down due to the effects of running on the low octane 'Pool' petrol that was mentioned earlier. With octane rating climbing to 80 in 1950 they began to increase. Bill Doran was fastest on the Sulby Straight at the 1951 TT, reaching 124.14 mph on his 500cc AJS that he brought into second place in the Senior race.

*

Bill Doran exits the dip at Governor's Bridge on his way to completing a lap of the 1951 Junior TT on his AJS 7R.

'The TT Special' continued to record average speeds on a stretch of the Sulby Straight and the published results were keenly scrutinised by everyone from the top 'works' rider to the privately entered Clubman. They were frequently the cause of debate and, occasionally, served to puncture the inflated claims that some riders made for their machine speeds.

*

In practice for the 1950 Clubman's, eventual winner Alex 'Jock' Phillip (Vincent) was fastest in the 1,000cc Class on his 3 year old, home-prepared, ride-to-work twin, when he was timed at 120 mph on the 'Sulby Mile'. Riding under a *nom de plume*, 'J Alexander' (Vincent) was next fastest at 110 mph on a new Black Shadow that he had ordered from Stevenage with the Clubman's race in mind. Not un-naturally, he was somewhat concerned as to why his unofficially 'works' prepared Black Shadow only averaged 110 mph, when Jock Phillip's home prepared 1947 machine with many thousands of ride-to-work and competition miles on the clock, managed 120 mph. Jock described the situation: *'On that particular afternoon the weather was good and the bike going really well. The real secret of a fast time on the Sulby Mile which included the last of the Quarry Bends, was to take these bends on the absolute limit! This gave you great momentum on the Sulby Straight and of course leaving your braking late was another great benefit. You can imagine my delight when The TT Special appeared with my bike averaging 120 mph with the mysterious J Alexander second fastest at 110 mph on the Works prepared Black Shadow. His immediate reaction was to take his bike to the Vincent* mechanics with the blunt instructions "I simply must have more knots". We nicknamed him Knots Alexander after that. He then asked me "Now then Jock don't tell me if you don't want to but just what maximum speed are you getting on Sulby?" I replied jokingly "to be honest I've never really been flat out" but I said, "if you really want a fast speed on Sulby you must take Quarry Bends absolutely on the limit then leave your braking until the last possible moment". His next question was "right then Jock, just where is your braking point before Sulby Bridge?" I said quite honestly "I genuinely never have any specific braking points and just rely on natural instinct. My danger point is when I see Marshals jumping out of the way!" The following article appeared in the next issue of Motor Cycling. "The mysterious J Alexander approached Sulby Bridge at a tremendous speed, unfortunately he left his braking far too late and was unable to take the corner - mercifully the slip road gate was open and the rider shot through and landed in the small river. As he did not have his fishing tackle and was fortunately uninjured he had to return to Douglas!"

*

An all-action shot of Alex 'Jock' Phillip during his winning ride in the 1,000cc Clubman's race of 1950.

Fastest times recorded at Sulby in the other Clubman's classes at the 1950 TT were: Senior 111 mph, Junior 103 mph, and Lightweight 89 mph.

*

In the same year's MGP, Don Crossley was fastest in the Junior at 112.50 mph on his AJS, whilst Harold Clark managed 116.13 mph on his Senior Norton.

It is hardly surprising that Alex 'Jock' Phillip set the fastest Clubman's time in 1950 for in another report from practice it was told that at the spectator-thronged Highlander *'He brought the house to its feet with a simply staggering performance. He took the whole section - down the hill, across the bump and out to Greeba Castle bends - with the throttle hard against the stop. The sight of the thousand twin roaring through the air compelled even the oldest inhabitant to confess that he'd never known anything like it'.* Alex and his Vincent went on to win the race.

*

Customers at The Highlander had always been able to combine drinking with spectating at what was one of the fastest parts of the Course, and there have always been a few devotees of the races who considered that TT stood for **T**avern to **T**avern.

*

Although the 1950 TT competitors were allowed to use petrol of 80 octane (except the Clubman's classes who were still on pump petrol), the fact that samples of the new fuel were not available until shortly

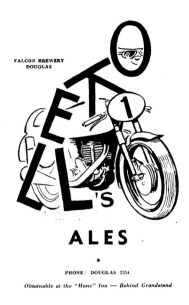

TT visitors consume their share of the local Okell's ales.

Harold Daniell collects his thoughts as he sits astride his featherbed-framed Norton before the start of the 1950 Senior TT. He earned the right to the number one plate by winning the previous year's race. Even 'works' riders like Daniell carried a plug-spanner tucked into the top of a boot.

before the races restricted the opportunities for engine 'tuners' to experiment and make the most of it. In perfect weather conditions on Senior race-day, Geoff Duke put the new petrol and his new feather-bed framed Norton with improved engine to good use by setting a new outright lap record of 93.33 mph. This beat the figure of 91.00 mph set by Harold Daniell (Norton) way back in 1938.

Norton 'Unapproachable'

Norton took 1st, 2nd and 3rd places in both the Senior and Junior races at the 1950 TT at record breaking speeds, and it was a year in which they truly lived up to the Company's long-standing slogan of 'Unapproachable'.

Norton employees were keen to share the successes of the motorcycles they helped to build and they organised their own trips to watch the TT races. Some 200 were estimated to have attended the Senior in the late 1940s. Given that most of the rest of the Norton work-force would listen to the radio commentary, little work got done at the Bracebridge Street factory on race-days.

*

The races were as popular as ever with the general public as the 1940s moved into the 1950s, particularly as petrol came off the ration in 1950 - although there were complaints about the cost having risen to 3 shillings (15p) for a gallon.

*

The majority of spectators travelled to the TT by boat, and the arrangements for 1951 were typical of the time. Besides the spectators who were fortunate enough to be on the Island for a one or two week holiday, the Steam Packet Co. put on seven midnight steamers to bring thousands of excursionists over just for the Friday Senior TT. Immediately after the race, seven steamers left for Liverpool and two for Fleetwood. In the period from the finish of the Senior race on Friday afternoon to early Monday morning, over 40,000 visitors were shipped back to the adjacent isles. For most people, holiday periods in the early 50s were far more regimented by their employers than they are today. You could take a week or a fortnight (probably your entire annual holiday allocation) but part weeks or extra days were usually out of the question, unless you were self-employed or could somehow arrange a sick-note. As has been seen however, the general restraint on taking casual days off was not enough to prevent those seven packed ferry loads of enthusiasts making the trip for Senior race day. There were of course plenty of people whose holidays were restricted entirely to a period prescribed by their employers - the Works Fortnight - that fell completely outside the TT period. They never got the opportunity to see the races, although they may have been amongst the many people who listened to the BBC's broadcasts, not only in the UK but also world-wide.

*

A 'works' ride was a dream come true for most competitors and in 1951 AJS signed promising young rider Mick Featherstone to ride 350 and 500cc bikes at the TT and selected International meetings. It is interesting to see that under the terms of their contract he kept prize money and trade bonuses, whilst the company retained start money. If his winnings were less than £1,000 by the end of the season, AJS guaranteed to make up the shortfall. In his only year in the TT he took fourth in the Junior on the 7R but retired the Porcupine in the Senior.

*

There were 13 practice periods for the 1951 TT of which 5 were for the National Clubman's classes and 8 for the International TT races that had been extended to include a Lightweight 125 cc class. The Lightweight Clubman's class was dropped. The new Lightweight 125 class attracted entries from several speedy foreign 'tiddlers' like Mondial, MV Agusta and Montesa, but it soon became clear in practice that the majority of British 125s would not be able to meet the 40 minute qualifying time for their race. Fortunately, the race-stewards agreed to increase it to 45 minutes.

*

Castor oils (such as Castrol 'R') were used by almost the entire entry for engine lubrication. Although Castrol 'R' has always been the best known variety, all the other manufacturers were able to supply a castor-based oil.

*

A good privateer of the late 1940s and early 1950s who made his living from racing was Phil Heath. He had an entry in the Junior and Senior classes of the 1951 TT but, come Junior race-day he suffered one of his recurring attacks of malaria (contracted on war-time service in the Far East). Normally these were not too severe: *'a slight giddiness which lasted 24 hours and as long as I stayed in bed or sat quietly and didn't move my head from side to side I was okay'.* It was a hardly a condition suitable for a rider to put in seven racing laps of the TT Course, but Phil was reluctant to lose his ride in the Junior event. Acknowledging that he shouldn't have raced, he recalls: *'I started okay and as* long as I kept my head steady looking straight ahead I could cope. Once I thought I heard a funny noise in the transmission and looked down, whereupon everything went topsy turvy but quickly I managed to get back to normal'. He felt very shaky at his pit-stop, had difficulty restarting, but once under way, he pressed on to the finish. Understandably riding slower than usual, he completed the race in 17th place. Although not well enough to attend the prize-giving ceremony held the same evening, he assured a concerned member of the local press from his 'sickbed' at the Howstrake Hotel that, by dosing himself with quinine, he would be fit for the Senior race. In the event, although he was fit to ride the entire race, his motorcycle only managed one lap.

Phil Heath takes Bray Hill in fine style during the 1952 Senior TT.

RPM

A rather more successful 1951 TT was enjoyed by Geoff Duke who won both Senior and Junior classes at record speeds on 'works' Nortons that were reputedly revving to over 8,000. Duke and Norton formed a powerful combination that proved too much for the opposition, and he became the first man to lap at over 90 mph on a 350 machine. The Lightweight 250cc was won by Tommy Wood (Moto Guzzi) who could safely use up to 8,500 rpm (but restricted himself to 8,000) and the Lightweight 125cc by Cromie McCandless on a Mondial. Cromie led Mondials into the first four places. He was taking his 13 bhp-engined bike up to 10,000 rpm on the level and touching 11,000 on some downhill stretches. All races were blessed with ideal weather and record crowds.

*

With their first four places in the Lightweight 125 race Mondial looked certain to take the Manufacturer's Team Award. Only one thing prevented them from doing so - they'd forgotten to enter in that category. The award went to D.O.T. with their Villiers powered two-strokes.

*

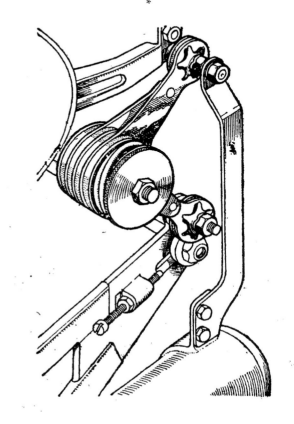

By the early 1950s all TT machines were now fitted with rear suspension that used twin hydraulic units and combinations of oil, air and springs to handle compression and damping, but Moto Guzzi retained the combination of springs and friction dampers that they pioneered in the mid-1930s.

Geoff Duke's Senior-winning Norton finished with an oily rear tyre - the last thing you would want on a racing machine! Incredible as it may seem to modern thinking, where all bikes have enclosed, gear-driven primary drives; racing machines of the 50s had exposed primary drive chains that were lubricated by a drip-feed of oil. This lubricant didn't confine itself to the chain of course and in an attempt to stop it reaching the rear-tyre it was common practice to fix an absorbent felt to the lower frame tube where it passed under the primary drive. It was a crude arrangement and not totally effective.

The clutches on race machines required air-cooling, but unlubricated primary chains ran much hotter than a roadsters that would be enclosed in an oil-bath. Failure to provide continuous lubrication to the primary would bring about early failure during a TT race, whereas thorough pre-race treatment with a lithium-based grease allowed the final drive chain to go the whole race without supplementary lubrication.

Although it was acceptable for chains on road-going bikes to be joined with a connecting link, for racing bikes a connecting link was considered a potential weakness. Renold chains always had representatives on hand to rivet the chains of racers before practice and racing.

*

Many riders sought to get two rides at the TT by entering a 350 in both the Junior and Senior classes, but in 1951 the race regulations specified that machines for the Senior race had to be from 351-500cc. This resulted in a rash of entries of 352cc bikes, and amongst them was veteran Bill Beevers. Bill had trouble in the Senior race on his '352' but eventually reached the finish, only to be challenged by Scrutineer Vic Anstice over the true engine size of his Norton. Admitting that it was only 346cc he was disqualified for having too small an engine. Bill was not impressed with this show of officialdom but consoled himself with the fact that he had at least managed to achieve his sought after second ride.

TTRA

From an idea mooted early in 1951 the TT Riders Association was formed in November of that year. Reuben Harveyson was the first Secretary and its objectives were to be *'purely social or benevolent in character'*. It is still going strong under the guidance of current Secretary, Allan Robinson, who took over in 1982.

*

The perennial topic of how much the ongoing improvements to the Mountain Course had contributed to Geoff Duke's high speeds at the 1951 TT was given an airing after the race and, predictably, no one could provide an accurate answer. An interesting twist was given to the usual arguments by Graham Walker. He speculated on the effect of changes to the Course since the first race was run over the Mountain in 1911. Winner Oliver Godfrey's average race speed was 47.63 mph and, with the use of his own practical experience and a good deal of imagination, Walker estimated that if Geoff Duke had been forced to ride his 1951 500cc 'works' Norton on the Course in 1911, he would have been pressed to average more than 62 mph - his average speed in 1951 was 93.83 mph.

A year later it was Geoff Duke who was addressing the issue of speed. In particular, he considered how many of the Mountain Course's 37 $^3/_4$ miles could be ridden with the grip hard against the stop in top gear. He reckoned the figure to be 15.2 miles, the longest continuous stretch being from Union Mills to Greeba Castle, a distance of 2.8 miles.

Bill Beevers rode in 42 TT races (solo and sidecar). Here he wheels his 350 Norton out for a damp practice session.

Chapter 6
THE ITALIAN CHALLENGE

The early 1950s saw British-built single-cylinder Nortons maintain their dominance of the Senior and Junior classes at the TT, even though the twin-cylinder AJS Porcupine of Bill Doran threatened in the 1951 Senior where it put up its best ever performance by finishing second. But British race fans were also aware of the challenge to Norton's supremacy from Italian twin-cylinder Moto Guzzis in the hands of riders like Bob Foster, and of the growing threat from the multi-cylinder machines of Gilera and MV Agusta. Graham Walker, in his role as Editor of 'Motor Cycling' wrote at the time: *'the supremacy of the single will probably be short-lived, but it will provide data which should make British multi-cylinder machines unbeatable in the world's classic events in due course'*. Those were the words of a man who correctly forecast the way ahead but who mistakenly assumed that British manufacturers would take the correct road.

Lightweights
Italian machinery already dominated in the Lightweight field, being victorious in each of the 6-lap massed-start Lightweight 250cc TT races through the late 1940s with bikes from Moto Guzzi and Benelli. In 1951 the 250cc race was reduced to 4 laps and reverted to an interval start. A 125cc race over 2 laps was introduced and the first four places went to the Italian Mondial marque whose ultra-lightweight racers were powered by high-revving dohc engines. Race distance for the 125s was increased to 3 laps the following year.

The road looks flat on the approach to Braddan Bridge but Len Parry has both wheels of his 125cc Mondial off the ground as he rides to third place in the 1952 TT.

The exciting single and twin-cylinder ohc Italian machines continued to dominate the Lightweight races, taking all the 125 and 250cc TT wins through the 1950s except for 1954 when German NSUs won both classes. Machines from the Italian Benelli, Moto Guzzi, Mondial and MV Agusta factories all had victories and monopolised the leader-boards, whilst Ducati tried for a share of the spoils in the latter part of the decade.

*

British factories did not produce a racing 125 or 250 at the time, (although Velocette had an experimental dohc 250). As 'The Motor Cycle' described it: *'national interest in the 250cc has touched rock-bottom'*. A few private runners campaigned pre-war 250 Velocettes or Excelsiors, and in some cases their own home-built racers but, although they put in creditable performances (Ron Mead finished 3rd on his 250 Velo in 1950), they dropped further 'off the pace' each year and finished well behind the Italian models. It was all very different from the pre-war Lightweight scene where, until the mid-1930s, British-built Rudge, Excelsior and New Imperial machines were usually able to beat their continental Lightweight challengers.

*

Had the rider of a British-built Lightweight been in a position to win a TT in the 1950s it is unlikely that he would have received a telegram of the sort sent to 1952 Lightweight 250 winner, Moto Guzzi-mounted Fergus Anderson. The President of Moto Guzzi, Dr. Giorgio Parodi telegraphed to Fergus: *'Bravo. Bravissimo. I kiss you'*.

*

Cecil Sandford gave MV Agusta its first TT win with his victory in the three-lap Lightweight 125 class in 1952. His double overhead camshaft, single-cylinder engine developed maximum power at 10,800 rpm and could reach 100 mph under favourable conditions. The Mondials of Carlo Ubbiali and Len Parry were second and third.

Heavyweights
The Italians were not satisfied with dominating just the Lightweight scene and MV Agusta brought their 500cc four-cylinder machine to challenge for the 1951 Senior TT. The machine was entered in the name of rider Jack Harding by Elmes Metals Ltd (Ernie

Les Graham on the 500cc four-cylinder MV Agusta at the 1951 TT. This photograph was taken during practice and shows (with 'C' plate) that he was riding as a reserve entry.

Earles), but 350cc World Champion Les Graham rode it for them. The MV retired from the Senior in 1951 but its inclined, across the frame engine with twin ohc and 'square' cylinder dimensions of 54 x 54 mm delivered 50 bhp @ 10,000 rpm, and its wailing exhaust note seemed to confirm the presence of abundant power. However, it was heavy and its handling left a lot to be desired.

An improved version of the four-cylinder MV from Gallarate returned in 1952 to take second place behind the winning Norton of Reg Armstrong. With Les Graham on board, the MV took over the lead in the closing stages after Geoff Duke retired his Norton with clutch trouble, but Armstrong fought back and snatched the victory. However, the luck of the Irish was with the Norton rider in that race, for as he crossed the finishing-line to beat the MV, the primary-chain snapped on his Norton. One of several post-war Irish racers who sported a shamrock on his helmet, Reg rode for Gilera the following year.

Norton 'Four'

Although still capable of winning the Senior TT with its single-cylinder Manx model, the Norton Company was aware that the future lay with multi-cylinder machines. In conjunction with the BRM car-racing firm it produced a design and preliminary castings for a compact four-cylinder, water-cooled, transversely mounted dohc engine with unit gearbox built in. Although a slave 125cc engine was built and subjected to bench testing - claimed to have delivered 11.5 bhp @ 13,000 rpm - Norton's proposed counter to the Italian multi-cylinder threat got no further.

A 'Motor Cycling' sketch of the proposed four-cylinder Norton racer.

It was not just MV Agusta which challenged the long-held dominance of the singles in the 500cc class, for the 500cc four-cylinder Gilera proved its worth by winning the World Championship in 1950 (a feat it repeated in 1952-55 and 1957), but it did not contest the Senior TT until 1953. By then the 'fire-engine' from Arcore with five-speed gearbox was putting out some 60 bhp at 10,000 rpm and with a three-man team comprised of past TT winners Geoff Duke and Reg Armstrong plus Alfredo Milani, the Gilera concern expected to win. However, although the Italians were fast getting to know all about four-cylinder power output, they still had some way to go to match the handling of a Norton Featherbed around the demanding TT Mountain Course. Geoff slid off his Gilera at Quarter Bridge on the fourth lap whilst leading the race, damaged his petrol tank and retired. This left Ray Amm (Norton) in the lead, and although he also slid off - at Sarah's Cottage on the last lap (and broke a footrest) - he remounted to win. Jack Brett brought his Norton into second place and Reg Armstrong was third on his Gilera.

*

Racing has always been about developing and improving machines to try and get ahead of the opposition. Seeking improvements to handling, MV Agusta experimented with Earles type front forks on all their race bikes. The MV did not have the easy-on-the-eye looks of a Manx Norton and could not match the Norton for handling, however, it returned for a crack at the 1953 Senior. Les Graham was the MV team leader and he came to the start of the Senior with one win already under his belt (the Lightweight 125cc) and a retirement in the Junior. On the second lap of the Senior Race, travelling at some 130 mph through the dip at the bottom of Bray Hill, Les lost control of his Earles-forked MV and crashed with fatal results.

George Brown was riding close behind Les Graham, and he watched mesmerised as Les fought unsuccessfully to control the wayward MV. George couldn't avoid the debris from the accident which burst into flames. He was flung from his Norton and finished in the branches of a roadside tree. Although he accepted it as a racing accident, George turned his back on racing and went sprinting and world speed record breaking, earning fame with the big Vincents that he named Nero and Super Nero.

Rising Stars
Despite (or perhaps because of) the danger of racing on the Mountain Course, there were plenty of entries

for the TT and MGP races in the early 1950s, with the MGP continuing to produce talented racers who went on to success at the TT. Names like Dave Chadwick, John Hartle, Derek Farrant and Bob McIntyre all took MGP and TT wins or podium places. 'Bob Mac' had his first Island race in the 1952 Clubman's TT where he finished second on an ailing BSA Gold Star. Riding in the MGP the same year on an AJS 7R, he won the Junior at a record race average speed of 85.73 mph for the 6 lap race. Two days later he contested the Senior MGP on the same Junior winning 7R. Growing familiarity with the Course enabled him to up the pace and average 87.67 mph in the Senior to take second place behind Derek Farrant on the twin-cylinder G45 Matchless, a racer developed from the G9 Matchless roadster.

*

Handsome but heavy, this is the twin-cylinder Matchless G45 in production form.

In the early 1950s visitors could still stay at large hotels like the Howstrake, Douglas Head, Falcon Cliff, Douglas Bay, etc. There they could rub shoulders with the 'works' teams who stayed at those same hotels and made use of their garages for race workshops.

*

For many a visitor their first lap of the TT Course on a motorcycle would be the fulfilment of a dream. Familiar names like Ballacraine, Ballaugh, Creg ny Baa and Governor's Bridge would become reality as the 37 ¾ miles unfolded beneath their wheels. Those who had been before were usually keen to put in an early lap and one such wrote in 1952: *'Immediate trip round the course at 6.30 a.m., passing a peacock, geese, two lots of cows and - on the Mountain - a Clubman's competitor on unofficial practice with a broken knee, a Norton and two dead sheep'.*

Alternative TTs
The Isle of Man Tourist Trophy races had a world-wide reputation and many other countries adopted

the title 'TT' and used it for their premier meetings, perhaps hoping that a little of the prestige and glory associated with the Island races would somehow be transferred to their events. One example was the Welsh TT. Somewhat removed from the one found on the Island, from 1922-27 it was a sand-race run on the wide-open spaces of Pendine beach and when it was revived in post-war years it was held at Eppynt, a former airfield.

Some of the more distant 'colonial' TT meetings were held over loose surfaced courses marked out with a few oil-drums. These were so different from the Isle of Man as to allow little comparison, but they were the making of many riders who went on to the TT 'proper' and rode the Mountain Course with distinction.

*

SPEEDS

'The TT Special' had used the Sulby Straight for its speed-timing for many years, but the other motorcycling magazines recognised that top-speed was also a topic of interest to their readers and they recorded figures on the fast drop past The Highlander between Crosby and Greeba Castle. The convivial atmosphere at The Highlander attracted members of the Press, the Trade and general public. Of a practice session at the 1952 TT it was reported: *'almost race-day crowds were gathered at this popular vantage-point to witness the winding-up of of the evening practising, the car-park opposite the pub and the new park in the adjacent field being jammed solid with coaches, cars and motor bikes'.* In another description that was full of TT atmosphere, renowned motorcycle engineer Phil Irving said of his first visit to the spot, *'at the popular Highlander, there was nothing between the riders and the customers but the glasses of Manx ale held in their hands'.* A large hump on the crest of the hill before The Highlander and further bumps on the curving downhill stretch tended to keep speeds slightly below maximum, whilst serving to provide increased spectator interest in the handling capabilities of the various makes of racing machine on view. Fastest that particular evening in 1952 were: Senior, Jack Brett, 126.80 mph, Junior, Bill Doran, 117.26 mph, Lightweight 250, Bruno Ruffo, 107.81 mph, Lightweight 125, Carlo Ubbiali, 97.57 mph.

*

'The TT Special' also timed riders down Bray Hill, and for those TT fans who wondered if the racers were really flat-out going down the Hill in the 1950s, (for it was difficult for the average motorcyclist to imagine that they could be), the figures obtained make for an interesting comparison with those achieved at The Highlander. The fastest speeds recorded over a half a mile stretch of the frightening descent of Bray Hill in 1952 were: Senior 127.69 mph, Junior 110.45 mph, and Lightweight 105.88 mph. Some riders got to know the location of speed-checks and rolled the throttle off a bit to 'fox' the opposition, but it is doubtful if fastest man down Bray, Jack Brett, was doing so on that occasion.

*

Riders were occasionally timed on the Mountain Mile, but as the stretch was subject to varying wind conditions it did not give truly comparable results. In 1951 when Bill Doran was fastest on Sulby Straight at 124.14 mph, he was timed at 133 mph along the Mountain Mile (with a very strong following wind).

*

Speeds continued to creep up as the following figures for Sulby Straight show. However, even there, true comparisons are difficult as conditions were rarely the same from one year to the next: 1952 TT - Senior, Les Graham (MV Agusta) 128.57 mph; Junior, Geoff Duke (Norton) 119.23 mph; Lightweight 250, Enrico Lorenzetti (Moto Guzzi) 111.82 mph; Lightweight 125, Carlo Ubbiali (Mondial) 91.85 mph.

The top men at the TT were generally quicker than those at the MGP where the best figures in 1952 were: Senior, Ken James (Norton) 122.48 mph; Junior, H.Pearce (Velocette) 113.95 mph.

In 1953 the effect of a strong side/tail wind at Sulby saw speeds of: Senior, Les Graham (MV Agusta) 137.43 mph; Junior, Jack Brett (Norton) 124.14 mph; Lightweight 250, Bill Lomas (NSU) 118.45 mph; Lightweight 125, Cecil Sandford (MV Agusta) 100.87 mph. The weather must have been similar at Sulby during the 1954 MGP when Geoff Tanner was clocked at 130.48 mph on his Senior Norton and Derek Antill managed 118.45 mph on his Junior AJS.

After one session of timing riders on the Sulby Straight the man from 'The TT Special' made his way to nearby Ginger Hall and afterwards wrote: *'Ginger Hall is a delightful spot for a pressman who wishes to combine speed with relaxation. He can sit on the steps of the hotel armed with a notebook, pencil and glass of ale - which is what this particular pressman did'.*

Another man who liked to call at the Ginger Hall for a refreshing pint between races was Travelling Marshal Jimmy Linskey. Now, a Travelling Marshal stopping and disappearing into the pub was not the sort of thing to escape the notice of the large number of spectators who usually gathered at Ginger Hall. On one occasion after downing a pint between races, Jimmy made a hash of getting back on the bike and finished in a heap on the floor. The result was a huge cheer from the crowd, several of who helped him to his feet, dusted him down and sent him off on his duties.

*

Reference was made above to the effect of wind on recorded top speeds. In their 37 ³/₄ mile circuits of the Mountain Course, riders find themselves travelling in all directions of the compass, so the benefit gained by having the wind behind on one stretch is usually cancelled out by having it in the face on another and as a cross-wind at other places. There probably is an optimum wind direction that offers the maximum benefit to lap speed; maybe it is the one that gives riders a push up the Mountain.

Fluctuations in wind speed and direction can bring about the need for changes of gearing, and its variable nature can make that a tricky decision. Well known tuner Francis Beart offered the advice; *'If at the end of practice you are not quite decided as to whether to go up or down half a tooth on the rear wheel sprocket, try and remember that the wind usually blows the wrong way on race day!'* Francis operated mostly in the days of four-speed gearboxes which made getting the right gearing ever more critical. No doubt he made a close study of the weather forecasts before making his final decisions.

*

The length and mixed terrain of the Mountain Course means that it is quite common to meet with varying weather conditions. During an early morning practice period for the Clubman's races in 1953 there was a strong wind and patches of mist on the Mountain, in Douglas it was raining hard and at Sulby it was dry and windless, but the bright rising sun was causing dazzle!

*

In the early 1950s riders began to dispense with using the old style tie-on number bibs that had been used for identification in both the TT and MGP races. During the 1930s the bibs were red, blue or green (relating to classes), although, with ACU approval, entrants could supply their riders with their own racing colours. With the spread of one-piece racing leathers in the early 1950s, it became the fashion for the piece of cloth with the rider's number upon it to be sewn onto the back of his leathers. Most one-piece leathers of the day incorporated a panel on the back for this purpose. The requirement to carry racing numbers on leathers was abandoned in 1978, for by then almost everyone carried race numbers on their fairings.

*

Visiting motorcyclists still had to pay for temporary Manx road tax when they reached the Island in the 1950s, (sometimes the formalities could be dealt with on the boat before arrival at Douglas) but, under the provisions of 'The Light Locomotives Temporary Licensing and Registration Order 1922 (Isle of Man)', race competitors could obtain exemption from paying duty on their machines, subject to some appropriate form-filling. This, of course, was at the time when the majority of competitors rode their bikes from their garages to the start of practice, and back at the finish. The use of vans was still uncommon. Even wheel-stands were a rare sight in the Paddock during the 1950s. It was customary for the organisers to provide a row of stout stakes for riders to lean their precious racers against.

Before the days when everyone used wheelstands, a Moto Guzzi mechanic parks one of the factory's racers against a post in the Paddock.

TT Garages

Many owners of private garages (and even business premises) in the Douglas and Onchan areas arranged to vacate all or part of them at TT and MGP time so that riders had somewhere to work on their machines. In return for such kindness, riders would bump-start their bikes outside their hosts' garages at 4.30 am and ride their unsilenced racers through the streets of Douglas up to the Grandstand for early morning practice! It was all illegal, as few were insured, but the police turned a blind eye. Thankfully, they also turned a deaf ear to the matter of noise (although in pre-war years they were not always so obliging, as several star riders discovered). After an accident involving a rider on an uninsured race bike in 1955, the police insisted from 1956 that machines had to have third-party insurance for riding to and from the Start. Eventually the organisers arranged this cover on behalf of riders.

*

Not all riders managed to get up for morning practice, but race officials and marshals had to be on duty. Concerned not to be a late riser, Travelling Marshal of the early 1950s Len Parry arranged with fellow marshal Fred Hawken (a reliable riser) to give him an early call. On retiring for the night in his hotel on the Promenade, Len would tie a piece of string around his foot and lower the other end out of his bedroom window. As Fred went past to where he garaged his bike, he would give the string a couple of sharp tugs to ensure that Len was awake.

NSU mechanics at work on their TT machines in a private garage on the Island.

Streamlining

In the quest for ever more speed, racing machines of the early 1950s began to be fitted with streamlining, something in which the Italian factories were well to the fore. There was little in the way of regulations to cover the topic but the FIM did insist that in the case of a rider falling off, he must be able to leave his machine. This ruled out the all-enclosing streamlining used by speed record breakers. It was a highly experimental business and many and varied were the early forms of enclosure. Starting with small fairings and screens to shield the rider, they gradually increased in scale to cover engine, front

Tarquinio Provini's Mondial shows its full streamlining as he speeds to victory in the 1957 Lightweight 125cc TT.

65

wheel, rear wheel and seat unit. Gilera, MV Agusta, Moto Guzzi, Mondial, NSU, and all the other top runners made use of such full enclosures. They were usually made of aluminium and were colloquially called 'dustbins'. Whilst streamlining generally increased a machine's speed, other benefits were that it improved fuel consumption and reduced rider fatigue. However, riders found that the customary benefit to be gained from engine braking was reduced, throwing more demands on the brakes and often requiring more use of the gearbox to slow for corners.

Norton seemed fully committed to the early experiments with streamlining, and they produced their share of outlandish shapes, including a long-nosed version nicknamed the 'proboscis'. As well as one or two variations on the 'proboscis' theme, they also produced a solo 'kneeler' in 1953 inspired by engineer Rex McCandless which Joe Craig called the Flying Dustbin. Then, at the end of the 1954 season, Norton suddenly declared themselves opposed to streamlining. Knowing that their machines would thus be outclassed the following year, they also declared that there would be no special 'works' models (they were working on mounting their engine horizontal in a new frame) and that they would only be supplying standard production racers. With Velocette having stopped manufacturing racing machines, the only other British racers (apart from one-off specials) were the AJS 7R and Matchless G45.

*

The early forms of full streamlining were not always suited to the TT Course, particularly in the windy conditions that could often be found on the Mountain. The result was that riders sometimes opted for just a small cockpit-fairing, so lessening the effect of strong side-winds.

Towards the end of the 1950s the FIM (who governed motorcycle sport) became concerned as to the way that streamlining was developing. In particular, they worried about the effects of sidewinds and about several unexplained accidents that could have been caused by the build-up of heat and fumes in the 'cockpit' affecting the rider. The result was that they banned the full 'dustbin' streamlining and permitted only the 'dolphin' type that left the front wheel exposed.

*

The introduction of streamlining was all part of the continued quest for increased performance that saw development of all parts of the racing motorcycle,

large and small. Racers needed to rev their engines to their prescribed limits when seeking maximum performance, but letting the revs go over the limit was a recipe for disaster. The chronometric type rev counters in use in the early 50s had a slight lag which meant that, under acceleration, actual engine revs were slightly higher than the figure shown on the dial. With the increase in high revving, fast accelerating engines, such inaccuracy was unacceptable. Accordingly there was a move to the use of magnetic rev counters that did away with the slight time-lag that occurred with the earlier chronometric pattern.

*

Norton used the image created by their racing successes in the advertising of their road-going machines.

1953 saw the last year of the 1,000cc Clubman's TT. This was despite the fact that there were over one million motorcycles on Britain's roads and that British manufacturers like Triumph, BSA, AJS/Matchless, Ariel, Royal Enfield and Vincent were all producing machines of over-500cc that might reasonably have been expected to show their sporting paces on the TT Course.

*

Last man away in the 1,000cc Clubman's race of 1953, Dick Madsen-Mygdal (Vincent) burns rubber as he rounds Quarter Bridge in pursuit of the rest of the field.

After looking at Dick Madsen-Mygdal's worn clutch dome, exhaust pipe and footrest rubbers after practice, one former TT competitor prophesied that he would do one of three things on race-day: *'throw it up the road, blow it up, or win the race'*. Dick was typical of many talented Clubman riders of the day. With holidays in short supply and a wish to get married as well as race, the two activities were combined and with his new wife on the pillion they set off on the Vincent for their first Island visit. A friend with a sidecar outfit was persuaded to bring a few of their additional bits and pieces with him. The set-up was the bare minimum with which to go racing and would be impossible to contemplate by today's competitors.

Having gone well in practice, the bike was treated to new tyres and plugs for the race. However, such pre-race expenditure stretched the newly-weds' finances to near the limit. Come race-day and it was a case of *'shall we, shan't we spend our last £5 on race insurance?'* Dick's wife, Stella, persuaded him to do so and it turned out to be a good investment.

Last man away but going into an early lead on corrected time, Dick had to pick off the 350cc runners

who had started ahead of the 'big uns'. All went well until the second lap when, approaching Brandywell very quickly, he shaped to take a slower rider on the outside. Instead of obeying the first law of racing and holding his line, the slower rider moved to the outside. Committed to pass but faced with a reducing gap, Dick eased as far to the right as possible and it seemed that he would get through. It was then that his wheels struck loose material in the rough outer edge of the road and the tyres lost their grip, throwing bike and rider down the road. The remainder of his TT and honeymoon were spent in a hospital bed. The bike was badly damaged in the crash but the last-minute insurance paid the £110 cost of having it repaired.

If the name Madsen-Mygdal sounds familiar to the present generation of TT enthusiasts, it will probably be due to the TT activities of Dick's son David, who has been an Island competitor for many years, with lots of Silver Replicas to his credit.

*

We are often fed with the derring-do and glamorous side of the activities of those in the racing spotlight but, as Dick Madsen-Mygdal's experience shows, there is another, darker side. Aiming to compete in the same race as Dick, another rider, Eric Ellis, came off in practice for the 1953 Clubman's just before Guthrie's Memorial on the Mountain climb. As a result, he was hospitalised for many months. In the latter part of the year, he wrote to friends: *'Even if I never stand up again I shall have no regrets. The 6 or 7 laps I did round that course were the most wonderful experience of my life and if I ever have the luck to be able to ride a bike again I shall don those leathers and show that Guthrie's Memorial a thing or two'*. Sadly, he was permanently disabled by the crash, and he never got to wear his leathers again.

*

The race organisers knew that they could not prevent accidents to competitors but they did all they could to minimise them. The organisers of the MGP were very conscious of the fact that they were dealing with relatively inexperienced riders, and they usually handed out advice in their programme. In 1953 riders were told: *'the speed at which any bend can be taken depends entirely on whether you have got the right line, and if you don't know the line ask some more experienced competitor or a Travelling Marshal. The Travelling Marshals are all very experienced and have had considerable success on this Course, and we have them for no other purpose than to help you'*.

'Crossley's Tours'
In another effort to help riders learn the circuit, former

A stylish Dennis Morgan riding his BSA Golden Flash on Travelling Marshal duty in 1953.

MGP winner and Travelling Marshal Don Crossley, took thirty of them on a lap of instruction. Travelling in a coach equipped with a PA system, they spent four hours on a detailed trip around the 37 ¾ miles. It was the first of what has become a traditional instructional coach-trip for MGP and TT competitors that still goes by the nickname of 'Crossley's Tours'. Don also received many personal requests for information that caused him to offer the following general advice. *'In the case of practically all the overseas riders who have been to me, I have stipulated at least 60 to over 100 laps at touring speeds no faster than 30 to 35 mph, so they could have a really good look at all the bends and corners, condition of the roads, whether good surfaces or bad, particularly the gutters on the approach to any corner and the exits'*. It probably sounded a hopelessly over-cautious approach to dashing young men wanting to make their mark on the Island racing scene, but Don Crossley knew what he was talking about because he, like others, had started his MGP career with a hefty crash due to the dangerous combination of over-enthusiasm and lack of Course knowledge.

Don Crossley was one of a number of experienced former competitors who made their knowledge available to newcomers to the TT and MGP races. Such assistance could be of great value to a rider who had hardly seen the 37 ¾ mile Mountain Course before being expected to go out at first light on a racing motorcycle in the close company of riders who were already well acquainted with it. The gaining of Course knowledge could not be rushed, but it could be accelerated by a good coach. In addition, machine preparation for the long and testing Island races has to be to a high standard. The correct gearing, carburation, plugs, suspension-settings, etc., all need to be established and pointers from someone who had done it before could save valuable time. A week or more of practice sounds plenty but if a rider has the wrong machine set-up, or repeatedly breaks down and spends most of the sessions sitting at the side of the road, the available practice time can disappear very quickly. Competing in the Island races is expensive and time-consuming. Failure to qualify is a bitter blow to a rider, but a good tutor can reduce the chance of that happening.

*

Organisation of both the TT and MGP races continued to run on tried and tested lines. Curwen Clague wrote in the local newspaper 'The Isle of Man Examiner' in 1949: *'so often has the job been done, so many people having done it year after year, that its magnitude today is sometimes overlooked because of the quiet manner in which everything falls into place at the right time. Race organisation is a thing that comes naturally to local officials and individuals, many of whom served their apprenticeship as marshals and Boy Scouts and their work for TT success is founded on an intense enthusiasm and a vast knowledge and tradition'.*

*

Riders still had to 'weigh-in' their machines before each race. At the TT this was done at the Grandstand and machines were housed overnight in a marquee. At the MGP the organisers used the garage premises of Messrs Fargher & Ashton in Westmoreland Road, Douglas (later Mylchreest Motors, now a multi-storey car-park), where they were lodged overnight in secure conditions. An hour before the start of each race, riders would collect their motorcycles and hope that everything was in order. (It wasn't unknown to find a leaking petrol tank, a flat tyre, or a reluctant starter, and panic would then set in for the unlucky rider). After firing their bikes up outside the garage, MGP riders were conducted on a parade through Douglas that took them along the Promenade and up to the Start area at the Grandstand. A breakdown van accompanied the Parade and it would collect any bike that expired and transport it to the Pits where, if he was lucky, the rider would fix the problem in time to start the race.

*

In the early 1950s the motorcycling press claimed that the TT races had developed into a great national and international sporting occasion, and that *'the man-in-the-street is as keen to know who pulls off the "Senior" as he is to learn the winners of the Derby, the Boat Race and the Cup Final'.* Budding racers who sought to emulate household names like Geoff Duke could buy a new Matchless G45 or AJS 7R for £366 ready for the 1954 season. Known as the 'Boy Racer', the 7R showed its reliability at the 1954 Junior TT where of the 29 private owner 7Rs that started, 26 finished the race. Of the non-finishers, one was a faller.

*

The TT meeting continued to hold its position as the premier event in the world road-racing calendar and both the Moto Guzzi and NSU concerns sang its praises in the Programme, rating a TT win above all others.

NSU impressed racegoers with their all-round efficiency both on and off the track. Rather than have mechanics sit blipping the throttles of their race-bikes for ten minutes to warm them up (and help wear them out?), they employed ducted hot air

blowers to help bring the engines up to operating temperature. Others filled their bikes with pre-heated oil just before the start, in an attempt to avoid the risk of early engine seizure when given maximum throttle from the word go. NSU lubricated their engines with an early type of Castrol synthetic oil.

Ban the 500s

In 1954 there were serious proposals at the FIM (the world ruling body for motorcycle sport), for the elimination of the 500cc class from international racing by 1956, to be followed by the 350s soon after. Whilst the powers that be played politics with the sport, the racers got on with the job of riding.

*

Clypse Course

Adjustments were made to the TT race programme in 1954 to cater for sidecars, for by then they had their own world championship class. Previously the last TT race for sidecars was in 1925. Seemingly concerned at the ability of the sidecars to cope with the Mountain Course, the race organisers created the new 10.8 mile Clypse Course for 1954.

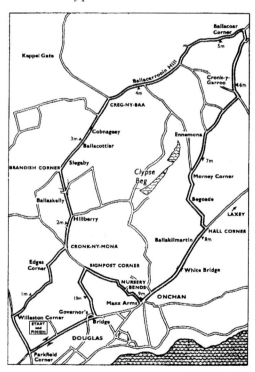

Map of the Clypse Course.

Narrow and twisty, the Clypse Course used the normal Start and Finish line, but instead of plunging down Bray Hill, competitors turned right at the top of Bray and headed through Willaston to Cronk ny Mona. There they joined the Mountain Course but ran in the reverse direction up to Creg ny Baa where they turned right towards Laxey, before returning via Onchan and again joining the Mountain Course, this time at Signpost Corner. From Signpost they ran the normal route to the Finish, although they omitted the dip at Governor's Bridge.

*

What are now called the Ultra-Lightweights (125cc), that were then known as the Lightweight 125s, also used the Clypse Course in 1954, and both the solo and sidecar events had massed starts for their ten lap races. Other changes saw the Junior TT still on the Mountain Course - but reduced from 7 to 5 laps, and even though the Clubman's were now just 500 and 350cc classes, the ACU found them ever more difficult to fit into the race programme and their races were run on the Thursday of practice week, resulting in wins for Phil Palmer (Junior) and Alastair King (Senior). Both were on BSA Gold Stars, as were the majority of the entry.

*

Weather conditions were mixed in practice and on the wet Friday morning 'Motor Cycling' reported that *'the most popular spots in the Island this morning were the Cadbury and Dunlop refreshment tents, to which the majority of riders hurried, shivering and emptying rain from their goggles, at the conclusion of each lap'.*

*

The race for the Lightweight 125s was the first to be run over the Clypse Course and victory went to Rupert Hollaus on his spine-framed NSU at 71.53 mph. (Les Graham had averaged 78.21 mph to win the same class on the Mountain Course the year before.) Eric Oliver and Les Nutt raced their Norton-Watsonian sidecar outfit to victory over the BMW opposition at 70.85 mph. It was a race that saw Inge Stoll-Laforge became the first lady to compete in a TT race as she passengered Jacques Drion to fifth place. Werner Haas gave NSU victory at record speed in the Lightweight 250 race over 3 laps of the Mountain Course. His little 250 was believed to be delivering 33bhp and its unusual streamlining allowed him to make full use of every one of them, whilst delivering 42 mpg. Haas raised the lap record by an incredible 6 mph to average 90.88 mph.

Rod Coleman gave the unstreamlined but redesigned AJS 7R with its three-valve engine its first TT win in the Junior. Experimenting with an outside flywheel, five-speed gearbox and 'proboscis' fairing on his Norton during practice, Ray Amm took a

This 1954 photograph shows four of the ultra-fast 250cc NSU twins with dolphin-type fairings.

controversial victory in the Senior over Geoff Duke's Gilera when, for the first time, the race was stopped on account of an earlier thunderstorm as the leader completed his fourth lap.

*

The adverse weather conditions at the 1954 Senior gave an interesting demonstration of the contrasting riding styles of the two main protagonists. Ray Amm, brought up on loose-surfaced race-tracks, would unashamedly trail a steadying leg in poor conditions as he rounded tricky spots like Ramsey Hairpin or Governor's Bridge. By contrast, Geoff Duke was always the immaculate stylist. Despite his proven off-road talents in Trials and Scrambles, when road-racing Geoff always kept his feet 'on the pegs'.

*

Although Moto Guzzi brought a 500cc version of their successful single-cylinder racer to contest the Senior race and MV brought improved 350-fours, Norton managed to keep them all at bay and with NSU's successes in the Lightweight classes, the Italian factories were noticeable by their absence from the list of TT winners in 1954. This proved to be only a temporary absence in the solo classes.

Despite the fact that Gilera and MV Agusta competed in the sidecar class on the Continent, the Italians never seriously challenged the Sidecar TT with their 'fire-engines', (although Florian Camathias did bring a Gilera-four outfit to the TT in 1964).

*

Early practice weather for the 1955 TT was unpleasant, and in the second session, antipodean John Hempleman stopped and joined the marshals at Ballacraine for no other reason than he was cold. Riders got used to climbing into damp leathers as the poor weather continued, and a new record for a low turn-out of riders was set in Friday morning's practice session on the Clypse Course. Despite a full complement of marshals, police, doctors, etc., only three 125's braved the foul weather. An hour later, only six 250's (for their race had been moved to the Clypse) turned out for their session. Press Secretary, Norman Brown, suggested mustering the Travelling Marshals for a race, for they were certainly on duty.

Day-Trippers
The effects of a train strike in the UK around TT time in 1955 hit the travel arrangements of many spectators and resulted in the cancellation of 'Motor Cycling' magazine's trips to the Senior. It was the first time this had happened since they started in 1914. One enthusiast wrote of these trips; *'the crowd filling the train had a strong flavour of motorcycles and was more reminiscent of Brands Hatch than British Railways'*. Most of the journey was no doubt spent chatting about motorcycling in general and TT races in particular. At Liverpool they would board one of the boats for the Island which, by the time it sailed, was full of recumbent bodies. The early arrivals had the soft seats, others made do with wooden benches and latecomers were out on the hard deck.

The early arrival of thousands of visitors in Douglas on Senior race day saw the Island's cafes awake and ready to receive them. Some would fit in a pre-race coach tour around the Course, or maybe take a leisurely breakfast. Others would take advantage of the free motorcycle show presented by thousands of machines parked along Douglas Promenade. Then it was off to secure a vantage point for the day's racing, perhaps taking a coach to a favoured spot on the Course, walking to the Grandstand or, for those with strong nerves, going to one of the accessible but truly frightening spectator spots like the bottom of Bray Hill.

After the racing had finished and the Roads Open car had been through, it was time for the day-trippers to start the journey in reverse. It would end with most of them arriving home shortly before their families were due to get up on Saturday morning. All in all, it was quite an exhausting way of attending the TT as most people would have done a full day's work before leaving home on the Thursday evening. Little sleep could be expected on the crowded ferries but enthusiasm for the racing would usually carry them through a largely sleepless 48 hours.

*

When each day's racing ends, the public is not allowed back on the roads of the TT Course until the official Roads Open car has passed. Although there were loudspeakers at popular vantage points around the Course, spectators at many other spots would remain in ignorance of the result unless they were doing their own timing of the top runners. The Roads Open cars of the 1950s often carried a board on the back with the main results from a race chalked on it - for those who were quick enough to read them.

*

Before the racing in 1955 there were 15 practice sessions that started on a Wednesday, and the Clubman's races (just Senior and Junior classes) moved to the Clypse Course. It was a move that reduced rider and spectator interest and left only the Senior and Junior TT races being run on the Mountain Course. Following yet another juggle with their race-regulations, riders in the Clubman classes had to carry full lighting-sets, speedos and centre-stands. After safety protests the ruling on centre-stands was relaxed.

One man who did not make the start of his Clubman's race was Alan Brodrick who fell during practice and dislocated his shoulder. Alan was employed in former World Champion Bob Foster's motorcycle shop and Bob, who was acting as a Travelling Marshal, was sent to investigate the incident. Seeing that Alan was not too badly hurt he limited himself to *'silly bugger, fancy coming all this way just to fall off'*, then told him to hop on the back and took him to hospital on the pillion of the BSA Shooting Star that he was using for his Travelling Marshal duties. Bob was a generous employer, for he allowed Alan and fellow employee Barry Cortvriend to buy new Gold Stars at cost price for the 1955 Clubman's. He then gave them a fortnight off work at the busiest time of the year, paid their boat fares and hotel bills, lent them the firm's van, two hack bikes to learn the Course, and let one of his mechanics accompany them to look after the bikes. Bob Foster spent half of the year in South Africa on health grounds and he gave generous support to riders from African countries like Ray Amm, Paddy Driver, Gary Hocking and Jim Redman, when they came to Europe to race.

100 mph Lap?
Qualifying time for Junior runners in the International TT race of 1955 was 34 minutes and for Seniors it was 33 minutes, an average speed of 68.60 mph. That qualifying speed was certainly set with the lesser riders in mind, because there was much talk about the possibility of the top runners getting round in a full ten minutes less and setting the first 100 mph lap.

On his Gilera that had improved handling and more power, Geoff Duke threatened the 100 mph lap during practice, and on race-day his many fans were delighted to hear that he had circulated in 22 minutes 39 seconds, which was announced as an average lap speed of 100 mph. Some 40 minutes later the timekeepers later amended his speed to 99.97 mph - an announcement that was roundly booed by those in the Grandstand - but Geoff did have the satisfaction of taking the race win.

Since the 1920s the ACU have regarded the length of the TT Course to be 37.7333 miles and they believed that their calculations of lap speed were correct to the nearest 0.003 mph. But, despite such apparent precision, all timing was done with hand-held watches. The whole issue of TT lap distance and times is a subject of great interest to some people. So much so that the topic could fill a book - but not this one!

*

Following victory in the 1955 Lightweight 250 race on an MV (that was only 203cc), Bill Lomas went on to win the Junior race with a non-stop ride on a Moto Guzzi from Bob McIntyre on a Norton. It was the first time that the Junior race had been won by a foreign make and it helped Bill to win four silver replicas in the week. His performance on the Junior Guzzi showed that when ridden by a top rider, a machine of modest power output could outperform more powerful models if it enjoyed the advantages of low build, relatively light weight, low fuel consumption, full streamlining and good handling. The Guzzi did and, although putting out only about 40 bhp, it repeated its win at the 1956 TT, ridden by Ken Kavanagh.

*

Geoff Duke and his Gilera on the Glencrutchery Road, heading towards the finishing line of the 1955 Senior TT in which they set new lap and race records.

Bill Lomas shows the low and streamlined shape of the single-cylinder 350cc Moto Guzzi on which he won the 1955 Junior TT and on which Ken Kavanagh won the 1956 event.

Moto Guzzi were pleased with Ken Kavanagh's victory in the 1956 Junior TT, and with their previous 10 TT wins.

As a young Australian, Ken Kavanagh was obsessed with a wish to ride the TT, having become convinced that it was *'the one race in the world that really mattered'* and regarding all other races as *'just stepping-stones to the Isle of Man'*. It took this tough Aussie six years and thirteen Island races to achieve his ambition of a TT

win, and when he did so he was not ashamed to shed a tear.

Australians do their share of ribbing the 'Poms' but Kavanagh was on the end of a bit at the weigh-in for the Junior. Seeing him arrive with his Italian Moto Guzzi, an ACU official called Guzzi team manager Fergus Anderson over *'just in case your rider doesn't speak English'*. Anderson replied *'He doesn't - he's an Australian'*.

*

Moto Guzzi had their own wind-tunnel and their brilliant designer Ing. Giulio Carcano treated streamlining as an integral part of the overall design, rather than something bolted on as an afterthought. In their never-ceasing quest to save weight, Moto Guzzi pioneered the use of lightweight magnesium fairings. Interested more in weight-saving than glossy appearance, they finished them with a single coat of dull protective primer.

*

Jumping back to the 1953 TT, a little story involving the 350 Moto Guzzi shows that sportsmanship was alive and well at the time. Guzzi had not put much development effort into the simple 350 in its early days, concentrating at the time on their complicated 500cc in-line, four-cylinder, shaft-drive, water-cooled, fuel-injected racer (that never appeared at the TT). But an easy early-season win at Hockenheim for the relatively unsophisticated '350' turned the factory's thoughts to the TT. The race regulations stipulated that a rider or machine could be changed before the race, but not both. However, factories enjoyed the privilege of being able to reserve entries and specify their riders at a later date. Moto Guzzi did not have an entry in the Junior TT but MV Agusta had three, although they only intended running two machines. Guzzi approached MV and asked them to nominate top Guzzi rider Fergus Anderson as the third rider of an MV. This was agreed and Anderson then did the permitted change of machine entry from MV to Guzzi. He went on to take third place in the Junior whilst the MVs retired. From then on there was no stopping the Guzzi which won the 350 World Championship from 1954-57.

*

An experienced TT rider, Terry Shepherd was on duty as a Travelling Marshal at the 1955 MGP. Velocettes asked him to use their prototype Venom model on his official duties, no doubt seeing it as an opportunity to give the new model some fairly strenuous test miles, whilst Terry saw it as an opportunity to keep his hand in on the TT Course.

Giving the Venom an unofficial run around the Douglas roads to sort out a slight carburation problem in the middle of practice week brought Terry a summons to the High Bailiff's' Court to explain why he was using this 'racer' on the roads. Unfortunately he was catching up on a bit of sleep (after early morning duty) at the time that he was supposed to be in Court so they sent an officer around to collect him. Anywhere else and he might have been for the 'high-jump', but the Court was quite understanding about the whole matter. Indeed, so understanding were they, that the policeman who had booked him was made to feel that he was the one who was in the wrong.

*

Terry Shepherd on the prototype Velocette Venom outside his Douglas 'digs' at the 1955 MGP.

The Venom was subject to test by members of the press whilst it was on the Island. The Mountain Mile was a particularly popular stretch for pressmen to put new sports models or actual race winning machines through their paces in early morning tests. Unfortunately they managed to blow the Venom's engine, so Terry borrowed an AJS 7R belonging to a friend, attached a pair of 'M' plates and completed several laps on that while the Venom was repaired. As this enabled him to sort out a few carburation and handling problems on the 7R, everyone was happy, except perhaps, Velocettes.

*

Several manufacturers of the day lent machines for use by Travelling Marshals at both the TT and MGP. Others were not ashamed to try and gain some of the glamour associated with racing by suggesting links with the TT in their advertising.

End of the Clubmans

Come the 1956 TT and the Senior and Junior Clubman's classes continued to attract good entries. It was a pity then that their practice sessions and races were pushed into the week following the main TT fortnight. A clear case of "After the Lord Mayor's Show . . .!". These two smaller classes had become something of a BSA Gold Star benefit and that seemed sufficient excuse for the ACU to put an end to them.

Having been introduced in 1947, the Clubman's races had then taken place amidst changing regulations that saw kick and push starts, cold and warm starts, individual and group starts, changes of circuit, changes to classes, changes to race days, countless arguments over eligibility and machine

This BSA advertisement from the 1950s for their 500cc Shooting Star hints at association with the pre-TT race activity portrayed on the quayside.

specification, etc. The Clubmans had stretched the ACU's organisation and race timetable and, notwithstanding their continued popularity with competitors, they dropped them after the 1956 event. Winner of both Clubman's races at the 1956 TT was Bernard Codd who took his Gold Stars to the first (and last) double win.

*

Carlo Ubbiali gave victory to the Italian MV Agusta factory in the two Lightweight classes in 1956 and John Surtees made it a hat-trick of MV successes riding his 500 with revised bore and stroke to what was his first TT victory, the 'Blue Riband' Senior event.

** John Surtees **

John Surtees was a TT winner who did not come up through the ranks of the MGP. John would probably have ridden the Manx if he had not ruled himself out by taking part in successful world speed record breaking rides on a Vincent in 1952. He served both his formal engineering and racing apprenticeships by working for the Vincent Company and racing its products, but his world record breaking rides for them meant that he was ineligible to compete in the MGP. Moving on to Norton machinery he was very successful on short circuits. However, he made an inauspicious TT debut in 1953 when the front-forks of his 125cc EMC snapped at Ballaugh Bridge and he broke his wrist. Returning in 1954 he gained respectable results on his own Nortons and in 1955, riding 'production' Manx Nortons supplied by the 'works' (something of a contradiction), he took 4th in the Junior but ran out of petrol in the Senior whilst lying 7th. Still very successful on short circuits (he won 68 races out of 75 starts in 1955), he was, nevertheless, serving a sensible TT apprenticeship.

John signed to ride for the MV Agusta team for 1956 getting a useful lift in salary from £500 a year (paid by Norton) to £5,000 from MV. He quickly earned his money by bringing not only his race skills but also his development skills to Gallarate. In an eventful TT practice in his first year on the Italian fire-engines he slid off the 350 at Creg ny Baa and in a later session hit a cow that jumped into the road just above Sarah's Cottage. Nevertheless, he achieved his first TT win in the 1956 Senior and led the Junior until he ran out of petrol on the last lap - imagine how frustrating that must have been!

MV Agusta team-mates John Surtees (in helmet) and John Hartle prepare for a practice session at the 1958 TT.

Although without a TT win in 1957, John took a further 5 TT victories (including the first 'hat-trick' of Senior TT successes between 1958-1960) and the 350 and 500 World Championships between 1958-1960. He then switched to car-racing and became Formula 1 World Champion in 1964, the only man to win a World Championship on two and four wheels.

Sidecars were allowed to make a clutch start (rather than run and bump) at the 1956 TT, and Walter Zeller gave BMW its best post-war solo TT finish when he brought his 'works' twin into fourth place in the 1956 Senior.

*

The Gilera team riders Geoff Duke and Reg Armstrong were missing from the 1956 TT due to their suspension from racing by the FIM after supporting a privateers protest over start money at the previous year's Dutch TT. Geoff still had an interest in the TT in the form of rider Jackie Wood who he entered on a 350 Velocette, he had also entered himself in the TT-time Isle of Man Grand National Scramble on a 175cc Gilera. To keep his hand in during the latter part of 1956, Geoff did duty as a Travelling Marshal at the MGP where he entered Frank Rutherford on a 500 BSA. He also found time to compete in the Manx Two-Day Trial on an Ariel. You can not keep a good man down!

*

The unmistakable style of Geoff Duke as he rounds Braddan Bridge whilst serving as a Travelling Marshal at the 1956 MGP.

Each TT produced technical innovations that aided development in all aspects of race-bike design. In 1956 DKW's three-cylinder 350cc two-stroke appeared with hydraulically operated linked drum brakes. Its rider, Cecil Sandford, also had to cope with three air-levers that could be used to regulate the supply to each carburettor. All foreign machines had five-speed gearboxes whilst the Spanish Montesa came with the only six-speed gearbox at the races. Others, such as MV, concentrated on handling issues with revised forks, whilst several riders of 500cc single-cylinder bikes tried to compensate for their power deficiency by using pannier-tanks within their fairings to get a non-stop run for the seven-lap race. Norton seemed to be constantly developing the brakes and refining other points on their 'production' Manx models, whilst Walter Zeller's BMW had an early form of hydraulic steering damper.

Technical advances may not have been so noticeable amongst the 'amateur' riders of the MGP but it was not unknown for manufacturers to use promising riders to put in development miles on prototype engine parts and the like. At the 1956 MGP Renold offered a new type primary-chain oiler that they claimed almost completely removed the danger of oil-splashes on the rear tyre, whilst Avon brought over a new front racing tyre.

Golden Jubilee

1957 was the Golden Jubilee of the TT races and there had been many changes since Charlie Collier and Rem Fowler took their single and multi-cylinder wins in the first event in 1907, (Rem setting the fastest lap at 42.91 mph on the St John's Course). The first 100 mph lap was confidently expected to be set in 1957 and Ferodo, suppliers of brake-linings to most of the entry, provided some supporting statistics. By their estimation, on a 100 mph lap a rider would apply his brakes 73 times and they would be on for some 2 minutes 50 seconds, which represented 4? of the 37? miles covered. For good measure, they added that a rider braking hard for Sulby Bridge would be looking to disperse 250,000 ft.lbs of energy.

*

Brakes were of little use to Eric Hinton during one fraught practice, for approaching Crosby the throttle on his Norton stuck wide-open. Left with no alternative but to pull in the clutch, he reported that *'just before the engine blew up the last thing I noticed was a reading of 11,500 on the rev counter'.*

*

The Gilera concern returned to the Island in 1957 with their 350 and 500 four-cylinder machines that by then delivered 52 and 70 bhp and came in fully streamlined form. Due to an early-season spill at Imola, Geoff Duke was sidelined and the Gilera riders at the TT were Bob McIntyre and Bob Brown.

*

To mark the special nature of the Golden Jubilee event the TT organisers increased the number of laps in the Senior TT from 7 to 8, giving a total race distance of 302 miles. Bob McIntyre was more than equal to the challenge and completed the race in a fraction over 3 hours at an average speed of 98.99 mph. Bob's only interest was in winning the race, but of greater importance to some was the fact that he became the first man to lap the Mountain Course at over 100 mph. In a convincing Senior TT win he broke the 100 mph barrier four times and left the lap record at 101.12 mph, so adding to his victory in the Junior event earlier in the week.

Bob McIntyre rounds Signpost Corner on his four-cylinder Gilera during his winning ride in the 1957 Senior TT.

Bob McIntyre received signals from four points on the Course in 1957, with the one at Sulby manned by the 1955 Gilera team of Geoff Duke and Reg Armstrong. The message they tried to get over to him in the closing laps was to slow down, for he had a healthy lead over second-place man John Surtees. Bob heeded their advice for, in his words: *'I knew they were right. There was no point in going faster than necessary - I remember thinking - I'll be told off for doing the lads out of Silvers if I go on like this!'* The point he was making was that (apart from the wisdom of saving the Gilera's engine), anyone finishing within a certain fraction of the winner's time was awarded a Silver Replica, so if Bob went faster than necessary, fewer people would get replicas thus making him unpopular with those who just missed out.

*

Second to Bob Mac in that record-breaking Golden Jubilee TT was John Surtees on his MV Agusta and, confirming the Italian dominance, Bob Brown brought the other Gilera into third place, while Dickie Dale rode the fabulous Moto Guzzi vee-eight to fourth, (despite the fact that it was only running on seven cylinders), and Keith Campbell brought his single-cylinder Moto Guzzi into fifth.

*

Whilst the 'Blue Riband' Senior event grabbed most of the attention at the 1957 TT the Lightweights and Sidecars contested their races over a shortened eight laps of the Clypse Course, with a win in the hard-fought 250 race going to Cecil Sandford (Mondial). The hard-luck story of the race was that of Sammy Miller. Having taken the lead on the last lap he slid off at Governor's Bridge and damaged his bike. Although it was only just under a mile from the finishing line, Sammy lost 5 minutes as he pushed his Mondial up the the Glencrutchery Road to take a gallant fifth place. It is history now that Sammy Miller turned to off-road sport, became the greatest British Trials rider of his era, collected Gold Medals in the ISDT, was no mean Scrambler, and now parades classic racing bikes whilst running a successful motorcycle museum.

The massed start Lightweight races on the Clypse Course always generated close and exciting racing, and the Lightweight 125 event saw a race-long fight at the front that finished in the order Tarquinio Provini, Carlo Ubbiali and Luigi Taveri.

*

Mixing two and three wheels at the 1957 TT and finishing ninth in the 250 race on an NSU was Florian Camathias. He did rather better in the Sidecar class,

The massed start to the Sidecar TT sees competitors streaming down from the Start to turn right onto the Clypse Course at Parkfield.

taking third place on his BMW behind winner Hillebrand and second-place Schneider, who were also on BMWs. Bill Beevers was a man who also mixed sidecars and solos for several years, usually riding in the Junior and Senior events as well as the Sidecar class. In earlier years, several riders who were known better for their solo exploits were also successful on three-wheels, Freddie Dixon and Graham Walker among them. But whilst some good sidecar drivers of later years also put up creditable solo TT performances (Sidecar TT winners Chris Vincent and Mick Boddice for example), solo riders doing well on chairs are now generally much harder to find.

*

It was not until 1957 that passengers in the Sidecar TT received Silver and Bronze Replicas on the same basis as their drivers.

Manufacturers Quit
At the end of the 1957 season the racing world was shocked by the decision of all the major

manufacturers, except MV Agusta, to withdraw from racing. This left MV virtually unchallenged and, as will be seen, they took full advantage of their position.

The Italian factories' withdrawal from racing resulted in a slowing of mechanical development on the racing scene. Bill Lomas says that Moto Guzzi had a 350cc V-8 and a four on the stocks, whilst other factories probably had their own development models.

*

Although the 1958 TT lacked entries from the 'works' teams who had withdrawn from racing at the end of the 1957 season, there were still plenty of competitors who wanted to take on the challenge of the Mountain Course. This meant that, as usual, in the Spring of the year the Isle of Man Highway Authorities commenced their usual flurry of activities to get the TT Course ready for racing. Road surfaces were repaired, bales put in place, kerbs painted black and white on the bends, warning signs erected, hedges trimmed, etc. Amongst all this activity there would be occasional sightings of visiting motorcyclists, for some overseas riders would arrive early and put in as many laps as possible in learning the Course on borrowed road-bikes.

*

It was debut year for Mike Hailwood, who came straight to the TT without a Mountain Course apprenticeship at the MGP. Competing in all solo classes on his first Island visit, he finished 7th in the Lightweight 125, 3rd in the Lightweight 250, 12th in the Junior and 13th in the Senior. It was an impressive performance, and one which earned him the Ray B. Westover Trophy as best newcomer.

*

Most TT fans recognise photos of Mike Hailwood by his gold and white helmet, but not so many know that in his early years of racing his helmet was red and white.

*

A young Mike Hailwood wearing one of his early designs of crash-helmet. This one was red and white and carried the motif 'Ecurie Sportive'.

Rhodesian Jim Redman was another debutant at the 1958 TT. Jim learnt that the bottom of Bray Hill was not the place to check your rev counter reading when, momentarily taking his eyes off the road to do so, he looked up to find himself on a brief but spectacular two-wheeled excursion along the pavement. Despite his later TT successes, Jim claimed that he always 'raced' with something in

hand on the Mountain Course.

*

The BBC continued its TT commentaries but in scaled-down form. In those days before videos, those who wanted the TT sensation to last for more than two weeks a year could take advantage of new long-playing records produced by Stanley Schofield Ltd. They contained introduction and potted commentary from Graham Walker, plus the sound effects of Lightweight MVs and Mondials, Manx Nortons, AJS 7Rs and the mighty MV fours. They could all be heard accelerating from the start, flat out through Glen Vine, etc, etc. Perhaps the most spine-tingling sound for armchair listeners was that of John Surtees going down through the gearbox under braking for Creg ny Baa, and then accelerating away towards Brandish.

*

A new 500cc Matchless single-cylinder racer made its TT debut in the hands of Jack Ahearn in 1958 and 'Motor Cycling' reported: *'if it is decided to go into production with it, it will become the model G50'.* Sharing the same stroke and flywheels of the 7R and of all-round similar appearance, it had a 90mm bore and was mounted in a 7R frame. The second G50 went to Manxman Jack Wood who later was Clerk of the Course for both the TT and MGP. G50 referred to the engine's output (50 bhp) just as G45 had done with the earlier Matchless twin-cylinder racer. The Matchless G50 was too new to have a selling price but the G45 was available for £403, as was the AJS 7R. The 350cc Model 40M and 500 Model 30M Manx Nortons cost substantially more at £481.

*

Although Norton claimed to be manufacturing only 'production' Manx Nortons, several specially prepared engines were made available to Keith Campbell, Geoff Duke, Alan Holmes (a 93 mm bore version), Bob Brown and sidecar-man Pip Harris at the 1958 TT.

Clean Sweep for MV Agusta

On his 'works' MV Agustas, John Surtees took comfortable wins in the Senior and Junior classes in 1958, although his race speeds were slightly down on 1957. Perhaps this was due to the changes in regulations that limited streamlining to the dolphin type, but it was probably because the combination of Surtees and the four-cylinder MV was a far superior package to the many single-cylinder ridden mounts that chased him home. Nortons filled the other podium places with former MGP stars Dave

Chadwick and Geoff Tanner in the Junior, and Bob Anderson and Bob Brown in the Senior.

*

On the Clypse Course Tarquinio Provini and Carlo Ubbiali took the Lightweight 250 and 125 races for MV, giving them a clean sweep of the four solo classes. It was the first time that had been achieved. The Lightweight 125 race brought interesting entries from new 'works' desmodromic Ducatis (that secured second, third and fourth places), and East German rotary-valved two-stroke MZs that finished fifth and sixth.

*

Enforcement of an FIM imposed minimum weight limit for riders in the 125cc class saw the diminutive Gary Dickinson having to load his MV with 23 lbs (10½ kgs) of lead to bring his weight up to the 9 stones 6 lbs (60 kg) minimum figure, with Swiss star Luigi Taveri taking on 21 lbs. In total, seven riders in the event had to add weight to their machines.

*

Walter Schneider emphasised BMW's growing dominance of the sidecar class with victory over fellow BMW-mounted Florian Camathias, whilst former World Champion Eric Oliver took a standard road-going Norton Dominator and Watsonian Monaco sidecar to tenth place at a race average speed of 59.95 mph.

British sidecar outfits had the 'chair' on the left, whilst Continentals invariably had the third wheel on the right. The sidecars still raced over the Clypse Course and, being very narrow in places, passing was not always easy. British crew Ernie Walker and passenger Don Roberts were lapped by race winners Walter Schneider and Hans Stauss towards the end. To draw attention to the fact that the Germans wanted to pass, Hans Stauss grabbed Don Roberts leg and shook it!

It sometimes happened that a sidecar passenger would change to another driver and machine during the TT period. However, a passenger who qualified in practice on a left-hand chair was not considered to be qualified to race in a right-hand chair.

Big Mileage

Being spread over two weeks and involving far more racing mileage than an average event, the TT has always been an expensive race meeting to take part in. A rider might well do 15 laps in practice and 6 in a race, making over 800 racing miles and bringing the need for major repairs. There was no start money

Taking to the pavement at Parkfield Corner on the Clypse Course are Carlo Ubbiali and Tarquinio Provini on their MV Agustas in the 1958 250 TT. Provini went on to win the race.

John Hartle's MV Agusta after it caught fire due to a petrol leak on the exit from Governor's Bridge during the 1958 Senior TT.

paid to riders in the 1950s and even the top runners found it difficult to pay their way, for the prize money for first place in the Senior was still a miserly £200 (going down to £3 for the 20th finisher). Fortunately the event was still well supported by the 'Trade', but the money they offered had to be earned. A few of the top riders would be on 'Trade' retainers, but tyre, oil and chain company bonuses were paid mostly on results. If a rider held a high race-placing until the last few miles of the last lap and then had the bad luck to retire, he might receive nothing for a fortnight's racing effort. The TT experience could easily be all expenditure and no income for many riders in its early years. Nowadays they all receive start money and can also receive some prize-money based on the number of laps completed in a race (even if they retire before the end) - but it is still an expensive business.

It was not just privateers who found the TT an expensive meeting. The 1958 event was a particularly

costly one for MV Agusta, because John Hartle's bike caught fire as he came out of Governor's Bridge on the fourth-lap whilst he was lying second in the Senior. It was totally burnt out.

It was Hartle who gave an experimental six-cylinder MV Agusta 500 its only race outing later in 1958. In the Italian GP at Monza he retired the MV whilst in 4th place, having pulled through most of the field after a bad start.

*

The FIM again gave consideration to removing the 500 and 350cc classes from TT and Grand Prix racing at the end of the 1950s. Maybe it truly was for safety reasons, but perhaps it was an attempt to give a higher profile to the lightweight motorcycles so successfully manufactured in Europe at the time. It is certainly fortunate that those running motorcycle racing in the late 1950s (when TT-winning speeds were just over 100mph) had no idea that forty years later the TT Course would be lapped at well over 125 mph!

Chapter 7
JAPANESE TAKE-OVER

As the 1950s drew to a close, the Isle of Man TT was still the world's greatest road-race and it continued to draw all the big-name riders and manufacturers. One result of this was that any motorcycle manufacturer who engaged in motorcycle-racing knew that to truly prove his product and to earn the respect of both the public and the racing fraternity world-wide, he had to subject his machines to the challenge of the famous TT races.

*

Although Honda motorcycles were only sold in Japan in the mid-1950s, Soichiro Honda's company was already the largest motorcycle producer in the world. Seeking a wider market he looked across the globe and decided to embark on a racing programme that would publicise the Honda name, gain the company prestige and so boost its export programme. It was a decision that changed the world of motorcycling - both road and race - forever.

Honda TT Debut

Back in Japan the Honda Company was aware that the TT was the best possible event in which to showcase its products to the wider world. It had achieved some racing success at home, mostly on dirt roads, and in the second half of the 1950s it sent representatives on fact-finding trips to the Isle of Man races. Armed with cameras, note-pads and many questions, their task was to discover everything they could about the TT Course and how best Honda could tackle the European racing opposition that had

mostly dominated the TT for its first fifty years. Such thorough preparation meant that by 1959 Honda were ready to make their TT debut.

*

As well as the customary programme of races for Lightweight 125s, Lightweight 250s, Junior, Senior and Sidecar classes, the FIM stipulated that at the 1959 TT there had to be Formula 1 races for 350 & 500cc machines. Not everyone welcomed the innovation (and even less people fully understood what Formula 1 was all about) but, in the words of Norman Dixon then Chairman of the ACU: *'Expressed simply, the machines in this race are the same as you can buy'*. Indeed, factory specials were really ruled out by the requirement that at least 25 of any model raced in Formula 1 had to have been built and sold.

*

The two classes in the first IOM Formula 1 event ran together, with the race taking place on the Saturday before traditional race-week. Victory in the 500cc class went to Bob McIntyre on a Manx Norton and first in the 350cc class was Bob's fellow Scotsman and friend Alastair King on an AJS 7R.

*

In his book 'Japanese Riders in the Isle of Man', Ralph Crellin tells how Honda entered the 1959 TT in the belief that they would be competing in a 'Formula' event. But, as their bikes were 125s and the 'Formula' race at the TT was only open to 350 & 500s, they found themselves competing in the Lightweight 125 racing class with their technically advanced

Bill Hunt (centre) and Honda's Ichioo Nitsuma (left) are shown over the Clypse Course in early 1959 by former Travelling Marshal Angus Herbert.

The first racing Hondas to appear on the Island were race-kitted road bikes and so retained something of a production racer look.

twin-cylinder RC142 models that were understood to deliver some 16 bhp.

*

Although they had prepared thoroughly, it was still a bold move for Honda to challenge the motorcycle world of the West at the Isle of Man TT. The small Island in the Irish Sea with the reputation of being the home of road-racing was half a world away from Japan in terms of distance, and an entirely different world in respect of culture, etc.; a fact the Honda team recognised by bringing their own cook and doctor.

*

Five Hondas were in the Programme for the Lightweight 125cc class of the 1959 TT. Four were entered by Honda Motor Co. Ltd. and were ridden by Japanese riders, whilst the fifth was ridden by American Bill Hunt. Although his entry was made in his own name, Bill worked for Honda in America and was the team's link with the West and served as Team Manager. All five were newcomers to Isle of Man racing and, although few realised it at the time, they were the pioneers of what was to become the take-over of motorcycle racing by the Japanese factories.

*

The 125cc Lightweight TT was held on the 10.79 mile Clypse Course which, although much shorter than the Mountain Course, still presented a demanding ride as it twisted its way through town and country. The Honda riders (wearing their futuristic jet-style helmets) arrived early and put in many course-learning laps in both the official practice sessions on their race machines, and at other times on road-going Hondas. Based at the Nursery Hotel, Onchan, the 12 strong team had the use of basic garage space and the Hotel yard, where their race machines were prepared

Honda machines and mechanics in the yard of the Nursery Hotel during the 1959 TT.

under the gaze of many curious westerners. Amongst the visitors to the Nursery Hotel were a few of the more perceptive riders of the day like Tommy Robb, Bill Smith and Luigi Taveri.

*

Practice times showed that the Hondas were unlikely to threaten Italian machinery during the race, and so it proved as Tarquinio Provini took his MV Agusta to victory at an average speed of 74.06 mph. However, in a hint of things to come, the Japanese machines did show commendable reliability. Only Bill Hunt failed to reach the finish and that was due to falling on the second lap. The four Japanese riders all brought their high-revving dohc machines to the finish, in the order:

6th	Naomi Taniguchi	68.29 mph
7th	Giichi Suzuki	66.71 mph
8th	Teisuke Tanaka	65.69 mph
11th	Junzo Suzuki	63.81 mph

Those performances were good enough to win the Manufacturers Award for Honda, and that was something they found enormously encouraging. It also indicated to astute TT watchers that such all-round reliability offered a sound basis for development and that Honda could well become a force to be reckoned with.

*

Whilst considerable attention was focussed on the Hondas at the 1959 TT, MV Agusta 'works' bikes again took wins in all the solo classes and BMW continued their domination of the Sidecar class. It was Geoff Duke's last year of riding in the TT and he finished fourth in the Junior race. It was his lowest ever TT finish!

The Wettest?

Poor weather caused the 1959 Senior race to be postponed from Friday to Saturday. Then, although it started in the dry, after the second lap the rains came and it turned into one of the wettest ever races and the slowest since 1949. Winner John Surtees was so wet, physically exhausted and trembling from the cold at the finish, that he had to be lifted from his machine. John maintained that the hailstones over the Mountain were severe enough to have stripped paint from his full-fairing. It was an even worse event for his team-mate John Hartle, for he threw his MV down the wet road in a big way at Glen Vine on the third lap, fortunately getting away with minor injuries.

Comparatively slow the 1959 Senior TT may have been, but other riders still spoke of Surtees

John Surtees corrects a slide as he goes through Hillberry on his MV Agusta in the very wet 1959 Senior TT.

howling past them in a cloud of spray from the four-cylinder MV.

*

The majority of the bikes used in the 1959 Senior TT were Nortons and it was still the custom for most competitors to ride their bikes up to the Start for practice and racing. When they got to the Paddock, riders parked their racers where they could, often leaning them against the surrounding chestnut fence. With so many identical bikes there was scope for confusion. It was veteran Albert Moule who found himself embarrassed after he accidentally took Terry Shepherd's bike from the Paddock for one practice session instead of his own. He realised his mistake by the time he got to Braddan Bridge and returned to the Start by side roads. There he found Terry standing in the Paddock scratching his head and muttering "I'm sure I left it here".

Seeding
An introduction in 1959 was that of 'seeding' the top riders in the Junior and Senior races and giving them early start numbers. The previous system of balloting for start numbers could see a top rider draw a 'late' number and so have the handicap of having to battle his way past many slow riders. This meant that he was not racing on equal terms with other top riders who may have drawn 'early' numbers and enjoyed relatively clear roads. (The one advantage of starting with a late number was that it did give a rider's support crew the chance to keep him more fully and accurately informed of his rivals' progress by way of signals.) From a spectator's point of view the new seeding system had the advantage of putting the top riders closer together on the road. This made it easier to measure the time intervals between them, so making it simpler (and more exciting) to follow the progress of the race. However, the top riders - whilst generally welcoming the 'seeding' system - had their own views. Some were happy to be in front, whilst others preferred to chase rather than be chased. The organisers generally leant a sympathetic ear to riders requests for slight adjustments to their starting numbers and by 1960 they decided the starting order of the 6 leading riders by ballot, (by 1961 the leading 10 were balloted and by 1964 it was up to the best 20).

*

With as many as a hundred entries in some races, it can happen that an up-and-coming rider who has been allocated a number down in the 60s or 70s reveals such good form in practice that he deserves a higher starting number. As there are usually a few non-starters in every race, the organisers sometimes allocate such a 'dark-horse' a revised number, perhaps in the 20s.

*

Having learnt much from their 1959 debut, Honda returned to the TT in 1960 with improved 125cc twins and new four-cylinder 250cc machines. Once again basing themselves at the Nursery Hotel, they enlisted the help of experienced Australian riders Tom Phillis and Bob Brown. There were six Honda entries in the 125 and 250 TT races and they extended their race programme in 1960 to include some of the European world-championship events.

Back to the Mountain
The organisers abandoned the Clypse Course for the 1960 TT and reverted to running all classes over the 37 ¾ mile Mountain Course. This meant that Honda and its Japanese riders had a fresh lot of learning to do in their second year at the races.

*

The new 250 Honda-four was basically a doubled-up 125. Both were over-square having cylinder dimensions of 44 x 41 mm, and their engines were now inclined in the frame to shift weight distribution and improve handling. With 16 valves, 6 speed gearbox, 4 flat-slide carburettors and revving normally to 13,500 (and able to take bursts up to 15,000), the new 'four' had an output of about 36 bhp and brought an exciting sound to the 250 class.

The four-cylinder engine of the 250 Honda with a white-gloved mechanic preparing to take the engine out.

While the Hondas were again reliable, with three of the four-cylinder bikes finishing, they were slightly down on speed. The fastest Honda rider was Bob Brown in 4th with a race-average speed of 89.21 mph, whilst first-time TT winner Gary Hocking sped to victory on his new twin-cylinder MV Agusta at 93.64 mph. That translated into a six-minute gap at the end of the two-hour race. Hocking was followed home by his team-mate Carlo Ubbiali with Tarquinio Provini on the Morini in third place.

*

Gary Hocking was a young Rhodesian hungry for success, but perhaps he let ambition overcome judgement by beating MV team-leader Ubbiali in the five-lap 1960 Lightweight 250 TT. Whatever, he suddenly found that promised rides on 350 and 500cc MVs in the Junior and Senior races were no longer available to him.

*

Honda's results in the the three-lap Lightweight 125 TT (held in a howling gale) were similar to those in the 250 race, and their achievements were solid but unspectacular. They were again short of power and could not match the pace of the Italian MVs and East German MZs. Honda riders took 6th-10th and 19th places.

*

The Japanese had a reputation for copying the West in the 50s, but in the 60s they also copied each other. In 1960 Suzuki decided that they would follow Honda's example and contest the TT. It is said that they sent a representative to the Island in February 1960 and, sitting on the bonnet of a Morris 1000, he made a cine recording of the whole 37 ¾ miles of the Mountain Course for those back in Japan.

*

Suzuki chose the 125cc class to debut their twin-cylinder two-stroke Colleda models that had separate alloy barrels with hard chromed bores, twin carburettors, a 12:1 compression ratio and ran up to 12,000 rpm on an 8:1 petroil mixture. The six-speed gearbox operated by going up from one to six, to neutral, to one, etc. Suzuki had two finishers, in 15th (Toshio Matsumoto) and 16th places (Michio Ichino), but their race-average speed was some 8 mph slower than the leading 125 Honda (that itself was some 5 mph slower than the race-winning MV Agusta). There was clearly a performance gap between the machines from the East and West but, whereas bikes like the small MV Agustas from Europe were nearing the limit of their development, the Japanese machines were at the beginning of theirs!

*

Whilst talking speeds, in the reduced to six laps (from seven) 1960 Senior TT, John Surtees pushed the outright lap record up to 104.08 mph when winning the race from team-mate John Hartle Positions were reversed in the Junior when John Hartle recorded his first TT win.

*

John Hartle speeds to victory on his MV Agusta in the 1960 Junior TT.

Norton, Matchless and AJS (all part of the AMC Motorcycles Group) still carried out limited development work on their single-cylinder racers but they did not enter 'works' riders, instead they passed their development models to respected private race entrants. With Norton that usually meant arch racing supporter Reg Dearden (who was said to have brought 22 Manx Nortons to the Island for the 1959 TT). Matchless and AJS entrusted their latest models to Tom Arter. Development of the many British single-cylinder racers that monopolised the larger classes was also pushed along by the efforts of private tuners like Bill Lacey, Steve Lancefield, Francis Beart and Ray Petty. Each had their own ideas of how to gain extra power, braking and handling, using modifications like needle-roller big-ends, coil valve springs, desmodromic valve-operation, 5-speed gear clusters, lightweight frames, hydraulic steering dampers and twin front brakes; whilst in the sidecar class the three-wheeler boys were dropping to 'kneeler' mode and experimenting with disc brakes.

*

During the 1960 Senior TT Derek Minter became the first rider to take a single-cylinder machine around the Mountain Course at over 100 mph. His lap speed was 101.05 mph on his Steve Lancefield prepared Norton, but he later retired from the race leaving Mike Hailwood (who also lapped at over the 'ton') to head the pack of British single-cylinder machines that chased home the Italian multis of Surtees and Hartle.

*

Most riders stopped once for fuel in what was now a 6 lap Senior race. Earlier experiments that involved the fitting of pannier-tanks on the singles for a non-stop race had mostly been dropped. A few fitted 7 gallon tanks in the normal position and hoped to complete the race without stopping. The multi-cylinder MV Agustas averaged about 22 mpg so a pit-stop was essential. The alternative of carrying 10 gallons of fuel would have made them almost unmanageable.

A Record Lap
Although 1960 saw records broken in the solo classes (all winners were on Avon tyres), it was the sidecar class where the lap record for three-wheelers was

Helmut Fath (BMW) on the approach to Braddan Bridge during his winning ride in the 1960 TT. The sidecar is fitted on the right-hand side of the outfit as was customary with drivers from the Continent. British drivers fitted their 'chairs' on the left.

well and truly shattered when Helmut Fath on his BMW added 28.61 mph to the previous fastest lap by a sidecar outfit on the Mountain Course. The reason for this huge increase was that the previous lap record was held by Freddie Dixon at 57.18 mph, which he set in the last Sidecar TT to be held on the Mountain Course way back in 1925. (When the sidecar class was reintroduced to the TT in 1954 it was to the Clypse Course.) As many had predicted, the sidecars' return to three laps of the Mountain Course took a heavy toll of machinery.

*

A man who was to go on to make a sizeable, and at times controversial, impression on TT history took his first Island win in the 1960 MGP. He was Phil Read and he won the Senior event by 1½ minutes, setting an impressive new lap record of 97.09mph on his unstreamlined Bill Lacey-tuned Norton.

*

At the 1961 TT the organisers adopted a policy of not recording the first lap times of each rider, the idea being to take some of the pressure away and allow riders to familiarise themselves with the Course. The first lap did count towards the number that they had to do to qualify. At least one of a riders laps had to be within the stipulated qualifying time for the class. They were; Lightweight 125 - 34 minutes, Lightweight 250 - 33 minutes, Sidecar - 38 minutes, Junior - 30 minutes, Senior - 29 minutes. The organisers dropped the policy the next year.

*

There were 15 practice sessions at the 1961 TT and they started on a Friday evening. For the first time ever at the TT, practice took place on Thursday afternoon instead of Thursday evening. The longer afternoon session was an already established feature of the MGP.

*

The FIM introduced an age limit of 55 for riders in International competition and this applied to the TT.

*

Following in the wheel-tracks of their compatriots from Honda and Suzuki, Yamaha brought 125cc RA41 and 250cc RD48 rotary-valved, air-cooled, two-stroke models to the 1961 TT. Yamaha had no dedicated testing facilities and most of their experimentation was done by riding their temperamental two-strokes along a nine-foot wide road bordering a river near their factory. They never found the 250's top-speed on that stretch! Like Honda, they had achieved racing success in Japan but they struggled against the rigours of the

Mountain Course in their first year of European racing, taking 11th, 12th and 17th in the 125 class and a more promising 6th with Fumio Ito in the 250.

*

Suzuki claimed to have improved their models for 1961 but one writer said of them: *'maximum revs are in the region of 11,000, and minimum revs do not seem to be much lower, judging by the speed the engine has to be run at when warming up'*. The racing two-strokes of the time all had narrow power bands and consequently needed many gears in the box (anything from 6 to 12) to enable the riders to keep them 'on the boil'.

*

Suzuki's 1961 TT was something of a disaster with constant mechanical problems in practice, the need to withdraw some of their riders from the races, and lowly finishes for those who did take part. The only bright spot for them was that they came into contact with the East German MZ team who were running their technically advanced two-stroke racers. Suzuki made the acquaintance of MZ rider Ernst Degner and

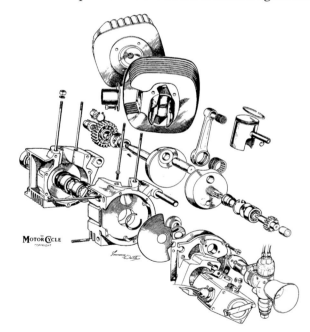

'The Motor Cycle' captioned this illustration by their artist Laurie Watts with: *'Mechanical simplicity and well harnessed resonances characterised the 1961 air-cooled MZ single, first one-two-five to reach 25 bhp. Note the half-moon squish band, short exhaust port, single piston ring, needle-roller con-rod bearings and cutaway inlet disc'*. Laurie Watts was allowed full access to all engine components and was even allowed to trace the shape of the ports.

later persuaded him to remain in Sweden after a race there, whilst his family was spirited out of East Germany and then they were all flown to Japan. Although it is said that Degner took many of MZ's race secrets with him to Suzuki, really there were no major secrets in the MZs' design. Everyone knew the principles involved in rotary valves and tuned exhausts, it was just that, initially, no one could match the East German concern (and their race engineer Walter Kaaden) in the application of them. Suzuki (and later Yamaha) spent fortunes in catching and overtaking MZ.

*

The year of 1961 saw European manufacturers begin to concede their position as makers of the world's best racing motorcycles. MV Agusta claimed to have withdrawn full factory support from racing but they loaned machines for the TT to Gary Hocking. He entered MVs in all four solo classes, with his bikes sporting a 'Privat' label to make the point that they were not fully works supported. Although the MVs showed that they were still quick enough for victory, Hocking suffered mechanical problems in all three of the races he started, (having decided not to race the 125), and his only finish was in the Junior where, on his ailing four, he finished second to Phil Read's Norton. In the previous two years MV had won all four solo classes at the TT.

*

Opposition to the Japanese in the Lightweight 250 class was further reduced when MZ found that they could not get their temperamental two-strokes to carburate properly over the ups and downs of the Mountain Course and so withdrew from the race. The stage was set for a Japanese take-over.

Honda Success

It was Honda who seized their opportunity at that 1961 TT. With much improved machines ridden by some of the best riders of the day, they swept to Lightweight victory taking the first five places in both 125 and 250 races. Although the opposition may have been weakened, these were not hollow victories, for they were both achieved at record breaking speeds. It was a stunning performance from a company that was making only its third TT appearance, and confirmation that Honda products were already amongst the best in the world. After the TT Honda went on to more sweeping victories in the continental Grand Prix and finished the year as world champions in the 125 and 250 cc classes.

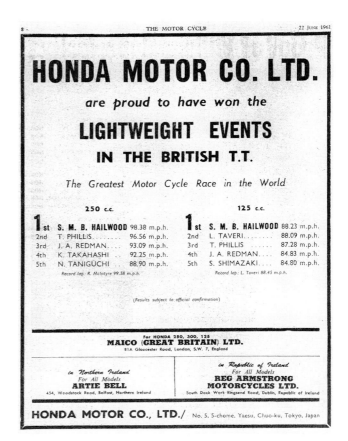

How Honda advertised their success at the 1961 TT.

Hat-Trick

Mike Hailwood was initially told that Honda could not supply him with a 125 cc machine for the 1961 TT, but after his formidable father Stan had explained his position as one of the UK's biggest motorcycle dealers, a 125 was found. So, on leased-from-the-factory machines, it was Mike who won both the 125 and 250 classes on the improved Hondas in 1961, and made it a hat-trick of wins (the first person to do so) by bringing his Norton home first in the Senior race at an average speed of 100.60 mph. Mike nearly made it a personal clean-sweep of the four solo classes but, after leading for most of the Junior race, his AJS engine failed towards the end of the last lap and let Phil Read (Norton) through for the Junior win in his first TT race.

*

In the thick of the TT action in 1961 was the great Bob McIntyre. He set the 250 race alight with a new record lap of 99.58 mph on his four-cylinder Honda RC162 before retiring whilst in the lead. In the Junior he held the early lead on a twin-cylinder Bianchi before retiring at Ginger Hall on the first lap, and in the Senior he chased Mike Hailwood all the way, finishing in second place on his single-cylinder Norton at an average speed of just under 100 mph for the six-lap race.

*

This sketch by an unknown admirer of Bob McIntyre shows him setting a new lap record on his 250 Honda in the 1961 TT.

Third finisher in the 1961 Senior race was Tom Phillis on the experimental twin-cylinder, push-rod Norton 'Domiracer' that generated much interest and plenty of performance, (lapping at over 100mph), but failed to receive much further development. However, the 'Domiracer' contribution at the 1961 Senior TT saw the first Norton 1-2-3 since 1950 and, with the Junior win, their last double TT victory.

*

Fred Stevens became the first to use an electric starter on a TT bike when he pressed the button to fire-up his modified Honda roadster and get away in the 1961 Lightweight race. Fred's quick start and departure from the line was in contrast to the traditional slower run-and-bump method used by the rest of the entry.

*

All 45 finishers in the 1961 Senior TT were on British machines. Of the 50 finishers in the Junior race, only 4 were on foreign makes. By contrast, the Lightweight 250 race had entries from 14 regular foreign manufacturers, plus a number of specials.

*

At the end of 1961 Norton announced that they had ceased production of Manx Nortons. A few new machines were assembled from spares in 1962 but it was, seemingly, the end of the line for the single-cylinder racer with a proud and successful pedigree. Racing is full of 'what ifs', but what if Norton had developed their plans for a four-cylinder racer in the early 1950s? Would it have been successful in competition against the Italians and Japanese, would it have boosted the sales of their roadsters as the Japanese factories' successes undoubtedly did? We shall never know.

*

Production of the Matchless G50 and AJS 7R ceased in 1962 although Jack Williams continued with development work on them at the factory for a few more years. Machines incorporating experimental features continued to be passed to Tom Arter and also Tom Kirby, who then made them available to selected riders.

*

The 1962 TT received 344 entries from 205 riders, 67 of who were from outside Britain. Derek Minter and Dan Shorey were the only two riders to start in all five solo classes. The Isle of Man Government made a direct grant of £15,000 to the ACU towards the cost of running the races.

*

SPEEDS

The performance advantage enjoyed by MV Agusta in the 500cc class was shown by the speed of 138.46 mph that the big MV clocked at Sulby. Next best was top privateer Mike Duff who managed 125.91 mph on his Matchless. On such a high-speed course where bikes are flat-out for long periods, there was no chance for the single-cylinder machines to make-up for the MVs huge power advantage by their slightly better handling. This was particularly so when the 'fours' were ridden by riders of the quality of Mike Hailwood and Gary Hocking.

*

'The TT Special' timed the sidecars at Sulby for the first time. Fastest was Florian Camathias on his BMW at 118.45 mph. They also clocked the 50cc runners and Luigi Taveri was best at 86.97 mph. Whilst that was highly creditable for a '50', ten of the 'tiddlers' were clocked at less than 60 mph at Sulby. Beryl Swain recorded 54.22 mph.

Tiddlers

An innovation at the 1962 TT was a race for 50cc machines, making the TT a six-race meeting. Although several small European manufacturers supported 50cc racing, including Kreidler with their 12-speed models, it was the Japanese who took victory in the two-lap race with Ernst Degner bringing his Suzuki home ahead of two Hondas at an average speed of 75.52 mph. It was the first win for a two-stroke at the TT since Kluge won the 1938 Lightweight on a DKW. The 50cc race also included the first lady competitor to race a solo in the TT, Beryl Swain, who took her Itom into 22nd place.

*

Although most solo classes were allowed six or seven practice sessions at the 1962 TT, the new 50s received only three. Starting his TT apprenticeship in the 50cc class, Bill Ivy appeared on his Chisholm-Itom but failed to finish. He was to go on to much greater things at the IOM races.

*

'Kipper'

A man who was to make his own piece of TT history and become the longest serving Travelling Marshal at the races was Manxman Allan 'Kipper' Killip. Allan did his first turn of duty at the 1962 TT and in the third practice session he was called into serious action. Equipped with an AJS Twin that he recalls as 'dreadful', he stretched the Ajay's performance to the limit as he sped to a major incident that involved top-man Gary Hocking and fellow Rhodesian, Graham Smith, who touched and fell at the very fast Ballacrye stretch, soon after Ballaugh. Hocking's MV burst into flames and despite a local farmer smothering it with wet sacks, it was badly damaged. Smith suffered a leg injury that put him out of the 1962 races but Hocking, although badly knocked about, rode in later sessions. A couple of well remembered but contrasting rider responses stick in Kipper's mind from that first big incident. The first was of Bob McIntyre stopping to offer assistance, taking a message and stopping again on the next lap to see that all was well. The second was of Jim Redman (fellow countryman to the two fallen Rhodesian riders) barely backing the throttle a fraction or lifting his head from under the screen as he passed. It is not difficult to guess whose action was most appreciated by the first-time Travelling Marshal trying to deal with a difficult incident.

*

Yamaha missed the 1962 TT but Honda maintained their domination of the Lightweights, keeping everyone else at bay and taking the first three places in 125 and 250 classes (all with European riders). In the same race as the 125 Hondas could be found private runners on tuned BSA Bantams. The rider of one such humble mount wrote later, *'A TT fortnight for riders of home-built Bantams is not passed in quite the same style of Hailwood and Redman - nor at the same velocity'.*

*

Winner of the 1962 Lightweight 250 TT on a Honda was Derek Minter. Riding as a privateer on a year old machine, Derek upset the Honda factory by beating their 'works' riders. Not a man to take orders, Derek tells that although he didn't rate his chances in the race "when a Honda representative told me to let the works riders pass, I decided to win". He did win, finishing two minutes ahead of Jim Redman.

Honda also entered a couple of 285cc fours in the Junior class, but victory there went to MV Agusta. Mike Hailwood rode MVs in the Senior and Junior along with Gary Hocking, Mike taking the Junior and Gary the Senior. There was a welcome win for a British machine in the Sidecar class where Chris Vincent and Eric Bliss took first place on their BSA Twin in a revamped race programme that saw the three-wheelers actually open race-week with their three-lap event. It was the first win for a BSA in an International TT race, although they had taken victory in earlier National Clubman's races.

*

Whilst racing to second place in the Lightweight 125cc race in 1962, Luigi Taveri set the first 90mph lap by a 125. Max Deubel (BMW) did the same in the Sidecar race before retiring on the last lap, and Gary Hocking set the first 100mph lap on a 350.

*

With top single-cylinder runners like Phil Read, Alan Shepherd and Mike Duff retiring from the race, Gary Hocking's Senior TT winning margin was nearly 10 minutes over Ellis Boyce who came in second. British fans were forced to face-up to the same dismal scenario that they had in the 250 class in the early post-war years. There, after previously dominating the class, lack of effort by home manufacturers saw their outdated products fall further and further behind the foreign opposition. The same situation now prevailed in the Junior and Senior classes and it looked like getting worse if Honda extended their efforts to the bigger classes.

Tragedy

As with other TT races down the years the excitement, spectacle, joy and glory of the 1962 series, was overshadowed by the death of a fine rider. Australian Tom Phillis was killed in the 350cc race at Laurel Bank when lying third on his 'works' Honda and trying hard to catch Hocking and Hailwood on their MVs. A popular figure who was much admired and respected, he also had an incredible desire to win. In those early 1960s, not only was there intense competition between opposing teams but there was also fierce rivalry between riders in the same teams, for the number of coveted 'works' rides were few while the number of riders who aspired to them were many. Tom Phillis's death had a major effect on his close friends in motorcycle racing. Fellow Honda teamster Jim Redman had serious thoughts of quitting but was persuaded by Bob McIntyre to keep riding. Gary Hocking felt that all the riders were being forced to press each other too hard and he persuaded Count Agusta to release him from his MV contract. The dreadful irony that ensued was that whilst Redman did continue racing, McIntyre was killed a few months later at Oulton Park and Hocking died in a car race in his native Rhodesia before the year ended.

*

Jim Redman (left) talks to Bob McIntyre at the 1962 TT.

For the first time at the TT riders received a small amount of start-money in 1963. It was £10 for the 50cc runners, £15 for other solos and £25 for sidecars. Prize-money remained at £200 for Junior and Senior winners, £100 for Sidecars and Lightweight 250s, £75 for 125s and £50 for 50s, whose race distance was increased from two to three laps.

*

Racing tyres adopted a distinct triangular shape in the early 1960s, the idea being to offer increased contact area when the bike was cranked over.

*

There were twelve practice periods in 1963 with the first one being on Saturday morning, and riders had to get used to the presence of a roundabout at Quarter Bridge.

*

One man who only just made TT practice in 1963 was Swiss sidecar driver Florian Camathias. Driving up through England his van broke-down near Hinckley. With his prime concern being to get to the Island he unloaded his BMW racing outfit, he and his passenger climbed into their leathers and they set off for Douglas on open pipes. There was a slight hitch at the Mersey tunnel when they could not produce money for the toll, but they were let through, made it to the boat, crossed to the Island and, for good measure, won the Sidecar TT!

*

Yamaha had not been idle during their year out of racing in 1962. In 1963 they returned to the fray with an improved 125 called the RA55, and the 250cc RD56 that was described as '*a rather more sophisticated version of the earlier RD48*'. Still air-cooled, it was sensationally fast, was claimed to deliver over 40 bhp at 11,000 rpm and really caught the eye with its TT performances. With Tony Godfrey joining Fumio Ito and Hiroshi Hasegawa, the Yamaha men stunned the Hondas of Redman, Robb and Taveri by holding first and second places on the first lap of the 250 race and clocking 140 mph through the speed-trap in the process. In a race that was held in blazing hot sunshine and on road surfaces that were slippery with molten tar, what would have been a fairy-tale victory for Yamaha was spoilt by Jim Redman's determined fight back, an extended pit-stop for Ito that relegated him to second place, and a life-threatening crash for Tony Godfrey.

and taking first three places at the 1963 TT with Hugh Anderson, Frank Perris and Ernst Degner. Thereafter, dominance swung from one to another of the three Japanese manufacturers and in their frantic attempts to maintain or recover their positions as top-dogs, they turned out evermore exotic examples of race machinery for the very best riders of the day to compete on and to set ever faster race speeds.

Helicopter Rescue

In an era that saw the greatest concentration of experimental machinery that racing has ever seen,

Jim Redman (Honda) rounds Signpost Corner as he heads for completion of another 37³/₄ mile lap of the TT Mountain Course in 1963.

It was Jim Redman's first TT victory and although he described it as *'a dream come true'*, he went on to explain that the race itself was a nightmare. In addition to the molten tar, his Honda overheated and the bike lost revs on each lap. He also had to put up with the contents of the oil-tank burning his leg throughout the race. Rarely does a rider take part in a long race like the TT without experiencing problems of some sort - even if he is the race winner.

*

The performance leap-frogging of Honda by Yamaha was to become a familiar characteristic of racing in the 1960s. Suzuki did the same to Honda in the 125 cc class, making incredible progress in development

such was the frantic search for performance and the pressure to win that manufacturers were constantly pushing the limits, and riders were sometimes carrying out an unreasonable amount of testing and development during competition. It was work that should have been carried out on the controlled conditions of the test-track and, mindful of this, riders of the ultra-rapid two-strokes always rode with at least one finger on the clutch lever, ready to counter the effects of an engine seizure. Although various theories were advanced, the reason for Tony Godfrey's high-speed crash at Milntown in the 1963 Lightweight 250 TT was never publicly revealed. But Tony, unknowingly, made a little bit of TT history with that mystery crash. With the assistance of Shell-Mex and BP Ltd the organisers had introduced a helicopter at the 1963 TT to speed the removal of injured riders to hospital so that they would receive early medical attention. Tony Godfrey was the first rider to make use of the new service.

*

Joining the fray with the Japanese two-strokes at the 1963 250 TT were several riders mounted on privately entered British-built Greeves racers. These Villiers-engined based machines had been running successfully in short circuit meetings for a couple of years, but this was their first attempt at the TT. The entries from riders like Reg Everett (whose earlier roadster-based Greeves racer sparked the Greeves factory's interest in producing a road race machine) caused factory boss Bert Greeves a few concerns. He wrote to each rider before the event reminding them that the Greeves 'Silverstone' model was an over-the-counter machine built specifically for short circuits and not for six laps of the TT Course. Asking the Greeves entrants to ride *'with skilled judgement and restraint'* at the TT, he nevertheless took a positive attitude and offered them his support. This took the form of a free steering damper, advice on brake linings and set-up, the manufacture of 3 gallon tanks, a front mudguard, an extended range of sprockets, and technical support on the Island from Bob Mills of the Work's Competition Department. In the event, six Greeves took part but only that of Allan Harris finished, albeit in a creditable eighth place.

*

Joe Dunphy was one of six Greeves riders in the 1963 Lightweight 250cc TT. Built for short circuit use, the Greeves were no match for the Japanese factory racers but they did achieve victories over the Mountain Course in the MGP races.

Greeves were just one of the **incredible 25 makes of** machine that contested the 1963 Lightweight 250 TT, but for all the noble efforts of these many concerns the real glamour and spectator interest was concentrated on the Japanese factory machines and their riders who, between them, created so much TT history in the 1960s. It was a time when the Japanese threw money and technology into racing and when now legendary riders like Mike Hailwood, Jim Redman, Phil Read, Tommy Robb, Bill Ivy, Alan Shepherd, Ralph Bryans, Stuart Graham, Mike Duff, Giacomo Agostini, Luigi Taveri, Ernst Degner, etc., were all young men in their prime. It is difficult to give such riders their dues in a book like this. Fortunately, many of them later wrote their own accounts of those heady days and the literary efforts of Tommy Robb, Jim Redman, Mike Hailwood, Phil Read, Bill Ivy, Mike Duff, Derek Minter and others, tell in detail of how TT and Grand Prix history was made.

Gilera Return

An event that gripped the public imagination and brought spectators flocking to the Island in 1963 was the unexpected return of Gilera to the TT after a six year absence. It was former world-champion Geoff Duke who persuaded the company to take their 1957 machines out of mothballs and contest the Junior and Senior events. 'Scuderia Duke' entered John Hartle and Phil Read (original choice Derek Minter being injured) but, for all the high expectations, it was clear from the outset of practice that they were going to find it difficult to match the pace of Jim Redman's Honda in the Junior race and Mike Hailwood on the sole MV Agusta in the Senior.

Redman duly took victory in what was a wet Junior race - Honda's first win in this class. Hailwood retired the MV and Hartle rode the Gilera (with gearbox problems) into a distant second place, nearly seven minutes in arrears.

Friday's 1963 Senior TT was preceded by the 50cc race and resulted in a win for Mitsuo Itoh on his Suzuki. It was the first TT to be won by a Japanese rider on a Japanese machine. The main race of the day, the 'Blue Riband' Senior TT, was run in dry conditions and saw John Hartle (Gilera) start at number 4 with Mike Hailwood (MV Agusta) getting away 10 seconds later at number 5. As they flashed through the start and finish area at the end of the first lap, a relaxed Hailwood was sitting tight on Hartle's tail and thus was some 9 seconds ahead on corrected time. Mike could have sat there for the rest of the

John Hartle prepares to take his Gilera out for practice in 1963. The AJS mounted Travelling Marshal in the background is Jack Harding.

race, but he soon drew ahead and eventually took the chequered flag 1¹/₂ minutes ahead of Hartle, having had a gear-change problem for most of the race. Riding the other Gilera, Phil Read took third place on a bike that he had *'never felt safe and confident on'* and, although they had been made to lap the Mountain Course faster than ever before, the Gileras went back to the factory at Arcore.

*

Mike Hailwood set a new lap record of 106.41 on his MV before the occurrence of the gear-change problems that slowed him in the 1963 Senior. The public were used to seeing lap speeds increase year on year and it was due to a combination of factors that included engine development, advances in tyre technology, improved fuels, and improvements to the Course. When looking at the improvements that have been carried out to the Mountain Course many race fans think that roads have been widened and corners eased solely for race competitors. That is not so. As in the rest of Britain, the increased demands of normal vehicular traffic on Manx roads brought

about the need for many of the changes that have contributed to increases in lap speeds.

*

Avon were among the top racing tyre manufacturers in the early 1960s and this is how they advertised their new 'cling' rubber in the 1963 TT programme.

Yamaha were desperate to achieve world-wide racing success to boost their sales of road machines and towards the end of 1963 they signed Phil Read to race for them in 1964. Phil was fully aware that the Japanese paid for results and that he would be expected to deliver. He had a lot of learning to do, for two-strokes were new to him as were seven-speed gearboxes, etc. However, he did deliver success to Yamaha and also played an important role over the next few years in what some people consider to have been a golden age of motorcycle racing. In his book 'Prince of Speed', Phil wrote: *'We swept through a show-piece of classic racing competition that was boosted by an open cheque-book, the like of which we may never see again'.*

*

Despite the open cheque-books waved by the Japanese manufacturers, the associated trade support of racing was beginning to shrink. At the 1964 TT competitors had to provide their own fuel during practice, although it was still supplied free of charge for the races. The following year Renold Chains made a nominal charge for the chains that they had previously provided free of charge. This was partly to bring about economies and partly to counter the abuse of their free service.

*

After a successful spell with Honda, Tommy Robb suddenly had his bikes taken away without explanation. Yamaha were looking for a third rider for the 1964 TT and Tommy was happy to accept a berth on one of their flying 250s. Suffering from chronic plug trouble through most of practice, he recalls in 'From TT to Tokyo': *'Things got really rough on one early morning practice when I stopped and ran out of plugs on the mountain - and believe me there is no*

Yamaha needed boxes of sparking plugs for their temperamental two-stroke racers.

lonelier place in the world at that time of the day! I had used my half dozen plugs and had begun to despair, when I spotted an old tractor in a field. I raced across with my plug spanner, took a rusty plug out of the tractor, put my Yamaha plug in its place, tried the bike; it fired first time, and was off again. The plug carried me back to the start, much to my relief'. Clearly expecting problems, the Yamahas carried spare plugs inside their fairings.

Yamaha teamsters Phil Read and Mike Duff both retired from the 1964 Lightweight 250 TT after Read set the fastest lap. It left Tommy Robb as the only Yamaha 'works' finisher. Honda took their customary first place with Jim Redman who finished with an oil-soaked rear tyre. He was chased home by Alan Shepherd on an MZ, with Alberto Pagani bringing an Italian Paton into a distant third place. Redman also won the Junior and, although they were Yamaha 'works' riders in the small classes, Read and Duff rode British machinery in the big classes and finished second and third to Redman on AJS 7Rs.

*

After missing the Junior with tonsillitis, Mike Hailwood rose from his sick-bed to win the Senior at the comparatively slow race average speed of 100.95 mph. It was still good enough to bring him home more than three minutes ahead of Derek Minter in second place.

*

Mike Hailwood (MV Agusta) at Keppel Gate during his winning ride at the 1964 Senior TT.

Although they never competed in the Sidecar class at the TT when in their prime during the 1950s, Gilera took one of their four-cylinder bikes out of mothballs for Florian Camathias to ride in three-wheeler form at the 1964 TT. He retired whilst lying second, leaving Max Deubel to take yet another victory for BMW, with Colin Seeley finishing second.

Mad Sunday

TT fans have always sought to emulate the riders whilst on the Island, and this was a fraught business when carried out amongst normal traffic. The Sunday before race week (not for nothing known as Mad Sunday!) is always particularly bad. In an attempt to ease the problem, the authorities introduced a one-way flow of traffic over the Mountain from Ramsey to the outskirts of Douglas, giving the ordinary rider an opportunity to play racers on this 11 mile stretch.

*

Those who, from choice or necessity, attend early morning practice for the TT in June find that it can be surprisingly cold. However, riders faced really unseasonably cold weather for the first few practice sessions at the 1964 MGP in early September. Even experienced riders must have been shocked when they looked at the information board displayed at the Start, for it told them that Course conditions were generally good *'except for frost here and there'*. A newspaper wrote of riders gathering for the same session *'in brilliant moonlight'*!

*

The 250 class had become so ultra-competitive in TT and Grand Prix racing that it began to steal some of the glamour from the 'Blue Riband' 500cc class, the latter having become slightly boring due to its domination by Mike Hailwood on his MV Agusta.

*

To combat the threat from the two-strokes of Yamaha and Suzuki in the Lightweight class, Honda unveiled their six-cylinder 250 model at the Italian Grand Prix towards the close of the 1964 season. Designed by Soichiro Irimajiri and said to deliver 53 bhp, it appeared too late to prevent Phil Read and Yamaha winning the 250 World Championship for 1964, but it became a major force in 1965.

*

Yamaha could not afford to lose status so they developed four-cylinder water-cooled 250 models for the latter part of the 1965 season. It was the sort of counter-blow that the racing fraternity had become accustomed to, and a look at Yamaha's production figures for road bikes in the 1960s illustrates why they were so keen to maintain their sporting image. In 1961 when they first raced at the TT they produced 130,000 bikes. By the end of the decade they were turning out 450,000 a year.

Phil Read was still running Yamaha's twin-cylinder racer at the 1965 TT and on the opening lap of the Lightweight race he set the first 100 mph lap by a 250, but his effort was not enough to prevent Jim Redman from taking victory on his Honda. The rasp from the new six-cylinder Honda's megaphones spilt far and wide over the Manx countryside, sending a shiver down the spine of anyone watching and momentarily deafening any rider that Jim passed. This victory gave him a hat-trick of 250cc wins, a feat which he equalled in the Junior where he also came home first. In the Junior race he was the only Honda 'works' starter. Was that due to super confidence on the part of Honda, or was it a sign that they were having to watch their racing budget on the motorcycling side as they increased their expenditure in the world of car racing? Whatever the reason, Honda could not have been too hard-up for they brought out a five-cylinder 125 to defend their position in that class.

*

Phil Read had a record-breaking win on his Yamaha in the Lightweight 125 race. Living up to his nickname of 'Speedy' both on and off the track, Phil found a way of quickening the process of dealing with the flood of youngsters who sought his autograph - he used a rubber-stamp.

*

Suzuki had also produced a four-cylinder two-stroke 250 that Aussie Jack Ahearn nicknamed 'Whispering Death'. Its handling left something to be desired, and rider Frank Perris offered to redesign the frame. When told that was not possible as the frame had been designed by a computer, Frank's immediate response was *'Then let the b . . . . y computer ride it'*

'Ago'

Making his TT debut in 1965 was a young Italian hot-shot named Giacomo Agostini on an MV Agusta. 'Ago', as he soon became known, had to comply with the new regulation that read *'Drivers entering the TT races who have not previously ridden on the TT circuit will not be allowed to commence practising until they have been on an officially conducted tour of the course or alternatively, have completed one lap of the course under the supervision of Travelling Marshals'*.

A coach-trip with 'Crossleys Tours' and Peter Crebbin commentating was the accepted way of meeting the new regulation, although Ago had potentially the best of all teachers available in MV team-mate Mike Hailwood. But, however much pre-race theory a rider takes on board, when it comes to his first practice lap he is on his own. Ago's first lap was ridden in extremely wet conditions and took him exactly half an hour, at a lowly average speed of 75.48 mph.

*

Chief Travelling Marshal Peter Crebbin (right) with a group of newcomers to the TT Course at Creg ny Baa. The need for such conducted tours was shown by another Travelling Marshal, Albert Moule, who was shocked upon attending a fallen rider at this same spot during practice in 1964 to be told by the rider "I forgot the corner".

The MV Agustas no longer had things their own way in the Junior race where Ago came a creditable third behind Redman (Honda) and Read (Yamaha) and Mike Hailwood set the fastest lap before retiring, although they were still in a class of their own in the Senior. But the TT Course is a great leveller and Mike Hailwood and Agostini were brought down to earth by treacherous road conditions in the Senior that saw them both spill above Sarah's Cottage (on different laps). Whilst Ago called it a day after his spill on the second lap, one lap later Mike picked up his fallen MV, kicked one or two pieces back into shape and, with broken windscreen, flattened exhausts and an oil-leak, he got back in the race, made two lengthy pit-stops and still rode to victory over Joe Dunphy (Norton).

*

Although it did not seem to receive a mention at the time, the circumstances of Hailwood's restart might well have brought about his disqualification. The uphill stretch above Sarah's is hardly the easiest place to push-start a racing bike, and eye-witnesses later told of Mike rolling it downhill (against the flow of the race) to bump it into life. Whilst he no doubt broke some regulation by so doing, the reality is that Sarah's is probably wide enough to perform such a manoeuvre without getting onto the racing line.

*

A slightly bizarre introduction for the sidecar class in 1965 was a 'no overtaking' zone on the narrow and twisting approach to Ballaugh. Indicated by internationally recognised roadsigns, the penalty for breaking the new rule was exclusion.

*

SPEEDS

By the mid 1960s the small capacity Japanese machines were faster in a straight line than the large capacity British singles. A classic example of this is shown in the speeds recorded at The Highlander by Mike Duff at the 1965 TT. Mike was by then a top-flight rider and his bikes were amongst the fastest in each of the four classes in which he rode. The figures he recorded were:

125 cc Yamaha	125 mph
250 cc Yamaha	143.4 mph
350 AJS 7R	122.9 mph
500 Matchless G50	137.1 mph

In several of the races, riders were timed over the first mile of the Course as they swept past the Grandstand at the start of the second lap. This yielded:

250cc	Bill Ivy,	Yamaha	129.52 mph
Junior	Jim Redman,	Honda	130.48 mph
Sidecar	Fritz Scheidegger,	BMW	113.22 mph

Mike Duff (Yamaha) at Quarter Bridge during the 1965 TT.

Giacomo Agostini's recruitment to the MV Agusta team was a dream come true for the patriotic Count Domenico Agusta, for he finally had a world-class Italian rider who had the potential to ride his Italian machinery to victory. However, instant success on the MV eluded Ago, for he was riding with the best rider in the world at the time - Mike Hailwood. When Count Agusta got a little impatient and suggested to Mike that in some of the later GPs of 1965 he might move over and let the young Italian have a taste of glory, Mike did move over - to Honda.

Chapter 8
HONDA TAKES
THE 'BLUE RIBAND'.

From their TT debut in 1959 when they arrived as oriental curiosities with roadster-based 125s, Honda had developed racing machines for the 50, 125, 250 and 350 classes and taken top TT and world-championship honours with them all. Yamaha and Suzuki were close behind in the small classes (sometimes even in front) and between them the Japanese manufacturers pushed the opposition to one side and dominated four of the five solo race classes at the TT. Honda's efforts to keep at bay the opposition from their fellow countrymen saw them develop five-cylinder 125s and six-cylinder 250s (with a 297cc version for the Junior class), and by 1966 they were ready to challenge in the Senior class. The 500cc (Senior) race had always carried the greatest prestige and had become known down the years as the 'Blue Riband' of the TT programme. Honda could hardly have chosen a better rider to challenge for Senior TT victory than World Champion Mike Hailwood, particularly as their long-time team-leader Jim Redman was out of the reckoning, due to a crash in Belgium that ended his racing career.

Despite their proven ability to produce racing motorcycles with ever-increasing engine outputs, Honda had frequently lagged behind in the handling stakes, wrongly believing that power was all-important. The new four-cylinder, 'across the frame', 500cc RC181 racer they produced for the 1966 season was particularly bad in that respect, indeed many people considered it downright dangerous, including Mike Hailwood. He was quoted in the book 'Hailwood' by Ted Macauley as saying: *'every time I rode the 500 I used to think on the morning of the race, I wish I didn't have to ride in this event. I wish it wasn't on. It wasn't just the usual matter of trying to win, it was trying to stay on the thing. It really was the most frightening experience . . . to try anything at all on the 500 I felt I was risking my life'.* That was the machine that Honda brought to the TT in 1966 in the confident expectation that Mike would tame both the bike and the Mountain Course, snatch the coveted 'Blue Riband' Senior race from MV Agusta, and thus complete their winning sweep of the solo classes.

*

Mike Hailwood has his Honda 500 on almost full-lock as he uses all the road at Ramsey Hairpin and begins to feed in the power for the climb to Waterworks. Note the massive front brake that almost fills the wheel.

What - No TT?

In 1966 the month of June was a strange one on the Isle of Man, for no TT races were run. As a result, the Island was bereft of the thousands of visitors who customarily made their annual pilgrimage to what they regarded as motorcycling heaven in the middle of the Irish Sea. The lack of races was all due to the effect of a lengthy seamens' strike that started in late Spring and forced the ACU to call-off their June event. Although they delayed for as long as possible, their decision to postpone was finally made on the 1st June, in the week before practice was due to start. That was time enough to allow most people to cancel their travel arrangements but too late to prevent a team of Yamaha mechanics flying in from distant Japan.

*

Apart from its adverse effect on the Island and its tourist industry, the postponement of the races posed a serious problem to the top riders and factories because the TT was a major event in the World Championship programme. By juggling with the dates of the MGP, time was found for the TT to be run at the end of August, just after the Ulster GP. Revised race days were Sunday 28th August, Wednesday 31st August and Friday 2nd September. The first race day had to be on a Sunday to allow many of the riders to make a quick dash by specially chartered boat to honour commitments at a major UK meeting at Oulton Park on the Bank Holiday Monday. New legislation had to be passed by Tynwald, the Manx Parliament, to allow Sunday racing.

*

Several manufacturers experienced problems at the 1966 TT that put them out of the event. Having seen the successes of their Japanese rivals at the Island's races, Kawasaki came with a 125cc machine for Toshio Fujii. Regrettably he crashed at Ramsey in the last practice session and was killed.

In a surprise move, the Gilera factory lent Derek Minter one of their old four-cylinder models and the services of a works mechanic, but Derek crashed at a damp Brandish Corner in the last practice session, breaking his arm and putting himself out of the race.

Italian ace Tarquinio Provini also had a major crash in practice on the sweeping bends approaching Ballaugh. Although it seemed to be accepted at the time that the crash was caused by his being dazzled by the low morning sun, twenty-five years later Provini told 'Classic Bike' magazine of the scarcely believable mechanical bodge to his 350cc four-cylinder Benelli that brought an end to his dashing riding career. In his words *The engine had broken on the Wednesday evening, and rather than stripping it completely, the mechanic removed one piston so that it could run as a three and we could do more laps the next day. A con-rod was sawn through just above its big-end. We ran the engine, and it seemed okay. But the remaining metal around the big-end eventually exploded, and a lump shot into the gearbox, locking the rear wheel'.*

*

The TT races may have been subject to delay in 1966 but that did not diminish the spectacle they eventually offered. No one was surprised that the man who created most of the headlines in 1966 was Mike Hailwood, for he rode 125, 250, 350 and 500cc Hondas and was 'flying' in every class. Pushing his 250 hard in Monday morning's practice, Mike had a con-rod poke through the crankcase of the six-cylinder machine at the Mountain Box and Honda had to fly in a new engine. The word went around that he would really be putting the rebuilt 250 to the test in the Thursday afternoon practice and everyone waited for the sparks to fly, including the Travelling Marshals stationed around the Course. One of them, Jimmy Linskey, was riding the Ballacraine to Kirk Michael section that afternoon and was very much aware that Hailwood was in the offing when, to his dismay, he realised coming through Glen Helen that his Triumph was throwing oil onto the rear tyre due to a missing oil-tank cap. Whipping up Creg Willey's Hill and along the Cronk y Voddy straight, he pulled in to where teas were served near the end of the straight, with the intention of finding a bottle cap that he could tape in place. No sooner had he stopped than Hailwood came through with the Honda absolutely on the limit. Jimmy heaved one big sigh of relief for, had he failed to spot his oil-leak and continued riding, he believed that Mike and the Honda would have been on him through the fast bends of the 11th Milestone that follow Cronk y Voddy, and if he had been cranked over with oil on his rear tyre he really believes that mayhem could have ensued. Hailwood set a record-shattering average speed of 104.79 mph on the fabulous 250-6 on that particular lap and it left everyone totally bemused. Just how did the man do it? Not only was he over 4mph faster than the official 250 lap record, but it was a speed that was also well in excess of the 350 lap record.

*

Riders frequently use the long Thursday afternoon practice to show how quick they are, often with the intention of 'psyching' the opposition prior to a race. Everyone tries to put in plenty of laps, there is much action, and racers and organisers treat it as a dress rehearsal. But the official logging of retirements in the 1966 Thursday session could have been better organised. (Information was generally posted on boards at the back of the Grandstand so that support crews could see them.) Rider George Cullen did not make it back to the Start and his mechanic set out to look for him without having being able to discover exactly where he had stopped. The result was a very slow trip around the Course in a van, with the mechanic looking in every gateway and pub until he found George at Ramsey. Loading the bike and starting for Douglas, they struck trouble with the van and eventually got back to the Grandstand in an unofficial lap-time of 5 hours and 13 minutes!

*

Mike Hailwood started his practice with the fearsome 500 relatively slowly, nevertheless he finished the week's preparations with a faster time than Agostini on his MV. He maintained his dominance of the Senior class in the race, winning by nearly 3 minutes from the still learning Agostini. In so doing he set a new lap record of 107.07 mph and won for Honda the coveted 'Blue Riband'. Mike also won the Lightweight 250, was the first Honda home in the Lightweight 125 in sixth (won by Bill Ivy on his Yamaha), but retired on the first lap of the Junior race at Bishop's Court with engine trouble, leaving Agostini to take his first TT win on the new three-cylinder MV, and debut-man Peter Williams to come in second on his AJS. Third in both Junior and Senior races was Chris Conn (Norton).

Honda's team of riders and mechanics at the 1966 TT. Riders in white T-shirts are (l to r) Jim Redman, Mike Hailwood, Stuart Graham, Luigi Taveri and Ralph Bryans. At Ralph's left shoulder is Nobby Clark, the only non-Japanese mechanic.

Sunday Racing

In the first ever TT race to be run on a Sunday, Fritz Scheidegger was excluded from first place in the Sidecar class for using Esso fuel instead of the Shell/BP provided by the organisers. After a protracted appeal he was reinstated as the winner. It had been an extremely close-fought race, with second place man Max Deubel less than a second behind Scheidegger. BMW showed their continuing dominance of the three-wheeler class by taking the first eight places.

*

There was still a race for the 50cc class at the TT but with grid numbers down to only one-third of what they were at the first running of the event in 1962, their Island days were numbered. In the first five years of the 50cc TT the little machines lifted their fastest lap times from 75.52 mph by Ernst Degner on his Suzuki in 1962 to 85.66 mph by Ralph Bryans on his Honda in 1966, and Bryans was to remain the ultimate (50cc) lap record holder, for the class was dropped after 1968.

Ralph Bryans brings his Honda 50 around Ramsey Hairpin prior to the long climb of the Mountain, on his way to setting a 50cc lap record of 85.66 mph. The little Honda used a bicycle type caliper brake at the front that acted on the wheel-rim.

Although there was a certain amount of mockery when the 50s were introduced, TT fans began to respect the tiddlers when they saw what they could do. Honda 'works' bikes eventually gave 11.8 bhp @ 21,000 rpm which meant top speeds of up to 110 mph and lap speeds in the middle-80s, while the Suzuki 50s finished up with 14 gears and peaked at 17,500 rpm. One of Suzuki's top runners, Hans-George Anscheidt, explained just how 'peaky' the little water-cooled RK67 two-strokes were, saying '*At 16,000 rpm you could just feel it pulling a bit; at 17,000 rpm it would begin to fly. Then, 500 rpm later, it was all over and you had to change gear again'.* That meant a gear-change every second under full acceleration.

Powerhouse of Suzuki's 50cc twin-cylinder two-stroke racer.

Whilst the outputs from such small engines were very impressive, real performance was only available from the genuine 'works' bikes and there was a massive speed differential between them and the privately entered machines. The FIM later ruled that the 50cc racers should be limited to one cylinder and six gears.

*

Dreams of a British world-beating racing motorcycle were fostered by the introduction of the Manx Hospital's Society Lottery that offered huge (for the time) cash prizes based upon the results of the Senior MGP and TT races. It was indicated that some of the proceeds from the Lottery would be available to create a British racer and ideas were invited for a prospective world-beater. In the words of respected engineer Phil Irving: *'Practically everybody who was anybody in the trade, and plenty of others who were nobody, weighed in with their pet ideas'*, but no world-beater emerged from them.

*

The 1966 MGP followed immediately after the rearranged TT meeting, giving the Manx people almost a month of continuous motorcycle racing over their roads. Amongst the newcomers at the 1966 MGP was one Dave Saville on a BSA. Dave was looked after by sidecar racer Fred Brindley and eventually swapped to racing three-wheelers himself, achieving TT stardom in the class. The Island's long month of motorcycling in 1966 was shared by the organisers, marshals, supporting Trade teams, the Press, etc.

Also putting in a month's work were the relatively new boys on the scene, Manx Radio, back for their second year.

Allan 'Kipper' Killip had a month of riding his BSA on the Mountain Course as he carried out Travelling Marshal duties in 1966. In this early morning shot he rounds the Gooseneck with only a few hardy spectators in attendance.

Manx Radio

In almost 40 years of existence Manx Radio has had a significant effect on the enjoyment and information that spectators and rider support teams have received from the TT races. Prior to its creation in 1965, spectators could only hear a full race commentary if they watched from one of the popular vantage points served by the limited public address system. The BBC had slimmed down its 'commentaries' to brief updates, so prior to 1965 even those who carried portable radios would miss out on the real details of what was going on if they were on a remote part of the Course.

An early advertisement for Manx Radio.

Based initially in a Portacabin behind the timekeeper's hut opposite the Grandstand, Manx Radio's commentator Peter Kneale could not even see the progress of the race on the main Scoreboard in his first couple of years for, despite their by now scanty reports, the BBC insisted on maintaining their pole-position in the Grandstand. From those difficult beginnings Manx Radio progressed to its own spot in the Grandstand in 1967 and the support of auxiliary commentary points at strategic positions around the Course. Those enabled it to offer what one writer of the time described as *'wheel by wheel, gear by gear, race-length commentaries'*. It was not only spectators who benefited from the greatly enhanced information that Manx Radio was able to transmit during the course of two-hour long TT races, because riders' support crews in the Pits and at signalling points around the 37 ³/₄ miles also received the timings broadcast over the air waves. They soon realised that the times and placings given out over the radio were up-to-date, accurate, and that the information could quickly be converted into very useful signals to riders, particularly if signalling teams were carefully positioned. Manx Radio's enhancement of support crews ability to inform riders of their own and their rivals' positions and timings at strategic positions around the Course has, without doubt, influenced the outcome of several closely fought TT and MGP races.

Peter Kneale was the anchor-man and voice of the TT in the Grandstand for Manx Radio commentaries from 1965 until his death in 2001. Geoff Cannell, whose voice was almost as well known, took over from him in 2002. Geoff had been the commentator at several round-the-course locations, before moving to the Start area and pioneering the use of the roving-microphone in 1988. In so doing he captured much of the high-octane drama from pit-stops in 'gasoline-alley' and shared it with spectators around the Course.

With such on-the-spot, mid-race reporting, plus his pre-race interviews that picked up the tension on the Start line and his immediate post-race interviews of the usually delighted (but frequently stunned) winners, Geoff and his radio-mike added a valuable new dimension to the race commentaries.

*

Geoff Cannell interviews a young Carl Fogarty in the early days of his use of the roving-microphone in the Paddock and Start area.

Whilst the Island was experiencing trouble with its strike-affected conventional shipping movements in 1966, there were also problems with an unconventional stationary vessel. The pirate radio station, Radio Caroline, anchored itself in Manx waters off Ramsey and beamed commercial transmissions to the UK, much to the annoyance of the British authorities.

Diamond Jubilee
The TT was back to its normal date in 1967 which was its Diamond Jubilee year and in attendance was the sole survivor of the 1907 races, Walter Jacobs. There was a little extra pomp in recognition of the Jubilee, a few more speeches, gold, silver and bronze Jubilee medals were awarded to the first three in each International race, and 2,500 pigeons were released from the Grandstand to compete in the 'Pigeon TT'. Of more importance was the introduction of a new Production machine race of National status with three classes (750, 500 and 250cc) over three laps.

*

The amount of time allocated for practice was increased (starting on Thursday) but the numbers out were small until Monday. One man who arrived on Saturday and was keen to make-up for lost time was Steve Jolly. He went straight from the boat to pre-race registration, had his bike scrutineered and rode two practice laps; all before going to check-in at his digs. By the end of practice, riders had put in a total of 2081 complete laps, a distance of 78,500 miles.

*

One disturbing feature of 1967 was that Honda had withdrawn its support of 50 and 125cc racing on the TT and World Championship scene. Suzuki fielded a three-man 'works' team and were strong favourites for the 50cc race which they wanted Yoshimi Katayama to win. That was fine in theory, but in the race Katayama had to make an early stop to change plugs. In his book 'Japanese Riders in the Isle of Man', Ralph Crellin tells how *Team-mates Hans-Georg Anscheidt and Stuart Graham rode as slowly as they could to let him catch up. Catching the dawdling pair at Ramsey, he took the lead up the mountain, but, looking back at his teamsters, he drifted into the ditch alongside the Mountain Mile and crashed, retiring unhurt, leaving Graham to win from a slowing Anscheidt*.

*

Bill Ivy had an unscheduled non-racing incident at Greeba Castle when he scraped his car on the roadside wall for a distance of 282 feet. It was no doubt a bit of a shock to his passenger, Mike Hailwood, and it also incurred Bill a £12 fine.

*

Mike Hailwood was still riding Hondas in 1967, indeed, he was their sole rider in the 250, 350 and 500cc classes. In one of his characteristically pithy comments he claimed that Honda were getting three men's work for one man's pay. As that was rumoured to be £25,000 a year (although Ted Macauley suggests £40,000, they were astronomical figures for the time – 'works' Suzuki rider Stuart Graham was getting £4,000), he was not doing too badly on the financial front. After a busy TT practice period, he then proceeded to show just why he was the highest paid motorcycle racer in the world by taking wins in the Lightweight (250cc) and Junior (350cc) classes on his 'works' Hondas. Using his favourite 297cc-6 cylinder machine in the Junior he set a new absolute lap record of 107.73 mph from a standing start, leaving machines from MV Agusta, Benelli, MZ, Paton, Norton and AJS well behind. It was his 11th TT victory and was the one that saw him overtake Stanley Woods record of 10 TT wins.

A Great Race
The Senior TT of 1967 was expected to be a close-fought race between the two main protagonists, Mike Hailwood (Honda) and Giacomo Agostini (MV Agusta). Although Mike might have been felt to have a psychological advantage over Ago following his stunning Junior win, everyone was aware that the 500 Honda was not an easy ride. Tension was high before the race and though the majority of spectators wanted Mike to win, for he was their champion and to many their hero, many were worried, because they knew he would have to give his all on the poorly-handling Honda, and so it turned out. Even hardened TT spectators who had seen many big TT tussles were impressed by the battle in 1967. Put briefly, Agostini started to claw-back the 30 second starting differential and held an early lead having lapped at 108.38 mph. Hailwood upped the pace (lapping at 108.77 mph) and dragged those seconds back until he was almost level on time at his pit-stop on the third lap. There he lost all that hard-earned time as he was forced to hammer a loose twist-grip back into place. For the two riders concerned, it was a typical 'against the clock' battle that is almost unique to the TT Course, and they saw each other only briefly at the pit-stop. Agostini left the pits with a 15 second lead, Hailwood gradually reduced, then went ahead on time - but only just. The epic battle came to an end

when Agostini's chain broke on the fifth lap at Windy Corner (he was the only competitor not using Renold chain) and Hailwood went on to win at a race average of 105.62mph, setting a new absolute lap record of 108.77 mph and recording a hat-trick of wins for the week. Perhaps Honda should have entered him in the other two recognised solo classes (50 and 125) that were won by Yamaha and Suzuki.

*

Maybe all the pre-race build-up for the Senior gave a spur to the British single-cylinder runners, for Peter Williams, John Blanchard, Malcolm Uphill and Steve Spencer all put in 100 mph laps, although not all lasted the pace. Williams (Arter Matchless) finished second and Spencer (Lancefield Norton) was third, having become the first man to set a 100 mph lap on his TT debut.

Production Racing

There were more than the customary five solo classes at the 1967 TT because the organisers introduced a Production race with classes for 750, 500 and 250cc machines. Run on the Saturday before normal race-week, it featured a Le Mans type start for each class. The 750s went first, followed five minutes later by the 500s and five minutes after them went the 250s, all over three laps.

*

Class winners in the 1967 Production race, from the left: Neil Kelly, John Hartle and Bill Smith.

Although there had been opposition to the introduction of the 'Proddie' race, spectators were kept on their toes by an event that was full of incidents and yielded many fine riding performances. John Hartle took victory in the 750 class on a Triumph Bonneville, Neil Kelly was first 500 on a Velocette Venom, and Bill Smith took the 250 class on a Bultaco Metralla by just 0.4 second from similarly mounted Tommy Robb after 113 racing miles in which they had never been more than a few yards apart.

*

BMW took their customary first three places in the Sidecar race, but leader Siegfried Schauzu's passenger Horst Schneider fell out at Governor's Bridge on the last lap. Uninjured, he climbed back aboard and 'Siggy' motored on to take the chequered flag and victory. Klaus Enders was second and Colin Seeley third.

*

Some riders take part in an unofficial competition to gain the 'honour' of being first away in the opening practice session of each TT and MGP meeting. At the 1967 MGP Tom Armstrong was determined to be that first man. To ensure his place at the head of the queue on Monday morning, he brought his bike and girl-friend to the Start before midnight on Sunday. He then left them to hold pole-position, while he went back to his digs to get a few hours sleep. Back at the Start in good time, it looked as though his girl-friend's stalwart effort might have been in vain when the practice session was put in doubt due to the foggy conditions. However, it went ahead, and Tom had the honour of going first.

*

Older race fans must have felt a touch of nostalgia when they saw entries in the 1967 MGP from Jimmy Guthrie and Stanley Woods. The latter-day Jimmy was the son of the great pre-war TT winner and showed his class by taking victory in the Senior. Stanley Woods could claim no such relationship to his honourable Irish namesake, and his race did not go so well when he had to retire from the Junior event.

Chapter 9
TT TRANSITION

The period spanning the late 1960s to mid 1970s saw many changes to the TT races, some had a greater effect than others, but all contributed to altering the nature and status of the premier event in the world of road-racing.

*

1968 got off to a bad start when Honda announced its withdrawal from the world motorcycle racing scene. The loss of such a major player was made worse when Suzuki followed suit, and before the end of the year Yamaha also dropped out. It seemed that their reasons were related to a need to reduce expenditure and to the FIM's intention to restrict the number of cylinders and gears in all classes. After almost 10 years of active participation at world-championship level, the seemingly ever-open cheque books of the Japanese manufacturers were snapped shut. The resulting lack of finance and non-availability of competitive

machinery persuaded several top riders to retire from the sport. Honda actually paid Mike Hailwood not to race anyone else's bikes in the World Championship in 1968, whilst providing him with bikes to ride in non-Championship events on a privateer basis.

*

Yamaha made the most of their last year at the TT with 'works' bikes in 1968 and, suspecting the end of their factory-rider status was near, Phil Read and Bill Ivy engaged in stirring battles in the World Championships, with Read eventually disregarding team orders late in the season and going for victory in every race. However, Ivy was at the top of his form on the Island and he stormed to victory in the Lightweight 250 TT, setting a new lap record of 105.51 mph before slowing but still leading Renzo Pasolini (Benelli) home by over two minutes. Read was the first man home in the Lightweight 125 race

---

** Mike Hailwood **

Although only 28, this man who was somewhat bemused by fame, had become a legend in motorcycle racing by the time that he 'retired' soon after 1968. Former editor of 'Motor Cycling', Bob Holliday, wrote of Mike in 'Racing Round the Island': *'Encouraged by a wealthy father, he had begun his TT racing with a quiverful of expensive machinery fettled by experts, but he soon showed he had those precious qualities that money can never buy, tremendous courage, outstanding skill and an inborn will to win. Yet SMB Hailwood won something of far greater worth than silver trophies - that rare accolade with which sportsmen love to honour their heroes, a nickname blending admiration with affection . . . "Mike the Bike".*

Whilst the financial influence of Mike's father on his early career was of immense benefit, Stan was a hard taskmaster and if Mike had not delivered success, the finance would have been withdrawn. Murray Walker wrote of Stan *'He could be utterly charming and, on the other hand, the most ruthlessly unmitigated bastard you ever met in your life'.* Although it may not have felt like it to this young man with a passion to race motorcycles, Mike actually served a tough apprenticeship. Racing in all the four recognised solo classes of his day (125, 250, 350 and 500), he would often compete in two race-meetings over a weekend and three at Bank Holidays. What with testing, riding in practice, heats and finals in all classes, there were few riders putting in more racing miles in the late 1950s and early 1960s than Mike Hailwood. When others took a winter break, his father arranged for him to go to South Africa for several months to race in their events and to toughen him up. It was those countless racing miles that further developed his natural racing skills and allowed him to take maximum advantage of the quality racing motorcycles that he was fortunate to ride to British and World Championships. When bored by having things all his own way on the 350 and 500cc MV Agustas in the early 1960s, he was desperate to get into the highly competitive action of the 125 and 250 classes and accepted rides on less-favoured EMCs and MZs before being brought into the Honda team to help counter the challenge from Yamaha. There he added further World Championships to those he earned with MV. Murray Walker knew Mike well and had a high regard for his talents. He described him as *'... unbelievably versatile. I've seen him at Brands Hatch get off a 500cc four-cylinder MV with right-foot gear change having won the race, walk across the grid and get onto a 125 single-cylinder two-stroke with left-foot gear change and win that, walk across the grid and get onto a 350cc single-cylinder AJS - totally different power and handling characteristics - and win on that'.*

Bill Ivy at Signpost Corner on his Yamaha at the 1968 TT.

on Yamaha's little four-cylinder, eleven-speed, water-cooled racer, but Ivy stole the glory with a 100.32 mph lap and a cheeky stop at Creg ny Baa towards the end to enquire of his race position (and to ensure that Read won in accordance with team orders). Being used to being top-man in the Yamaha team, Phil Read did not take kindly to the fact that Ivy had been promoted into his place. A proud man, he wrote of the obvious slowing down incident by Ivy in 'Phil Read - The Real Story', saying *'I think I'd have preferred it if he had won'.*

Agostini Dominates

In 1968 Giacomo Agostini started on a sequence that was to see him take 9 out of the next 10 races in the Junior and Senior TT classes. With double wins on his MV Agustas in all but one race over a period of 5 years, race fans got used to reading headlines like *'Easy Win for Agostini'*, both on the Isle of Man and in the other world championship events. He achieved those wins with varying degrees of ease and never felt the need to get anywhere near the 108 mph lap speed that he recorded in his titanic struggle with Mike Hailwood in the 1967 Senior.

*

British singles in the hands of Brian Ball and Barry Randle followed Agostini home in the Senior race in 1968, whilst fellow Italian Renzo Pasolini rode his four-cylinder Benelli to second in the Junior.

*

Renzo Pasolini (Benelli) was a rider with an individual riding style - he stuck both knees out when cornering.

Santiago Herrero brought his Spanish Ossa 'works' bike to contest the Lightweight 250 TT. As he was a newcomer he borrowed an Ossa Trials bike to ride a preliminary lap. Unfortunately, no one told him which direction the Course ran and he rode his first lap (on open roads) in the reverse direction to the one taken by the racers. However, by race-time he had a fair idea of how the corners were strung together. He may not have had the experienced riders' detailed knowledge of line, camber, manhole covers, shiny bits, lingering damp patches, changes in road surface, etc., but 'Santo' learnt well and showed his quality by taking 7th in his debut year and 3rd the following year. His death in the 1970 TT was a sad loss.

*

A 750 sidecar class was brought in to join the 500s in 1968 and the big boys competed for the Fred W Dixon Trophy. The new class attracted 69 starters but only 26 finished. The other 43 were left scattered around the 37 3/4 mile Course suffering from various forms of mechanical mayhem. More than a few were made aware that standards of preparation sufficient for short circuit racing were simply inadequate for the TT. In 1969 each sidecar class was given its own race.

*

The organisers were thrown into panic before the 1968 Sidecar race when the Bell Textron Jet-ranger rescue helicopter was unable to be used, due to being grounded world-wide on the orders of the manufacturers. After much deliberation, the Sidecar race went ahead without the services of the rescue helicopter. That would not happen today, for the rescue helicopter is seen as an essential part of the organisation. Indeed, there have been instances of late where the visibility for riders has been good but mist hanging above the Course has meant that the helicopter could not see its landing sites. The result has been delayed or cancelled practice sessions.

*

Tyres have always been vital to motorcycle racers and designs were changing. Lower profile tyres that gave a bigger contact patch were being developed for racing by the tyre companies. Their rounded shape was designed to give a smoother transition between vertical and lean, and they were able to handle increased power.

*

Development also took place in the braking area. Yamaha had used bigger and bigger drum brakes that eventually almost filled the wheel, but experimental disc brakes were being tried and they eventually became standard fittings on race machinery.

*

As with the world championships as a whole there were few 'works' bikes at the 1969 TT, and the

Kel Carruthers (left) with his Benelli in the winner's enclosure after his victory in the 250cc TT of 1969. Frank Perris (right) brought his Crooks Suzuki into second place and here congratulates Santiago Herrero on achieving a fine third place on his Ossa.

missing bikes and their top riders took a little gloss off the event. Ago was still equipped with his factory MVs, and they allowed him to win by something like 10 minutes in Junior and Senior classes. Phil Read and Kel Carruthers had 'works' Benellis for the 250 race. With four-cylinders and an output of 50 bhp they were too quick for the opposition, although only Carruthers made it to the finish - in first place.

Phil Read claimed that Benelli offered him the 250 ride in 1969 so that he would not be in a position to challenge their 'works' runner, Carruthers, on any other machine. He also claimed that they then provided him with a 'dog' of a bike which, in his words: *'never looked like finishing, let alone winning'*. Speed-trap figures lent some weight to the claim, showing that Carruthers bike reached 133 mph and Read's 129 mph.

*

The 750 and 500cc sidecar machines were given separate races, each over three laps. Wins went to Siegfried Schauzu (750 BMW) and Klaus Enders (500 BMW). The fastest sidecar was clocked at 127 mph past The Highlander and there was not a great difference in top speed between the 500s and 750s (although some of the BMWs were only of 520cc).

Kawasaki Win

Dave Simmonds won the 125 race on a Kawasaki, (a

first TT win for them) and all the main TT races were won at much slower pace than in previous years. It was a different picture in the Production TT, at least in the 750cc class, where Malcolm Uphill hustled a Triumph Bonneville around to average 99.99 mph for the three laps, and to set a new lap record of 100.37 mph. So pleased were Dunlop with Uphill's performance on their road-going K81 tyres that they instantly renamed them 'TT100s'.

*

Making its name on the general racing scene was Yamaha's production racer. Given the title 'production' to distinguish it from the 'works' machines, it was an out-and-out racer based on their earlier twin-cylinder, air-cooled model. By then available in TD2 (250cc) and TR2 (350cc) form, in the next few years the Yamaha two-strokes went on to transform the general racing scene and the TT and MGP races. They, together with an increasing number of four-stroke Aermacchis, filled the grids as the British singles had done in earlier years.

*

Making his Isle of Man racing debut at the 1969 MGP was future multiple TT winner Mick Grant. Showing little signs of the talent he was later to display, Mick finished last on an ailing 500 Velocette.

*

The TT was still popular with spectators, and they would come as individuals, with a few mates or, sometimes, with their local motorcycle club who would take-over a complete hotel for a week or fortnight, so adding a strong social side to the thrill of watching the races.

*

Few would deny that racing on the TT Course can be a dangerous affair, but the perception of danger is a personal thing. Everyone has their own level of risk beyond which they are not prepared to go, although, quite clearly, the acceptance of risk by TT riders must be very much higher than average. All the casual talk of *'the throttle works both ways'* (suggesting that all a rider has to do is shut-off) is nothing more than talk as a rider fights a bouncing and snaking race bike through one of the many wall-bound corners on the TT Course. To shut the throttle in such a situation could spell disaster, he may well have to open it to get out of trouble!

Discontent

The TT was still part of the World Championship and some of the regular championship riders had formed themselves into a Grand Prix Riders Association with the aim, amongst other things, of increasing prize

money and improving track safety. Many were dissatisfied with both of those aspects of the Isle of Man races. Whilst readily acknowledging that the TT was the longest established of all race meetings, riders were saying *'tradition is no longer enough'*. Although difficult to believe, the financial reward for winning the Senior TT was still only £200, a figure that had remained the same for forty years - yes, since 1930. Because the TT was a championship round the organisers knew that top riders were obliged to attend but the rumbles of discontent grew louder, particularly as 'works' and 'trade' support was now very scarce and even many of the stars had to pay much of their own way. Although the fact that the TT was over-subscribed with entries may have made the organisers complacent, there was still an urgent need to stifle the rumbles from star riders with a significant injection of cash to boost start and prize money. Had that been done the organisers would have protected their event; but they missed the chance.

A fine Trophy for the victor Bill Ivy at this presentation ceremony, but he received only £200 for winning what was claimed to be the premier event on the World Championship calendar - a TT race.

Criticism of the TT's finances persuaded the ACU to make public the cost of running them. Using the figures from 1967, they showed that the meeting had incurred a loss of £1,493. Overall cost of running the event was over £30,000, and the Manx Government gave the ACU £20,500. Income from entry fees was £4,200 (of which £4,069 went on riders' personal accident insurance). Riders received £12,500 in prize money and expenses, but wanted more.

*

Financial discontent took second place to concerns over safety at the 1970 TT, when a total of six riders were killed during practice and racing. It was a high price to pay for sporting entertainment. In his book 'Honda Conquerors of the Track', Christopher Hilton wrote the moving words: *'There is a very great emptiness when brave men who have the choice accept it, balance it, ride it through, and don't come back'.*

*

Overshadowed by the huge cloud of emptiness created by the deaths of those fine riders, wins in the established racing classes in 1970 went to Agostini (MV Agusta), Kel Carruthers (Yamaha) and first-timer Dieter Braun (Suzuki), whilst Siegfried Schauzu and Klaus Enders secured a win each on three-wheels. A wide variety of machines contested the three Production classes (now of International status and over 5 laps) and wins went to Malcolm Uphill (Triumph), Frank Whiteway (Suzuki) and Chas Mortimer (Ducati).

*

The sidecars often offered interesting solutions to the problems of racing, and a prime example was shown in the 750cc class of 1970 where there were two entries from Vincent powered machines. But Vincent never made a 750 of any sort - their nearest to the size were 500cc singles and 1000cc twins - yet one of the Vincent entries in 1970 was a single and one was a twin. For the average mortal just taking part in an Isle of Man race is a pinnacle too hard to climb, but some people like to make things difficult for themselves! Approaching the problem of creating 750cc Vincent motors from opposite directions, Mick Farrant ran a heavily bored and stroked single-cylinder engine, whilst John Renwick appeared with a sleeved down twin-cylinder version of the Stevenage product.

*

Another incident involving a sidecar came in practice when Ron Small stopped at Crosby with petrol-pump problems (most 'chairs' carried their fuel-tanks in the sidecar, thus requiring a pump). A friendly AA man offered his services, cured the problem, and quickly had the outfit on its way.

*

Spectators used to watching motorcycle racing on short circuits that utilised massed starts, sometimes

John Renwick and Pete Kennard round Quarter Bridge on their 750cc Vincent outfit in 1970.

112

claimed that it was difficult for them to maintain interest in TT races that had riders starting at intervals. Perhaps in an attempt to appease them, the ACU experimented with starting arrangements for the 1970 solo events. Their plan was to start riders in groups of 9 at 90 second intervals. Although the idea was tried in the Thursday afternoon practice session, it did not find favour and, for the races, riders were despatched in pairs at 10 second intervals.

New Rules
Under an FIM ruling, 50cc machines were by now limited to one-cylinder, 125 and 250cc machines to two-cylinders, 350 and 500cc to four-cylinders. All classes were restricted to a maximum of six gears.

*

Despite the many questions that were being asked about the events, the TT and MGP races went on, and they continued to attract talented newcomers. The 1971 TT saw a young Barry Sheene with entries in the Lightweight 125 and Production 250 races. Barry could have become a TT star if he had been prepared to work at it. Instead, he decided that the requirements of racing in the TT exceeded the level of his personal risk threshold and he never returned. In contrast, fellow short circuit racer Charlie Williams came to his second MGP in 1971, won the Lightweight race and went on to become a multi-TT winner (and a star of the short circuits).

*

Other 'new' names to be seen on the TT leaderboards of the early 1970s were Alan Barnett, Paul Smart, Tony Jefferies, Ray Pickrell, John Williams, Chas Mortimer and Mick Grant. There were also some who had served longer apprenticeships and were now beginning to shine, such as Tony Rutter, Rod Gould, Jack Findlay and Peter Williams.

*

The qualifying lap-times that riders had to achieve in practice to be eligible to take part in the main TT races of the early 1970s were reduced and became: Senior, 28 minutes, Junior, 30 minutes, Lightweight 250, 30 minutes, Lightweight 125, 34 minutes, Sidecars, 35 minutes, and each rider had to complete a minimum of four practice laps.

*

Though many riders still wore the original 'pudding-basin' style crash-helmets, the jet-style had become increasingly popular and there were even a few full-face ones in use in the early 1970s.

*

The Mountain road was fenced for its entire length to

In his first year of duty as a Travelling Marshal in 1971, Des Evans had to 'make do' with this Triumph Trophy, while his colleagues rode the faster Triumph Tridents. Des was the first Travelling Marshal to wear a full-face helmet and he was to serve in the job at every TT and MGP until the end of 2002.

keep away wandering sheep, but they occasionally found a hole and it was still a fairly regular job for Travelling Marshals to remove any that were found on the road before the start of early morning practice. Experienced Travelling Marshal Jack Harding was called on the telephone by Race Control shortly after he arrived at Ramsey one morning in 1971 and told to fire up his Triumph Trident and deal with sheep on the Course at the 29th Milestone. Jack was not a natural born shepherd, and the sheep at the 29th knew it. Travelling Marshals received instruction on how to deal with sheep, but first they had to catch them. After chasing ewes and lambs up and down the road with limited success, Jack became worried, for he knew that the first riders would soon arrive. Fortunately, Race Control judged that he was having trouble as he hadn't reported in from the Bungalow (the next Travelling Marshal station), so they ordered fellow Travelling Marshal Albert Moule away from

These Triumph Tridents outside Horsman's of Liverpool are bound for the Isle of Man to do duty as Travelling Marshals' machines. Fitted with non-standard Fontana front brakes (one has experimental discs and stanchions), close-ratio gearboxes and higher overall gearing, they were very carefully assembled and offered an exhilarating ride.

Ramsey to help. Between them they managed to clear the road just as they heard the wail of Agostini's MV coming up the Mountain. Seconds later, he sped past.

*

It was not only sheep that got on to the Course and Dave 'Crasher' Croxford encountered a pig in the road when rounding a slowish bend. However, all was well for, in his words his JPS Norton *'had the edge on acceleration'* over the pig.

*

Agostini suffered a rare mechanical failure on his MV Agusta in the 1971 Junior race. Nearest challenger, Phil Read, was by now a privateer and riding Yamaha production racers. Phil set the fastest lap in the Junior but was also forced to retire. Victory went to Tony Jefferies on a Yamsel. The Yamsel comprised a Yamaha engine in a Seeley frame, the latter being made by former top sidecar racer Colin Seeley who

also took over the production rights for Manx Nortons (sold on to John Tickle) and AJS and Matchless racers. Colin also turned out complete Seeleys with 350 & 500 AJS/Matchless based engines.

*

Senior race victory did go to Agostini in 1971 but the 'manufacturers' award was won by Ray Cowles who entered a team of three riders on G50 Matchless models under the 'Cowles-Matchless' title. His three runners all finished in the top ten, with Selwyn Griffiths in fourth place, Roger Sutcliffe in sixth and Tom Dickie in ninth. All three were former Senior MGP winners.

Formula 750

The Production race of 1971 was reduced to 4 laps and top man was Ray Pickrell on a three-cylinder Triumph Trident. Honda took the 500 and 250 classes with CB450 and CB250 models ridden by John Williams and Bill Smith. The TT continued its process of change with the addition of a new three-lap Formula 750 race aimed at accommodating the 750 machines of Triumph, BSA, Norton, Honda, etc. The regulations were similar to those administered by the American Motorcycle Association at Daytona. They allowed the 750s to throw off the performance restricting shackles of Production rules and to howl around the Mountain Course on open-pipes in the hands of dashing riders like Tony Jefferies, Ray Pickrell and Peter Williams. The first staging of what can be seen as the forerunner of today's Superbike racing, saw Tony Jefferies speed to victory on his Triumph 'three' at an average of 102.85 mph. The official report on the race said *'it is the opinion of the Stewards that racing for machines of this new type has a very exciting future'*.

*

The addition of the National Formula 750 race in 1971 made the TT an eight-race meeting (counting the three Production machine classes as one race), which was double the number of the immediate post-war period and, not surprisingly, the total entries accepted increased from about 250 in the early 1950s to 530 in 1971. The percentage of riders who finished their races across all classes varied from a high of 69% to a low of 43% in the years 1952-71. Percentage finishers in the Production machine classes were slightly higher.

*

Although the TT organisers eventually bowed to rider pressure and offered increased prize-money at the 1971 meeting (the Senior TT winner taking £750 instead of £200), the groundswell of discontent with the TT amongst a few of the top riders continued to gather force and would not go away. The respected former editor of 'Motor Cycling', Bob Holliday, described the 1972 position in his book 'Racing Round the Island' with: *'an undercurrent of anti-TT feeling that had been rippling among some of the leading riders for several seasons burst into flood after Gilberto Parlotti crashed his 125cc Morbidelli into a concrete post on the misty Mountain. His death, and the conditions that caused it, had an immediate emotional effect. Agostini declared that he would never ride the Mountain course again. The only reason he came was to gain Championship points, otherwise he would not make the long journey and spend so much time practising when he could be taking part in events whose shorter courses would be better protected. He wanted the TT removed from the World Championship, and he was supported by a number of other prominent riders, including Phil Read, Rod Gould, Barry Sheene and John Cooper'.* Parlotti's death was a particularly sad business because although early morning practice sessions were temporarily abandoned at the 1972 TT (evening sessions and Thursday afternoon were extended), it could not be claimed that he did not know the Course. He completed 50 laps on a hack bike, went out in every official practice, had personal tuition from Agostini and made it clear that he was thoroughly enjoying his first year at the TT.

Missing Stars

Early morning practice returned to the 1973 TT but Agostini, Read, Gould and other 'names' did not, even though it meant them losing the chance to earn World Championship points and the possibility of winning what had become a £1,000 first prize in the Senior race. Reading the comments and opinions expressed about the TT by star riders before and after 1972, it is difficult to believe that they were made by the same people. Unfortunately they were, and they showed that the top riders had gone through massive changes of attitude. Whereas before they had been very much for the TT, by 1973 they were very, very much against. Phil Read even took it upon himself to write a letter of complaint to the Patron of the ACU, the Duke of Edinburgh. Whilst some of the undoubted glamour that top names brought to the event was missed in 1973, it did not affect the number of spectators attending, nor the fast and exciting racing served up for them to watch by a new generation of riders striving for TT honours. And, whatever the views of a few big-earners (Agostini was reputedly on £50,000 a year from MV Agusta), taking part in the TT was still the height of ambition and peak of their riding careers for many riders.

*

Top sidecar men like Klaus Enders, Siegfried Schauzu and Rolf Steinhausen were happy to continue racing at the TT and Enders took a double victory (500 and 750cc classes) in 1973, (Schauzu having been the first man to attain the sidecar double in 1972).

Tony Rutter and Charlie Williams took the Junior and Lightweight 250 wins, with the evergreen Jack Findlay bringing his twin-cylinder, water-cooled Suzuki home first in the Senior (first two-stroke win in the Senior since 1913) and Tommy Robb crowned his long TT career with a win in the Lightweight 125 category.

Peter Williams' second place in the Senior on his outdated Arter Matchless was a tribute to his riding,

Klaus Enders (BMW) rounds the Gooseneck in this shot from the 1972 Sidecar TT.

but it heralded the last meaningful result by a British single at the TT. Production winners were Tony Jefferies, Bill Smith and Charlie Williams, while Peter Williams brought his Norton home at the head of the Formula 1 field at an average speed of 105.47 mph and a fastest lap of 107.27 mph. His was by far the fastest speed of the week, although his Norton was not the fastest machine. An understanding of how he

managed to lap at 107+ can be gained by reading his personal account of a lap on the Norton. It contains many graphic phrases like *'hard against the stop . . . flat on the tank . . . the front wheel comes off the ground . . . ride it through there on the back wheel . . . ignore the bumps . . . can usually do flat out . . . power on early . . . back wheel could suddenly go . . . the front wheel just touches the road here and there . . . properly set up with all the power coming on . . . couldn't believe I could take it flat . . . just heave on the bars . . . I sit up here but only because I don't like my head bouncing on the tank at 145 mph!'* It was a straight-from-the-saddle account that left ordinary mortals in envy of Peter's immense talent to exploit the handling of a machine to the full. However, he still gave the Course the respect it deserves, writing *'I don't like using quite all the road because its nice to have a bit to spare in the Island'.*

*

Although they were not present on the Island in 1973, the views of sundry 'star' riders could still be read in the press. They were losing championship points by not racing there so they continued their campaign to have the TT stripped of its World Championship status. Most (but not all) of the critics had proved themselves by their past TT

Tommy Robb at Quarter Bridge on the way to winning the Lightweight 125 TT of 1973.

performances and their words carried the weight of genuine experience. They were saying that the Mountain Course had had its day. Well, maybe it had for them, but over 30 years later, riders are still queuing to sample it.

*

Not for the first time, there was talk of finding a short, alternative circuit to the traditional Mountain Course on the Island. 'The Motor Cycle' conducted a survey to find out what race fans thought of such a move and found that 98% were opposed.

*

One bright note in 1973 was the 'The TT Special' was still going strong and conveying TT news far and wide, as it had done for over 45 years.

The long-running newspaper 'The TT Special' had been reporting on the races since 1927.

More Money for the TT

The ACU and the Island authorities had woken up to the fact that the TT's World Championship status really was at risk, and they doubled the financial grant to the races in 1974. Had their action been taken five years earlier in the late 1960s, when it should have been obvious that factory and trade support was disappearing and riders were finding it harder to pay their way at what was a particularly expensive race meeting, injection of the substantial amounts of prize and starting money that they belatedly made in 1974 may well have been sufficient to maintain the TT's status on the world's racing scene. But by 1974 its championship days were numbered.

*

The extra money pumped into the event meant there were plenty of riders seeking what had by now become a good pay-day, even though the top stars stayed away. But it was not just money that attracted

riders to Island racing, for three months after the TT the Manx Motorcycle Club had 1,000 entries for 456 places at their MGP event - where no prize-money is paid.

*

Recognising that there was still much prestige to be gained from an Island win, Suzuki provided four-cylinder 500s for Paul Smart and Jack Findlay to ride in the 1974 Senior. Even with new frames, the searching TT Course showed that their handling was poor and this was despite Findlay becoming the first person to use one of the new breed of slick racing tyres on his machine. It was a similar situation for Chas Mortimer who brought one of Yamaha's 'point-and-squirt' four-cylinder 700cc racers to the Island for the 'International Open Formula 750 "Classic" Race' (where Suzuki fielded three-cylinder machines). After some frightening incidents in practice Chas (who was also a regular contestant in all World Championship events) decided that the Yamaha was not suited to the Mountain Course.

*

Veteran Aussie Jack Ahearn came out of retirement for one last year at the TT and had a conrod break on his 500 Honda during practice. Jack told how the engine was *'holed top, bottom and dead-centre'*.

*

In an unusual incident, John Williams was fortunate to get away with light injuries after a very heavy crash at Kerromoar on his Suzuki. As he set up to physically heave the bike over for a change of direction, the twist-grip rubber came off in his hand. Rubbers are usually wired in place but such an incident showed the need for extra-thorough machine preparation at the TT. The course puts above average demands on a machine and if mechanical failure does occur, the absence of run-off areas can turn an 'incident' into a tragedy. John had been involved in another strange happening earlier in the week. A boot sole came loose while he was riding in practice and in wriggling his foot around, his boot fell off. He returned to the Pits wearing only a sock on one foot.

*

After some juggling with the 1974 race programme, the Formula 750 race was given top billing on the Friday of race-week, thus ousting the Senior from its traditional spot. Unfortunately, like most of the other solo classes, the F750 race showed the changing face of racing and was hi-jacked by 'small' Yamaha two-strokes. Their incredible rise (by now in TZ water-cooled and disc-braked form) was shown by the

Mick Grant takes Ballaugh Bridge in fine style on the Triumph Trident known as Slippery Sam.

results in: Lightweight 125cc - first 4 places, Lightweight 250cc - first 12 places, Junior 350cc - first 39 places, Senior 500cc - first 8 places, Formula 750 - first 3 places. Only in the bigger Production races (now open to 1,000cc machines) did any other make get a look-in. There Mick Grant brought 'Slippery Sam' to his first and 'Sam's' third TT win. By then owned by Les Williams, Triumph Trident 'Sam' was to achieve two more wins before passing into TT history.

BMW showed their pace in the same Production race with Hans-Otto Butenuth and Helmut Dahne taking second and third places. In the Sidecar races BMW four-strokes took wins in both classes with Luthringhauser (750) and Schauzu (500). But George O'Dell's two-stroke Konig came a close second in the 750 class and Rolf Steinhausen (Konig) set a new lap record for three-wheelers of 98.18 mph. The Konigs were developed from high-performance boat engines.

*

It did not go unnoticed at the TT that on the weekend between practice and racing, the safety conscious Giacomo Agostini and friends were competing in a non-championship meeting held on a 6.55 mile public roads circuit at Chimay in Belgium.

*

Coming half-way round the world to compete in his first Sidecar TT in 1975, seven times Australian champion Alex Campbell hit out at critics of the TT, saying *'My feeling is that money is not the thing you should be racing for. Racing should be for the sport'.* For Alex and many others, racing was for sport, but those who were in it just for money had very loud voices and they were more easily heard in the corridors of power.

*

The organisers kept the classes strictly segregated during practice in 1975 and while this was generally welcomed, some riders were frustrated that their time on the track during the lengthy Thursday afternoon session was far more restricted than usual. 'The TT Special' did not support the segregation of classes, making the point that practice was just what it says, and that it was not a race. There had been complaints the previous year about the massive speed differential between 750s and 125s when they were out in the same practice sessions. The 125 race was dropped for 1975, but the difference between the fastest and slowest (250 Production) was still considerable, and segregated practice avoided them being out together.

*

There were fewer practice sessions than usual and whilst the arrangement was probably welcomed by those who found early morning practice sessions to be a drain on their stamina, it must have been hard for riders who were competing in several classes to find enough practice time to get their machines set-up properly.

Changes

There were yet more changes to the TT programme in 1975. The Lightweight 125cc class was dropped and the 750 Sidecar class was increased to 1000cc. The Production race became a 10 lap event with two riders sharing each machine, and a handicap system that saw the 250s doing only 9 laps. That was not a problem to 'Slippery Sam' who came home first in the hands of Dave Croxford and Alex George having averaged 99.60 mph for the 3 hours 47 minutes and 17.2 seconds of the 378 mile race. The Formula 750 race was now the International Open Classic TT with riders making clutch starts in pairs at 10 second intervals. Mick Grant took the chance to break Mike Hailwood's eight year old outright lap record on his three-cylinder Kawasaki at 109.82 mph in the 'Classic'. The effort was perhaps too much for Mick's 'Kwacker' and he retired, letting John Williams take the win and £1,500 first prize on a Yamaha at an average speed for the six-lap race of 105.33 mph from Percy Tait and Charlie Sanby. Consolation for Mick Grant was that he won the Senior on his 500 Kawasaki from a horde of Yamahas.

*

Lucas were just one of the component suppliers who were glad to advertise their association with the bikes used in the Production races.

Regular World Championship racer Chas Mortimer was quite happy with the TT Course (he had raced every year since his MGP debut in 1966), and felt that with the prize money now better than at any other Grand Prix, all the other big-name riders would still be racing on the Island if they hadn't made such loud and public criticism of the Course (when prize money was low!). Chas had a successful (and profitable) 1975 TT with a win, two second places and a third.

*

In a move that did not endear him to those World Championship contenders who stayed away from the TT 'on principle', Grand Prix runner Takazumi Katayama entered the 1976 TT on Yamahas, seeking extra points to boost his World Championship challenge. Showing his talent he took second in the Lightweight race, fourth in the Senior, ninth in the Junior, and 17th on a shared RD250 in the Production race. (He finished the season in second place in the 250cc World Championship).

*

A first at the 1976 TT was the all-Japanese sidecar crew of Matsato Kumano and Isao Arifuku. They struggled with a twin-cylinder Yamaha four-stroke engine and brought up the rear of the field in practice and retired from the race at the end of the first lap.

*

'The TT Special' concluded its reports on the 1976 TT by announcing it as *'the best ever'*. Helping to justify that claim were record breaking performances in the postponed Production race (with BMWs taking the first three places in the 1,000cc class), plus new lap and race records by Mac Hobson in the Sidecar race, who took his Yamaha round at 99.96 mph to give Yamaha their first win in the sidecar class. The constantly improving John Williams took his Suzuki to a record-breaking Senior lap of 112.27 mph, but then lost the lead after running out of fuel on the last lap and pushed in to finish seventh. This let Yamaha-mounted Tom Herron through for a win, and he was followed by five other Yamahas to complete the top half-dozen finishers. Yamaha monopolised the other solo events in similar fashion, except for the 'Classic' which went to John Williams and his three-cylinder 750cc Suzuki in a start-to-finish win.

*

All the record-breaking and close finishes to races in 1976 were witnessed by ever-increasing numbers of spectators. Seeing the event as an all-round success, 'The TT Special' concluded its report on TT fortnight by asking *'who needs the so-called stars?'*

Chapter 10
PARTING OF THE WAYS

At the end of 1976 the FIM announced that the Tourist Trophy races would no longer count towards the World Championships. It really came as no surprise, for the influential star riders who wanted to race only on artificial tracks were taking the sport further and further away from racing on natural road circuits. Now it was all out in the open and riders could decide which element of the sport they would compete in. Many were still happy to do both, but for those of a different mind-set the FIM's decision confirmed the parting of the ways. Taken from the Isle of Man, the British round of the World Championship moved to the flat and featureless former airfield circuit at Silverstone. A greater contrast with the TT's Mountain Course could scarcely be imagined and it just served to emphasise the gulf that had arisen between road and circuit racing.

*

Pessimists forecast that the TT's loss of World Championship status signified the beginning of the end for the Manx races, whilst optimists regarded it as the start of a new era. In support of the latter view it was announced before the end of 1976 that the race budget for 1977 would be increased to £150,000, with £100,000 set aside for start and prize money, thus making it far and away the richest race meeting in the world.

More Changes
The organisers felt that another juggle with the race programme was called for in 1977, so the 350cc class was dropped and their traditional race title of Junior was given to the three-lap race for 250s, which previously raced as the Lightweight 250 class (sometimes known as just the Lightweight after the earlier demise of the Lightweight 125 class).

The Production TT was also dropped for, in the words of Ray Knight the event had lost its way *'due to convoluted rules that permitted manufacturers to build any bike to specification especially written by themselves for the race'*. To fill the gap in the programme the organisers created four-lap races for new classes of TT Formula I, TT Formula II and TT Formula III, catering for high-performance road-based machines of specified capacities that were available for sale to the public through normal commercial channels. Various performance and safety enhancing alterations were permitted, although many were

only practical or affordable to 'works' entries. Four-strokes were encouraged by giving them a capacity advantage over the two-strokes, in that Formula I was for two-strokes of 350-500cc and four-strokes of 600-1000cc. These races developed into their own World Championship (usually referred to as 'Formula TT'), involving rounds on circuits in Belgium, Holland, Ireland, Portugal and the Isle of Man. It was a commendable attempt to give the TT its own form of Championship but in the words of journalist Mick Woollett: *'they swelled the entry lists but blurred the image of the races'*.

*

Other changes for 1977 saw the two Sidecar races opened-up to 1,000cc machines. A winner of each leg was declared, plus an overall winner based on the best results from the two legs. Both races were of four laps. As it was the seventieth year of the TT and Queen Elizabeth's Silver Jubilee, there was also a four-lap Jubilee TT. All of the above came with the previously announced increases in prize money that attracted good entries and helped keep the TT in the headlines.

'Works' Return
An event that certainly made the headlines in 1977 was the return to the Island of multiple World Champion Phil Read and, of even more importance, the return of Honda with 'works' machines for him to ride. Read was one of the most voluble of the top riders who boycotted the TT after 1972, but he then had to stand aside for the next few years and watch as the TT's prize-money soared far beyond that paid at any of the conventional World Championship meetings he contested. As Read's world title efforts went seriously off the boil in 1976 compared to his early Yamaha successes and those of his MV glory days of 1974 and 1975, he decided that it was time to return for another TT pay-day. In explaining his almost unbelievable about face, he claimed that now the pressure was off to compete for World Championship points the TT was once again acceptable to him. However, that did not mean that he was acceptable to a large number of TT fans, to marshals, or to many Manx people. Fans expressed their opinions of what they saw as a purely money-orientated return in letters to the press, some static marshals tried to persuade their colleagues to strike

Phil Read returned to the TT in 1977 on the 'works' Honda to contest the new Formula I class.

while others made clear that if he fell in front of them they would not pick him up. Phil also tells of backlash from the Manx public in the form of being refused petrol at filling stations and the like.

For all the genuinely strong feelings raised by Phil Read's return and the accompanying hot-air that it generated, it was actually good for the TT to have him back, and it was even better to have Honda back. But Read certainly was not the only quality rider in the event and although most were British there were plenty of top name foreign runners of the day, among them being Pat Hennen (USA), Jon Ekerold (SA) and Stu Avant (NZ).

*

Come the races in 1977 and Phil Read showed his class with victory on a Suzuki in the Senior event, lapping at 110.01mph before the race was stopped one lap before its scheduled distance due to bad weather. Continuing his winning return he also took first place on a Honda in the new Formula 1 race. Visually it seemed to spectators that his four-cylinder

'works' Honda was derived from the roadster models that many of them were riding and it helped them to relate to the race. The production-derived four-cylinder machines played an ever increasing role at the TT in the years that followed.

*

Although Phil Read was glad to pocket the prize-money from his Formula I and Senior race wins (plus substantial start-money), he looked forward to further earnings from the richest race of the week, the Classic. But it was not to be. Engaged in some unofficial open roads testing, he fell at Brandish, damaged his shoulder and put himself out of the race.

*

The Suzuki RG500 with which Phil Read won the Senior TT was a model that had been around since 1974, and it replaced Suzuki's TR500 water-cooled twins. Used with success on the Grand Prix circuits, this was its first major win at the TT. A water-cooled, disc-valved, square-four, two-stroke, it initially offered just under 100 bhp but that gradually increased as the engine was developed. Offering useable power in the 8-11,000 rpm range, the RG500 became the mainstay of 500cc racing from the mid-1970s to the early 1980s, filling the grids in the manner that the Manx Norton had done in earlier years.

*

A late Suzuki RG500 without its race fairing.

By now an established star on the TT scene, Mick Grant took his Kawasaki to victory in the 1977 Classic race with the fastest time of the week, averaging 110.76 mph for the six-lap race distance and setting a new absolute record of 112.77 mph. It was a far cry from Mick's Island debut in the 1969 Senior MGP where he finished last on an ailing Velocette. Another rider who had started his Island racing career at the MGP was Charlie Williams (Yamaha). He was by now an established TT star and in 1977 he won the Junior and came second to Mick Grant in the Classic.

*

Renold advertised their 1977 TT successes in the motorcycle press.

Top riders who run several machines are generally guaranteed a very busy time during TT practice. They will often complete a lap, pull in, pass the bike to a mechanic, exchange a few words and take out another bike of different size in an attempt to fine-tune gearing, suspension, steering, etc. It can be very frustrating to such a rider if he breaks down somewhere inaccessible and has to remain there for the rest of practice. Riders and support crews know most of the back roads and junctions where a 'rescue' of a stranded rider can be effected, but it is not always possible. One year Mick Grant's engine exploded at the remote 33rd Milestone and Klaus Klein, who was following, came off on the oil. Seemingly unhurt, Klaus was still taken away by helicopter for a check-up. Being an opportunist, the unintentional perpetrator of the accident, Mick Grant, hitched a ride in the helicopter back to Douglas and so was able to take another bike out in the same practice session.

*

Stunt rider (and much more) Dave Taylor entertained crowds during the interval between races in 1977. On his modified Honda moto-cross bike he attempted a complete lap on the back wheel, and almost succeeded. Not to be outdone, Barry Roberts did a lap backwards on his Bonneville. This does not mean that he rode the Course in reverse but that he was standing on the footrests of his bike and looking over his shoulder as he rode in the normal direction.

Joey Dunlop's First Win
The event that rounded-off TT week in 1977 was the Schweppes sponsored, four-lap Jubilee Race. Joey Dunlop was in only his second year of TT racing and was allocated riding numbers in the 30s by the organisers in the races that he entered - obviously they did not rate him too highly! Entry to the Jubilee Race was by invitation only and Joey would seem not to have received an invite, for his name did not appear in the programme for that event. However, a few strings must have been pulled, and when Jubilee race-day arrived he was on the starting line. Come the finish of the race and he was on the top step of the podium, having taken his privately entered Yamaha TZ750 to his first TT victory. It was a winning feat that Joey was to repeat another 25 times in his TT racing career.

100 mph Sidecars
Dick Greasley and Mick Skeels set the first official 100 mph lap for sidecars in the opening race for

Joey Dunlop (Yamaha) on the way to his first TT win, the Schweppes Jubilee TT of 1977.

three-wheelers. George O'Dell had achieved the 'ton' in practice, but records set in practice don't count - although that didn't prevent George from having an all-night celebratory party in his hotel. Proving that his 'non-official' 100 mph practice lap was no fluke, hard-charging George lapped at 102.80 mph in the race and came home first ahead of Dick Greasley. That offered the best possible reason for yet another party! Less cause for celebration was his crash in the second race that left him with a broken leg.

*

In its first year as a non-Championship event, the 1977 TT meeting was judged a success. The Isle of Man was already trying to shape and style the TT period as a fortnight of activities that encompassed more than just the racing. No doubt the large number of spectators who attended in 1977, including many with foreign registration plates, pleased the organisers and the many Manx concerns that benefit from the extra business that comes their way over the TT period.

*

Happy Families

For many riders, taking part in the TT is a family affair and they bring wives, children, fathers, uncles, etc, to the Island in June. Sometimes these family members just come for the holiday but in most cases they are actively involved with race preparation and support of the rider. A popular expression amongst motorcyclists down the years is that 'racing gets into the blood' and there have been plenty of instances where families have shown this to be the case. Sons have followed fathers into the TT, brothers have raced together, wives have passengered their husbands in sidecars, and there have been a couple of solo races where husband and wife rode against each other.

*

Family involvement can start at a young age as Andy Molnar and son show.

From the very first TT race in 1907 through to 1914, talented brothers Harry and Charlie Collier competed together on the Matchless models that they produced. Although they suffered several retirements, neither finished in lower than fourth place in the nine races in which they were classed as finishers. That was an impressive record for those early days.

*

There have been other combinations of brothers such as the Twemlows who each rode the TT from 1924-1930, with Ken taking one win and Eric taking two; the Pike brothers in the pre and early post-war years, and the Simmonds in the 1960s on predominantly Japanese machinery that included Tohatsus and early Kawasakis. The 1969 MGP was unusual in having three sets of brothers entered, the Dowies, Kirwans and Bilsborrows, whilst twins Peter and Ron Hardy formed a sidecar crew at the 1970 TT. Particularly successful brotherly riders in recent years have been Bob and Bud Jackson and, surely the most successful family racing relationship of all, Joey and Robert Dunlop who comfortably won more TTs than any other pairing.

*

Many sons have followed their fathers into TT racing and in some instances they have competed against each other. 'Pa' Applebee was riding in the Senior TT of 1912 that was won by his son Frank on a Scott. George Cowley (Snr) and (Jnr) both rode in the same races in the early 1920s, as did John and Ossie Wade in 1926.

*

Les Archer was a well-known competitor in pre-war years and in the early post-war period his son, also Les, joined him in the Island races before going off to become European Moto-cross Champion. The 1960s saw sidecar racers Bill and Mick Boddice in the same event, whilst father Fred Hanks and sons Norman and Roy were also sidecar racing in the same era (Roy still is!) and on several occasions all three were in the same race.

*

Father and son entrants Ossie and John Wade enjoy a relaxed moment before the start of practice for the 1926 TT. Both rode HRDs fitted with JAP engines. Ossie rode the TT from 1920 to 1926 and John from 1926 to 1928, so this was the only year they rode together.

In a few cases, particularly talented fathers and sons have both achieved TT wins. Les and Stuart Graham did so, as did Tony and Michael Rutter, Bill and Ian Simpson, Tony and David Jefferies.

*

The Jefferies family, almost a dynasty, is amongst the most successful of TT families. Patriarch Allan Jefferies was a talented all-round motorcyclist who rode in the MGP in the 1930s and in the first Clubman's TT of 1947. His eldest son Tony started his TT career in 1969 and, riding in various classes, he took victory in the 1971 Junior on a Yamsel and the 1971 F750 on a Triumph. Brother Nick started his Island racing career in the MGP of 1975 and rode to four third places before winning the Senior MGP of 1983 and moving on to the TT. Thereafter he was a consistent leaderboard finisher and, in his best ever ride, won the Formula 1 race at the 1993 TT.
Even greater TT glory was to come the way of the Jefferies family with the representative from their third generation, David. The brilliant riding of David Jefferies, son of Tony, has surpassed that of other members of his family and has already put him on a par with the TT greats.

*

Amongst other honourable TT family names are Jack and Peter Williams, plus George and Carl Fogarty. There have been TT/MGP father and son riders like George and Tony Brown, father and son MGP winners like Roger and Ralph Sutcliffe and, uniquely, father, mother and daughter competitors over the Mountain Course in John, Hilary and Gail Musson.

Hilary, John and Gail Musson at the 1978 TT where Hilary and John both rode in the Formula III race finishing in 14th and 15th places. Gail had to wait a few years before her MGP rides.

In what sometimes seemed like an attempted take-over of the MGP, five Kneen brothers competed in the event through the 1980s and 90s.

*

There have been many husband and wife sidecar teams. Obviously, their aim in each case was to ride together and work as a team, but the husband and wife combination of Peter and Sandra Barnett were in opposition, for they both rode solo Yamaha R1s in the 2000 Production TT. With Sandra already being the fastest lady around the TT Course, few were surprised when she finished ahead of Peter.

*

Family involvement with the TT is not limited to riders, for it also extends to marshals and officials. Indeed, current Clerk of the Course for the TT and MGP, Neil Hanson, follows in the footsteps of his father who was Clerk of the Course for the MGP in early post-war years.

Surprise!

The few people who noticed it were somewhat surprised when Mike Hailwood appeared at an evening practice for the 1977 MGP mounted on a Padgett's Yamaha fitted with a Travelling Marshal's 'M' plates and a camera.

Behind the borrowed leathers, helmets and camera is Mike Hailwood, about to take an 'M'-plated Yamaha for a lap during evening practice at the 1977 MGP.

Mike duly completed a lap, with a few stops for interviewing, filming, etc. and, on completion, expressed himself a little shocked at the speed of the Yamaha. Understandable really, as Mike hadn't ridden a proper racer around the Island for 10 years. Anyway, he then disappeared and everyone thought that was it - a one-off ride by the twelve-times TT winner, with a bit of filming done on the way.

*

The 1977 TT had been a very good year for race-fans and, as they often do, many of them booked their hotels and guest-houses for the following year before they left. They were the wise ones, for by the time of the 1978 TT, every establishment was showing a 'No Vacancies' sign. The reason was that 'Mike the Bike' returned to race at the TT in 1978. It was eleven years since Mike Hailwood had ridden an Island race and for spectators it was just too good an event to miss. His legion of older fans flocked to Mona's Isle to see his return, while those who were too young to have known him in his hey-day were just as keen to see what they had been missing. Television crews and journalists flew in from all over the world.

Although Mike (and the other riders) had only six practice sessions, no one could have been disappointed at the outcome of his return. In a stunning display of riding skill, Mike took an unfancied Ducati to victory in the Formula 1 race, leaving experienced opponents like Phil Read, John Williams, Alex George, and Chas Mortimer trailing in his wake, plus what journalist Ted Macauley

Mike Hailwood gets his Ducati under way at the start of the 1978 Formula I race that he went on to win.

described as *'a pack of youngsters on thoroughbred race machinery, howling after his reputation'*. It was truly a quality win, because the Ducati twin had no TT history and delivered probably 20 bhp less than the main opposition. But Mike was a master of getting into a fast and smooth race rhythm, and his reward was to stand on the top step of the winners podium once again.

Mike Hailwood's victory in 1978 saw him set race and lap records for the TT Formula 1 class, and in doing so he lapped faster than he had done in his prime, even though, in his words: *'Truthfully, I was well within my safety limits, seven-tenths, well below 100 per cent effort, and with plenty left in hand had I needed it'*. It was a highly emotional time for all involved, and Mike's performance served to both confirm and add to his already legendary TT status.

*

Having taken on petrol at Windy Corner on the last lap of the Senior race that was won by Tom Herron, Mike declined the Silver Replica that he was called up to be presented with at the prize-giving, for he knew that receiving 'outside assistance' was against the rules. So, the great man was a sportsman as well as a hero! Confirming that status, he went to Mallory

Park's Post-TT meeting and, although getting a poor start on his Ducati, he pulled through the field passing riders like Phil Read and John Williams to take the Formula I win.

*

Ducati were a bit half-hearted with their support of the 1978 TT and most of the effort on Mike's machine was put in by Steve Wynne and Pat Slinn of Sports Motorcycles. They carried out the whole operation on the strength of a handshake with Mike - no contract. Yamaha did seem to realise the publicity value associated with his return and provided three 'works' bikes for him to ride in races other than the Formula I class. However, despite the fact that this was the first time they had given unqualified factory support to the TT for ten years, the Yamaha effort failed to impress and their bikes were sidelined with niggling problems.

*

An early experiment with computerisation of TT race results was dropped when, after the 1978 Formula I race, they showed the winner to be Mike Hailwood on a Vespa at a race average speed of 240 mph. Well, at least they got the winner's name right!

*

Mike could not help hogging the headlines in 1978 but, as at every TT, there were plenty of other more mundane things going on. In a minor change to the rules, riders competing in their first TT were obliged to wear fluorescent jackets during practice to advise others of their status. They also had to prove to TT Safety Officer Alan Mullee that they had inspected the entire course prior to practising.

*

Amongst all the triumph of the 1978 TT was tragedy. Three riders were killed in the first Sidecar race. Mac Hobson and his passenger Kenny Birch died after they lost control over a bump at the top of Bray Hill and Ernst Trachsel died in an incident at the bottom of Bray. Sidecar racers are a tough breed, but hearing the tragic news at the finish of the race, many had to struggle to control their emotions. Tragedy also struck in the Senior event. Top American Pat Hennen had set the race alight with a record-breaking lap of 113.83 mph (becoming the first man to lap in under 20 minutes), but on the last lap it is believed that he was struck by a bird at Bishop's Court and in the resulting crash he received injuries which he survived but which prevented him from racing again. Once again racing on the Mountain Course had shown that there was a price to pay for all the speed, excitement and glamour that it generated.

*

It almost went un-noticed that 350cc World Champion Takazumi Katayama sacrificed his chance of a Silver Replica in the 1978 Senior race by stopping and assisting at the Pat Hennen incident.

Manx Millennium

The year of 1979 was a special one for the Isle of Man as a whole, for it was its Millennium Year, an occasion which recognised one thousand years of unbroken parliamentary rule by Tynwald. The TT did its best to give the Island an event to celebrate, although the weather during practice was very unworthy of the occasion.

*

Expected to be amongst the race winners in 1979, Mick Grant arrived on the Island on crutches after a spill at the North West 200. Although he was just about fit for a first practice on the Thursday afternoon (along with 260 other riders) by the end of practice he did not feature in the top twelve in any class.

*

World sidecar champion George O'Dell crashed in practice near Ginger Hall and broke the same leg that he had done in his crash at the Bungalow the previous year.

World sidecar champion George O'Dell at Greeba Bridge in the 1978 TT.

Paddock Hotel

Racing at the TT was still an expensive business and there were complaints from those riders who make up the field behind the star names that a small proportion of riders were getting a disproportionate amount of the start and prize money. Many ordinary riders could not afford to compete without the unseen financial help of friends, families, workmates, local motorcycle firms, plus the hotels and individuals on the Island that gave them free accommodation for the races. Not all are lucky enough to get such accommodation and many have no choice but to make use of the 'Paddock Hotel'. This is not a multi-storey edifice on a par with the Hilton. In fact, it is the riders name for the campsite at the side of the Paddock that, for race fortnight, is filled with multi-coloured tents, vans and modest motor-caravans.

Race-team transporters occupy the foreground with the many-coloured tents and vehicles of the 'Paddock Hotel' in the background.

It is no joke living and preparing race machines under such conditions. Wind, rain, mud and lack of basic workshop facilities can be a real test of fortitude at an event like the TT when there are many other pressures for race-teams to contend with.

*

One man operating on the proverbial shoe-string at the 1979 TT was Freddie Broadbent. He bought his 250 Formula III Suzuki as an insurance write-off six months before the TT for £130. A battered wreck it may have been, but he rebuilt it to FIII specification and was on the Island for his first TT race.

*

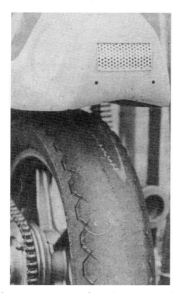

Helmut Dahne was a regular TT competitor, initially with BMWs. In 1979 he rode a Honda in the Formula I race and this was the condition of his rear tyre at the end. No tread left and down to the canvas.

With a slightly better supply of race machinery than Freddie Broadbent, Mike Hailwood returned for another foray at the races he first rode in twenty-one years before. Ducati showed a little more interest in Mike's efforts but they turned out a bike that was probably worse than the one used in 1978, doing helpful things like reversing the direction of the gearchange. Mike was determined to enjoy what he announced as his last TT, and although he narrowly lost out to Alex George in the big-money Classic race (by 3.4 seconds), he took a comfortable win on his Castrol Heron Suzuki in the Senior, setting new race and lap records, and again recording his own personal fastest laps of the TT Course. Second place man was the experienced Tony Rutter who told Mike after the race *'When you came by, I tried to keep up with*

you, but no-way . . .'. With the Senior win giving him his 14th TT victory, Mike's legion of fans must have wondered just what he would have done to the record books if he had not been absent from the Island races for eleven years. Those same fans greeted with mixed feelings the news at the 1979 event that he was finally retiring from racing at the TT. Of course, they would have liked to have seen him race again and add to his total, but they were aware of the dangers of the Mountain Course, and so many were secretly happy at his decision and wished him a safe retirement. Two years into that retirement, Mike was killed in a car accident when returning from a family errand. It was a cruel twist of fate that a lifelong racer on two and four wheels should meet his death in a road traffic accident.

*

Mike's 1979 Senior winning machine is now owned by the Manx Government and is intended for display in a proposed TT Museum that is to be up and running by the event's centenary in 2007.

*

Although Mike Hailwood's rides at the 1979 TT once again made the headlines, there were many other fine performances. Trevor Ireson and Clive Pollington won both Sidecar races, Alex George added the TT Formula I to his Classic win, Alan Jackson took his third consecutive win on a Honda in the TT Formula II and Barry Smith bought his Yamaha home first in the TT Formula III. In winning the Junior race that was back to six-laps, Charlie Williams (Yamaha) beat the eleven-year-old lap record of Bill Ivy. It was a record that Bill set in 1968 at 105.51 mph. Leading from start to finish, Charlie lifted it to 106.83 mph.

Winners Alex George and Trevor Ireson both put out a plea that there should be no further alterations to the TT Course. Alex felt that by making things smoother they were making things more dangerous in places where, previously, a bumpy surface had served to naturally govern speed. Trevor agreed, even though smoothing of the Cronk y Voddy straight had at least rid the sidecar men of the affliction that he called *'Cronk y Voddy Cronkiness'*. He explained: *'It was so bumpy that if you took it flat out, by the end you had double vision, a mild form of concussion I suppose'.*

*

Another name from the past who appeared at the 1979 TT was John Surtees. John took part in a 'Millennium Parade' of machines and riders from former years. After 18 years out of the saddle he completed a lap at 95 mph from a standing start on a

John Surtees leads Phil Read into Ramsey. Both riding MV Agustas, they are shown during the Classic Parade at the 1979 TT. Although both John and Phil won World Championships on MVs, they rode in different eras.

500cc MV Agusta. It served to reawaken his interest in riding motorcycles and he has raced and paraded them ever since.

Black-Flag

It is not unknown for riders to strike machine trouble in a race, such as a loose exhaust or oil leak, and be unaware of the problem, even though it may well have been noticed by course-side marshals. It is at such times that the organisers employ the black flag procedure. At selected points the marshals are equipped with a blackboard on which they chalk the rider's number. As he approaches, the blackboard is displayed and the black flag is waved to attract his attention and indicate that he must stop. Black-flagging is invariably done at a point where a Travelling Marshal is stationed and it is he who carries out the machine inspection and determines

whether a rider can continue or whether he must retire. In the 1979 Senior race young hot-shot Steve Ward, winner of the 1978 Junior MGP, was black-flagged at Ramsey but, after inspection, was allowed to continue the race. The business of slowing, stopping and accelerating away again had obviously cost him time and the timekeepers carried out their standard practice of crediting him with the time they estimated he had lost. Then a problem arose, for after his time credit was taken into account Steve was shown as having broken the lap record! A hasty adjustment was made to his time credit and Steve eventually finished in a fine fourth place.

*

The 1979 Millennium TT races were attended by the largest ever crowds and they brought to an end on a high note a decade that had caused more than its fair share of troubles for the event.

Chapter 11
TT FESTIVAL

After the tribulations of the early 1970s, the TT had lots of hard work and considerable sums of money pumped into it, giving rise to the claim that at the end of the decade it was *'the richest motorcycle event in the world'*. As a result, organisers the ACU and funders the Isle of Man Government had, by the start of the 1980s, an undeniably successful event on their hands. This extended beyond the racing that had seen the welcome return of 'works' machinery and increased entries, for it was now claimed that 'TT Fortnight' offered something for everyone, whatever their motorcycling interest, and that it had been transformed into a 'TT Festival'.

*

TT FESTIVAL

It is a surprise to find out how little time some visitors to the Isle of Man at TT-time spend watching the actual racing. Indeed, many do not visit with the intention of doing so, for they get their enjoyment from just being among their own kind and being part of the overall TT 'scene'. The traditional 'TT Fortnight' always had subsidiary attractions - motorcycling and other - for the entertainment of race visitors, but over the past twenty years this aspect has been much developed. The list of subsidiary events is now so huge that it takes up several pages in the official TT programme and visitors can be heard complaining of clashes of times/dates that prevent them seeing all that they want to. Fitting in everything that takes place in practice week can be hectic enough, but TT week can get seriously frenetic!

There is truly something for everyone - enthusiasts for individual makes find that most 'Owners Clubs' hold get-togethers, and these can vary from the huge Honda Day at Peel to the gathering of a few like-minded Morini owners at a small pub in Laxey. Manufacturers put on demonstration rides of their latest machines (on and off-road), motorcycle magazines have special promotional events that include organised ride-outs, etc. On the competition side the main TT races are supplemented by the Pre-TT Classic Races run on the Billown Circuit during practice week and the Steam Packet Races run at Billown immediately after TT. Events like Trials, Moto-cross, Beach-races, Hill-climbs, Enduro, Super Moto and Sprints also take place around the Island. For those who want to emulate the tarmac racers there are Track-Days at Jurby, and there is a week of events for Vintage bikes, parades of Classic machines around the TT Course, and the firing-up of exotic old racing machinery to pound and delight the ear-drums in unlikely locations like the historic Castletown Square.

There is always a good selection of vintage bikes to be seen at the TT.

Most visitors look forward to getting in plenty of riding, including a blast around the Course on Mad Sunday when the Mountain section is made one-way for the day.

No worries about riding the wrong side of the white line on Mad Sunday, for the Mountain section of the TT Course is made one-way so that race-fans can enjoy taking the racing line.

When the bikes do get put to one side for a while, visitors can take in the free show of thousands of bikes parked handlebar to handlebar along Douglas Promenade, the stunning displays of the Red Arrows, fairground rides, bungee jumps, stunt-riders, mini-bike racing, organised street parties, tattooists, the zany antics of the Purple Helmets, motorcycling film-shows, meet the riders and chat-shows, and any amount of evening entertainment offered by Pubs, Bands, Discos, Barbecues, Firework Displays, etc., that are all geared to bikers' tastes and needs. Add to that the many impromptu and private events that take place and you really have a full fortnight of activities.

It is very easy to describe an event as a 'Festival', but it is not so easy to achieve the atmosphere that such a title demands. The TT does so, by the tankful, and it is all offered against the high-octane background of the world's greatest road races.

For all the 'side-show' activities available to visitors, racing motorcycles over the Mountain Course is what the TT is really all about. Massively over-subscribed entry lists for the seven-race programme proved the popularity of the races in 1980 but must have meant disappointment for the many entries that could not be accepted. (The following year there were over 1,000 entries for 550 available places.) No doubt a good few of the entry had their eyes on a share of the £200,000 prize fund, but for others the aim was simply to take-up the enduring challenge of racing motor-bikes over the TT Mountain Course, as earlier generations of racers had done over the preceding 75 years.

*

The 'TT Formula I' event that opened race-week in 1980 was keenly contested both during and after the race by the Honda and Suzuki 'works' teams. Indeed, a bit of needle crept in even before the start when, in a tactical move, Suzuki-mounted Graeme Crosby managed to take over the riding number of the no-show American Dave Aldana (moving from 3 to 11) and thus put himself in a position to keep an eye on the race progress of Honda's Mick Grant (No.12). The lead chopped and changed between the two of them during the race, but at the finish Grant was declared the winner by 11 seconds. Fourth finisher, Gordon Pantall, then submitted a protest claiming that the petrol tank on Grant's Honda was of greater capacity than the 24 litres permitted by the regulations. Honda admitted that the tank was capable of holding 28 litres but explained that they had put air bottles and table-tennis balls inside to reduce its petrol-holding capacity to regulation size. Mick Grant had done his bit to help matters in that direction when, at the end of the race, he brought his fist down onto the aluminium tank with considerable force in what he described as a spontaneous gesture of celebration. Suzuki saw the resultant capacity reducing dent somewhat differently, but their protest was dismissed and the win stood to Honda.

*

In a race in which the first four places did go to Suzuki, Graeme Crosby won the Senior (and his first TT) after a race-long battle with Ian Richards who dropped out towards the end. Steve Cull was second, Steve Ward third, and Stan Woods set the fastest lap.

*

In the six-lap Classic race (confusingly, it was for modern machinery, not for 'Classic/Vintage' machinery as the term is used today) Joey Dunlop won on a two year old Yamaha TZ750 supplied by Rea Racing, leaving the 'works' Hondas of established runner Mick Grant and rising star Ron Haslam to take second and third places. Riding under what was to become his favoured number 3, it was not an easy ride, for the strap holding the eight gallon petrol tank broke on the first lap and Joey had to hold it in place with knees, arms and chest. Despite this handicap, he set a new absolute lap record of 115.22 mph on his way to first place and showed Honda that he was by now a formidable TT runner. Honda wisely decided that they would rather have him riding for them than against them, and were soon supplying him with race machinery.

Graeme Crosby (Suzuki) at Parliament Square, Ramsey, during the 1980 TT.

133

The sidecar spoils in 1980 were shared by the pairings of Trevor Ireson / Clive Pollington and Jock Taylor/Bengt Johannson, with each taking a win and second place.

Charlie Williams (Yamaha) won the Junior race that was reduced to 4 laps (due to delayed starts to the Formula II and Formula III races earlier in the day), and in second place was Irish newcomer Donny Robinson just 12 seconds adrift. In third place amongst the customary swarm of Yamahas was Steve Tonkin on a British made Cotton, the same make of bike that Stanley Woods made his TT debut on in 1922.

*

Joey Dunlop, the man Honda decided they would rather have riding for them than against them.

One man who could not get enough high-speed action was Belfast's Ernie Coates. A couple of years earlier he rode in every TT race, solo and sidecar. In 1980 he contented himself with putting in 100+ mph laps on his 250 Cotton and 350 Yamaha. He also averaged over the 'ton' while acting as passenger to sidecar-driving brother, Wallace.

*

At the 1981 TT the customary Thursday afternoon 'dress rehearsal' practice was held on Wednesday afternoon to accommodate the Grand National Moto-cross meeting. As luck would have it, the weather on Wednesday was good for racing, whilst on Thursday it was fit only for Moto-cross.

One Careful Owner

By the end of practice week, riders in all classes had completed 1824 laps and 68,820 miles. One man who put in his share of practice miles only to be left bitterly disappointed at the end of the week was Eddie Roberts. His Honda blew its engine in the final practice session and it looked as though he was out of the opening Formula I race. Then a German visitor offered him a ride on his road-going Z1000 Kawasaki, complete with high-rise handlebars. Eddie did not even get to learn the generous visitor's name before he raced the bike to 28th place at an average speed of 91.96 mph.

*

After complaints in previous years, a slightly more equitable distribution of prize-money saw lesser lights (the backbone of the races) receive an increased share of the prize fund in 1981.

National newspapers were aware that their readers wanted to know about the TT and several ran TT-time competitions and provided race reports and results in their daily issues. The Daily Mirror even involved itself in activities on the Island.

Those who could afford them were using quick-fillers at their petrol stops, which meant they need only be stationary for about ten seconds. Joey Dunlop was riding for Honda but his second stop in the Formula I race was a bit longer because, in a first at the TT, he had a rear-wheel changed (to get the benefit of a new tyre), whereas Ron Haslam, also on a Honda, used one tyre for the whole race. Amongst private runners seeking to gain advantage from the use of quick-fillers, Neil Tuxworth arrived with one made from a milk-churn and Derek Huxley utilised a beer-keg.

Protests

What had been needle between the Honda and Suzuki 'works' teams at the 1980 TT turned into bad feelings and worse in 1981. New Zealander Graeme Crosby on his Suzuki was in the thick of it again in Saturday's Formula I event, the 300th TT race to be run on the Mountain Course. Waiting on the start-line in mixed weather conditions, 'Croz' made a last minute decision to fit a slick rear tyre and missed his

number 16 starting spot. As a result he was made to start at the back of the field with no allowance being given for the time he had lost. Honda teamsters Ron Haslam and Joey Dunlop duly passed the finishing line in first and second places, but with a storming ride Crosby finished third (even with his time handicap). Simple arithmetic showed that if he had received an allowance for the time lost at the start he would have won the race. So, Suzuki slapped in a protest. This time it was upheld, Crosby was declared the winner, Haslam and Dunlop were relegated to second and third, and Honda were furious!

*

When the time for the Classic race arrived, Honda were still fuming over Crosby and Suzuki's Formula I win. In an attempt to register their displeasure with the organisers decision they appeared for the Classic race with their machines painted black and their riders dressed in black leathers (actually made from blue leather painted black). It was a protest that aroused mixed feelings among spectators, and one

Honda teamsters dressed in their black 'protest' leathers, take it easy before the start of the 1981 Classic race. From the left: Alex George, Ron Haslam and Joey Dunlop.

135

that did nothing for Honda's performance in the race. Indeed, Graeme Crosby took his Suzuki to a record-breaking win, becoming the first man to complete a six-lap race in under two hours. Mick Grant (previously dropped by Honda) brought another Suzuki into second place, with the all-black ensemble of Alex George and his Honda in third. Although Joey Dunlop (Honda) set a new outright lap record of 115.40 mph, he ran out of petrol. Perhaps Honda put too much effort into staging their 'all-black' protest and not enough into fundamentals like providing Joey with sufficient fuel. Overall, the nature of their protest did not win them many friends.

*

In his book 'Honda - The Complete Story', Roland Brown quotes one of Honda's advertising slogans as *'Honda Enters. Honda Wins'* and described it as *'brilliant in its simplicity, outrageous in its arrogance, ruthless in its clarity'*. But, whatever Honda's widely advertised level of past performance, Suzuki reminded them that they should take nothing for granted at the TT. Honda did not come across as good losers in 1981, particularly when the modified advertising slogan (below) got into circulation.

*

A modified version of Honda's famous advertising slogan that circulated at the 1981 TT

For all the problems that the mighty Honda team felt they had in the opening Formula I race, a man with a real problem in that event was privateer Ray Knight, for he was reported as retired *'with a broken handlebar'*. Just imagine the high-speed trauma that bald statement probably concealed! A similar

problem befell Charlie Williams when his right clip-on snapped at the 33rd Milestone. Competing in the TT will reveal weaknesses, as manufacturers have discovered down the years, and such component failures are the thing that riders dread most of all when riding the Mountain Course.

*

Steve Tonkin won the Junior on an Armstrong at a record race average speed after Graeme McGregor (Kawasaki) set a new lap record but dropped out on the last lap. Second was a man who had just moved up to the TT from the MGP, Bob Jackson, and his was a name that was to feature in many more TT results. Flying Scotsman Jock Taylor had Bengt Johannson in the sidecar as they took a double win, setting a new lap record for the three-wheelers at 107.95 mph.

*

The Senior race was hit by rain and stopped at the end of the second lap without a result being declared. Chris Guy was in the lead at the time but in the following day's re-run he fell at Braddan Bridge and victory went to Mick Grant (Suzuki). Another faller at Braddan was the usually consistent George Fogarty, father of Carl 'Foggy' Fogarty. The TT continued to attract new and talented riders from both short circuit and road-racing backgrounds, amongst the high-placed finishers in the Senior were names like Donny Robinson, John Newbold, Billy Guthrie and Con Law.

*

As with the TT Formula I race, lap and race records were set in the TT Formula II and Formula III races, where victory went to Tony Rutter (Ducati) and Barry Smith (Yamaha).

*

Barry Sheene had established himself as a vociferous critic of the TT down the years (after just one ride in the event), and so it was a puzzle to racegoers in 1981 to see Bernard Murray entered on a Yamaha under Barry Sheene's name in the Senior and Classic races.

'Croz'
In contrast to Sheene's professed dislike of the TT, one top Grand Prix runner (5th in the 500cc World Championship in 1981, 2nd in 1982) who was very much for the TT was Graeme Crosby. He explained in 'Classic Racer' that what he liked about it was *'The way the racing is spread out over the ten days, the enthusiasm of the fans, dawn practice, hard partying on the days off, the history of the place . . . it's magic, really, but it's so hard to explain the place to people who've never been there'*. Crosby was a favourite with many fans

and knew how to entertain them. On his TT debut in 1979 he was pulling monster wheelies out of the Gooseneck on his big Moriwaki Kawasaki fitted with high bars and only a cockpit fairing. He did this while still putting in 109 mph laps. Not bad for a first-timer! After upsetting Honda at the 1981 TT with his controversial win over Ron Haslam in the Formula I race, 'Croz' upset Yamaha later that year by accidentally taking Barry Sheene out at the British Grand Prix. Within the Suzuki camp he was (in his words) the subject of a successful campaign by Randy Mamola to have him dropped. Thus it was that for 1982 he was down to race a Yamaha in a team run by Giacomo Agostini. With Ago's anti-TT attitude, this automatically meant no TT races for straight-talking Crosby, a source of regret to him and his fans. However, 'Croz' did not want to miss all the TT action in 1982 so he showed up on the Island for a ride in the Classic parade lap, acted as pit-attendant for Norman Brown and, no doubt, managed to fit in attendance at a few parties.

*

The TT celebrated its 75th anniversary in 1982 and the Isle of Man Postal Office issued a set of five postage stamps to celebrate the occasion. They featured solo riders of the past: Charlie Collier, Freddie Dixon, Jimmy Guthrie and Mike Hailwood, plus the sidecar crew of Jock Taylor and Benga Johannson. In addition, the Manx Treasury minted 75,000 coins of 50p face value that featured Mick Grant.

*

Despite the heavy cost of racing at the TT, entries continued to be over-subscribed. To soften the financial burden every entrant received a minimum of £100 towards their expenses, and the organisers operated a system whereby riders who had taken part in the event during the previous three years were credited with points that entitled them to more financial support - a form of loyalty bonus.

*

The weather was particularly good for practice in 1982, allowing riders the maximum time in which to ensure their machines were in the best possible race trim. One man keen to complete a practice lap during the Monday evening session was Phil Lovett. When his Kawasaki ran out of petrol at Hillberry he obtained a lift to the Pits via back roads, collected some petrol, got a lift back to Hillberry, topped up his tank and completed his lap. This was duly recorded as an official time of 1 hour 41 minutes 33.2 seconds.

*

Ron Haslam's first TT appearance had been in 1978 and was greeted with apprehension by experienced TT watchers, for he used a pure short circuit scratching style that seemed to allow no margin for error.

Ron Haslam's short circuit scratching style is still evident even though he moved to 'works' Hondas for the TT in 1979.

Ron survived those early years, steadied a little and, after being 'robbed' of first place in 1981, he finally gained an undisputed TT victory in the Formula I race of 1982 on his Honda Britain machine, at a record race average speed of 113.33 mph. Mick Grant was back with Honda and led in the early stages, setting the fastest lap at 114.93 mph before retiring. Another Honda Britain man, Joey Dunlop, was second. It was the only podium finish that Joey achieved at the 1982 TT.

*

A first-timer at the TT, 22 year old Norman Brown astounded regular runners by taking victory in the Senior on his Suzuki entered by Hector Neill Racing, and second place in the Junior on a Yamaha. Norman's rise to success was particularly rapid. He made his first Island racing appearance just 9 months earlier as a Newcomer in the MGP. There he won the Junior Newcomer's class and came second in the Lightweight race. Although that made his move to the TT almost a certainty, he showed wonderful talent in taking the Senior win in his first year amongst the big boys, particularly as he finished with an oil-soaked rear tyre. His performance was reminiscent of Geoff Duke's early Isle of Man racing days, but Norman's prospects of emulating Geoff and of a glittering TT career were ended later the following year, when he was killed in an accident in the British GP at Silverstone.

*

In a move that served to emphasise the fact that the Senior race was no longer the 'Blue Riband' of the TT meeting, the organisers split the entry into 500cc and 350cc classes for 1982. Tony Rutter won the 350 class from Phil Mellor and Manxman Graham Cannell.

*

It was an unlucky year for Charlie Williams, for despite leading three races and setting three new lap records he did not manage a podium finish. Typical of Charlie's bad luck was the Senior race. Forced to stop at the Sulby Hotel with a mysterious mis-fire, he assumed his race was over and accepted the offer of a pint. Before he could settle down with it to watch the race, he suddenly spotted a kinked fuel line. A few moments later he was back in the race, set a new lap record of 115.08 mph, but had lost too much time to threaten the leaders.

*

Although the organisers did not normally issue riding number 13, Chris Guy made a point of asking for it and was happy to ride under this unlucky number, but he had a troubled TT in '82. Another unlucky man was veteran of 77 TT races Bill Smith. In an unusual accident his Honda seized on the approach to Ballaugh Bridge in the Formula II race and he was badly injured. Although Bill recovered to race again at the TT, he found it difficult to get back to his former pace and had to be satisfied with his pre-accident total of 49 TT Replicas.

*

There was a strange incident in the Senior when Dave Dean saw a spectator waving a red jacket at Glen Helen and, because he had just passed a two-machine accident at Doran's Bend, took it as a signal that the race had been stopped. He toured to Kirk Michael before waking-up to the fact that the race was still very much on. Although the Clerk of the Course was willing to credit him with the three minutes that he was estimated to have lost, the International Jury would not do so. Dave therefore finished 15th instead of 10th.

*

Phil Read was still looking for another big TT pay-day but his only result of the week in 1982 was a decent fourth place in the Senior. He did a bit of showing-off and treated the crowds to a spectacular wheelie at the start of the Classic, but did not manage to finish the race. Mick Grant was asked before the Classic if he thought that Phil posed much

of a threat and rather perceptively replied: *'Pose, yes. A threat, no!'*

*

Another new name was added to the list of TT winners in the Classic race when New Zealander Dennis Ireland won on a Suzuki. It was a race of attrition for established runners like Charlie Williams, Mick Grant, Ron Haslam and Joey Dunlop; but Dennis was there ready to inherit victory at the end of the six-lap race. Second in the Classic and the Senior was 350cc World Champion Jon Ekerold from South Africa. The ACU paid good money to try and boost the TT by attracting stars of Ekerold's world standing, and he always gave full value on the Island. Indeed, he achieved his second spot with a broken gear-lever.

*

A line-up of classic racing machinery prior to parading around the TT Course.

Before the Classic race there was a parade lap of 'Classic' machines headed by Stanley Woods on a

138

500cc KTT Velocette. In this case the term Classic had vintage connotations, although a few modern bikes managed to work their way in, including a couple of Hondas ridden by Ron Haslam and Joey Dunlop. Were those two stars riding simply to give Honda a bit more publicity, or could they have been getting a useful pre-race look at the damp conditions before their rides in the Classic race proper that followed the parade?

*

In another race that showed the TT Course was as demanding as ever, numbers 1-10 were all forced to retire in the Junior race. This left Con Law, who had been beset with mechanical problems during practice, to win on a Waddon. Like the Armstrong that won in 1981 and the Cotton that came third in 1980, the Waddon was a British machine powered by an Austrian Rotax twin-cylinder, two-stroke engine. Also on a largely British machine was Neil Tuxworth on a 250cc Wicks.

*

Although he had been competing at top level for many years, a sidecar win at the TT still eluded Mick Boddice. He dropped out after leading both races in 1982, leaving Trevor Ireson to take the first leg, Jock Taylor the second and Roy Hanks to get the overall win based on the results of both races.

The TT Course is particularly demanding on sidecar outfits and some drivers ran different machines on the Island to the ones they used on short circuits. Ken Sprayson ran a free welding/repair service at the TT for many years on behalf of Reynolds Tubes. When they withdrew their support, Shell backed his efforts for a few years. Ken's services were certainly needed, for in 1982 he did over 160 different repairs and claimed that more than half of the sidecar entry availed itself of his free service.

A Short Circuit TT?

Although the TT was synonymous with the Mountain Course, well-meaning attempts had been made down the years to find a site for a short circuit to GP standards on the Island. With an abundance of short circuits available in mainland Britain, it was difficult to see how such a project would succeed, but that did not prevent the idea being raised at regular intervals. The Island's Tourist Board even created a Short Circuit Sub-Committee and in 1982 and 1983 it received several proposals. Well known racers such as Geoff Duke, Phil Read and even Barry Sheene lent their names to schemes, but despite agreeing that

'further investigations should take place into the feasibility, desirability and viability of such a project', it went no further.

*

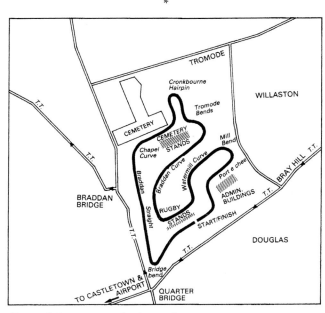

One of the proposals for a short circuit on the Isle of Man that was considered in the early 1980s.

To most motorcyclists the TT remained firmly linked to the Mountain Course. For them, attendance took the form of an annual pilgrimage and they were prepared to go through any hardship to achieve it. One enthusiast wrote of this annual migratory need: *'To lack this urge . . . to go to the TT races . . . is, I suggest, to lack an essential quality as a motorcycle enthusiast'.*

Some spectators book their TT visits in very good time, others, due to work/family commitments, cannot do so and sometimes it can be a last minute decision to go. That can cause problems in getting a boat crossing, finding accommodation, etc. One such enthusiast of the mid-1980s also wanted to keep the cost down and decided to go by 'moped'. But this was no ordinary moped for it was powered by a clip-on type engine of the 1950s attached to a folding paratrooper's bicycle of the 1940s. Taking advantage of a cheap rail and boat excursion fare, the intrepid fan took the folded machine in a bag as hand luggage, re-assembled it in Douglas and had cheap transport for a few days stay. Unable to resist doing a lap of the Course, the otherwise trusty moped suffered slippage of the roller-drive in a wet ride up the Mountain and the resulting lap time was measured in hours rather than minutes.

Breakdowns on the way to the Island have beset

plenty of motorcyclists down the years, and many a TT fan has been towed onto the boat with a dead bike, aiming to fix it in Douglas. The 'must get there' tales are legion. Like the one about the rider from East Anglia who set off for the Island but broke-down just a few miles from home. He picked up the local paper, rang about a bike advertised for sale, bought it and set off again, all on the same day.

Inevitably, with such a high concentration of speed-hungry motorcyclists on such a small Island there are accidents at TT time, some serious, some not so. Falling off a bike (fast or slow) can be expensive in repairs. Occasionally one sees an unlucky faller who has left his battered machine outside his digs on Douglas Promenade, complete with a notice explaining how it got to this state and a bucket inviting contributions toward repairs. No doubt reflecting that 'there but for the grace of God go I', many enthusiasts throw in a few coins to ease the unlucky rider's financial pain.

Higher and Higher

The year of 1983 gave the TT crowds more high-speed racing with records broken in several classes. Con Law took an EMC (another Rotax based bike) to victory in the Junior at a record race speed. In doing so he also achieved the first over 110 mph lap on a 250cc machine, at 110.03 mph. Tony Rutter added to his TT Formula II wins and set a new record lap of 109.44 mph on his Ducati, Joey Dunlop brought his 850cc V-four Honda to victory in the TT Formula I event with race and lap records, leaving the former at 114.03 mph and the latter at 115.73 mph. Winners Tony and Joey were relatively old at 41 and 31 years, but victory in what had become the TT's premier race, the 'Senior Classic TT' (opened-up to 1000cc machines), went to 24 year old Rob McElnea (Suzuki) at a record race speed of 114.81 mph, whilst Norman Brown (Suzuki) set a new absolute course record of 116.19 mph before running out of fuel.

*

Although the Junior TT remained for 250cc machines, a Junior 350 race was also run for bigger machines (taking the place in the programme of the TT FIII race that was dropped). Jon Ekerold led in the early stages but retired, and the race was won by Phil Mellor (Yamaha), although race and lap speeds were slower than in the race for 250s.

Boddice Wins!

In the Sidecar class Mick Boddice showed that he had at last got the right balance between speed and reliability, winning the second sidecar race after trying (and so nearly winning) for 14 years. Mick was to get that balance right many times more in the years ahead and become a multi-TT winner. But the speed of the sidecar outfits was a cause for concern, not least for some of the passengers. Drivers generally built-up

Mick Boddice at Ginger Hall in 1983, on his way to the first of many wins in the Sidecar TT.

speed during the week of practice, and after the Thursday afternoon session former winner Trevor Ireson was informed by his passenger that he had reached his personal limit and could not go on. By the end of practice a couple more passengers had given up. One of them just disappeared without trace, leaving his driver to assume that he had departed the Island and returned home.

*

The MGP was still proving a prolific breeding ground for future TT riders and anyone with a crystal ball would have found the results of the 1983 Junior Newcomer's MGP particularly interesting. They were:

1st Robert Dunlop (Yamaha)
2nd Steve Hislop (Yamaha)
3rd Ian Lougher (Yamaha)

*

In a revamped programme at the 1984 TT the Junior 350 race was dropped and there was no 350 class in the Senior event. A three-class Production race was brought back, the maximum capacity for Formula 1 machines was reduced to 750cc, a two-class 'Classic Bike Historic' race was introduced, and qualifying times were stiffened.

Production Return

Ever since the first event in 1907, the TT has been run to accommodate both the sporting interests of competitors and the commercial interests of manufacturers. Spectators' views were occasionally taken into account and it was down to the organisers to devise a programme that balanced the varied interests. When, in 1984, they announced their intention to run the reintroduced Production race on the Saturday before race-week, the manufacturers, in a rare show of solidarity, made joint representations and achieved a revised race time of Friday afternoon, making it the last race on the week's programme. As this was the same day as the Classic race, it indicated just how important the Production race was to the manufacturers. Previous Production races had proved difficult to administer and became notorious for the protests they generated. It was seasoned competitor Ray Knight (himself a winner of the 500cc class of the Production TT in 1968) who summed up the problem with the words: *'A Production race fails completely if everybody is not quite convinced that the machines are as you can buy . . .'*. In an attempt to discourage illegal performance enhancing modifications, it was proposed to include a 'claiming rule' whereby it was possible for a winning machine to be purchased by a

fellow competitor for a fixed price at the end of the race. Whatever problems they created for the organisers, the wide variety of Production machines available meant the new race had the potential to be technically interesting and very good for the TT.

*

Practice for all the 1984 races was even more hectic than usual, with well-known names like Steve Tonkin, Neil Tuxworth and Steve Henshaw suffering high-speed spills. Indeed, the rescue-helicopter ferried 17 riders to hospital over the TT fortnight.

*

Come race-week and Joey Dunlop took the second of what were to be many Formula I wins for Honda on his V-4 RS750R. Joey lost out in the Senior after breaking the absolute lap record of 118.47 mph on his three-cylinder, reed-valved, two-stroke NS500 Honda, which ran out of fuel on the last lap. (That was the official reason giving for his stopping, but some seasoned TT watchers believed that he had a major mechanical problem that Honda did not want to admit to.) Senior victory went to Rob McElnea on his Suzuki RG500 (the eighth year in succession that the RG500 had won the Senior) and Rob also took a hard-fought Classic win for Suzuki, holding off the challenges of Joey Dunlop and Mick Grant.

*

Regular speed readings were no longer published in the motorcycle press, but Joey was reported to have been travelling at 175 mph past The Highlander during the TT Formula I race. That was not the sort of time and place that a rider would want to experience a mechanical failure but, inevitably, they do happen at the TT. Malcolm Lucas had the front tyre of his Suzuki fail at Greeba Bridge and that is a quick enough spot for most people. But, after picking himself up from the resulting crash, Malcolm's first words were: *'Thank God it went there and not somewhere really fast'*.

*

The new three-lap Production race of 1984 did not disappoint and Geoff Johnson (Kawasaki GPz900R) won the 751-1500cc class, Trevor Nation (Honda CBX750) the 251-750cc class by just 2.2 seconds from Helmut Dahne (Honda VF750), and Phil Mellor (Yamaha RD250LC) was first 100-250cc. The Japanese manufacturers went away satisfied that they had made their point in the Production classes, just as they did in the racing ones.

*

Australian riders have featured at the TT for many years. After finishing second in the Junior of 1983,

Helmut Dahne (Honda) at Whitegates during his ride to second place in the 1984 Production TT.

Graeme McGregor from down-under won the 1984 Junior on an EMC and, the same day, the TT Formula II on a Yamaha. Charlie Williams finished his highly successful TT career with second place in the Junior.

*

New names appeared amongst the TT leaderboard finishers every year and Roger Marshall, Nick Jefferies, Brian Reid, Gary Padgett, Robert Dunlop and Ian Lougher featured in 1984. All the riders performances were logged by a new computerised recording system.

Historic TT
The Historic race was for what were regarded as vintage machines and brought the first TT win for an American rider, when Dave Roper was fastest over the three-lap event on his 500cc Matchless G50. First Historic 350 was Steve Cull on an Aermacchi. The heavily bearded Dave Roper quickly earned a reputation as a hard-charging rider on the Historic bikes that he rode for Team Obsolete. It was a necessary style, for Historic bikes did not have the surfeit of bhp enjoyed by the race machinery of the

day. As a result, every mph had to be protected by the maintenance of high corner speeds and a degree of boldness in passing manoeuvres. The Historic Race was only run for one year at the TT but the MGP, that had started the ball rolling with what they called Classic Races, run theirs to this day. Dave Roper contested the Classic MGP events for a number of years and Travelling Marshal Keith Trubshaw (a man who had taken four second places at the MGP) had first-hand experience of Roper's forceful riding style in the late 1980s, for the bearded American passed him on the inside when both were cranked over at Kate's Cottage. Keith thought it was a bit close and perhaps Dave did too for in the Paddock he went over to Keith and enquired if he was the Travelling Marshal that he had passed at Kate's. Receiving a nod Dave said: 'I saw that you'd left me a gap on the inside'; which was not quite the way that Keith had seen it.

*

In 1985 many spectators were faced with a major change to established travelling arrangements, when most of the Isle of Man Steam Packet Company's

142

sailings to the Island were switched from Liverpool to Heysham, some fifty miles further north. Such a change of port did not affect the many TT enthusiasts who travelled from Ireland, amongst them being Joey Dunlop. But Joey did not travel to the Island by Steam Packet boat anyway, instead he made arrangements with a friend who owned a fishing boat to bring him, brother Robert, some of their racing bikes and a group of friends, from Belfast to Douglas. In 1985 this resulted in what Joey describes as the most frightening experience of his life when the boat, 'Tornamona', sank just outside Belfast, taking the bikes to the bottom. Although passengers and crew were thrown into the water, they were all rescued and, eventually, so were the bikes. It was hardly the most promising start to a TT fortnight, but a mere thirty-six hours after the sinking, Joey was out in practice on 'works' Hondas, setting the pace, re-acquainting himself with the Course and experiencing the usual changes that included major road improvements at Quarry Bends.

*

There were several consequences to Joey and friends' ship-wreck. A specially enlarged tank for Joey's 250 was recovered by a diver and he used it in the race. Although the petrol tank for Robert Dunlop's 250 was not on the boat, the keys to the filler-cap were!

*

More changes to the race programme were introduced in 1985. Out went the big Classic race and the Senior event recovered its former prestigious top billing. Out also went the Historic races, after only one year. On the organisational side, quick-fillers were banned and everyone used the standard gravity-fillers supplied by the organisers.

*

The top Production bikes were shown to be hitting 155 mph on the drop from Creg ny Baa to Brandish, with Tony Rutter's 750cc GSX-R Suzuki faster than the 1000cc Hondas. (The big Hondas had been fastest the previous year at 147 mph and the quickest 750 had reached 136 mph.) In the 250 class the fastest recorded speed was 123 mph, set by Phil Nicholls and Michael McGarrity. The 'Roads Open' Jaguar XJS was clocked at 143 mph.

Joey's Hat-Trick

Despite his 'shipwreck' on the way to the Island, by the end of practice in 1985 it was clear that Joey Dunlop was in top form. Carrying that form through to race-week, Joey sped to victory on his Hondas in the Formula 1, Junior and Senior races, so becoming

only the second rider to achieve a hat-trick of wins in one year. Brian Reid had looked a likely winner of the Junior on his Yamaha until he ran out of fuel at Hillberry on the last lap. Joey knew all about running out when leading a race and in this instance was happy to snap up victory. In doing so he gave Honda its first 250cc win since 1967.

*

Veteran Tony Rutter continued his winning ways and took his fourth Formula II victory in five years on his Ducati, whilst Mick Boddice and Dave Hallam were the sidecar winners. Production wins went to Geoff Johnson (Honda), Mick Grant (Suzuki) for his seventh TT win, and journalist Matt Oxley (Honda) who was able to write a first-hand account of his Production Class A (100-250cc) win in the pages of 'Motorcycle News'.

New Grandstand

With the arrival of the 1986 TT came a major change for those who liked to spectate at the Start and Finish area. Gone was the 60 year old timber and steel

The Tower of the new Grandstand that houses Race Control's office on the top floor.

Grandstand and in its place was a new Grandstand and Control Tower of brick, concrete and stainless steel. Showing the Island's confidence in the future of the races, it was a structure that was obviously built to last, although spectator seating was still open to the elements. At least Race Control's accommodation at the top of the tower now kept out the weather and it was equipped with the latest telecommunication and computer technology. The press-room had similar high-tech facilities, plus one all-important traditional one: a bar serving Okell's ale.

*

A heavy overnight gale early in the meeting made conditions very difficult for competitors staying in the 'Paddock Hotel'. It also blew down the Scrutineers' tent and, more importantly to some, did the same to the beer tent. It was to be another year before permanent scrutineering bays were provided in the Paddock, and when they arrived all bikes were scrutineered on race-days, the practice of 'weighing-in' the day before was dispensed with, as was the MGP tradition of competitors parading through Douglas to the start.

*

A pre-event worry for the organisers at the 1986 TT came in the shape of new rules from the Civil Aviation Authority that threatened the use of the rescue-helicopter and, therefore, the races, for the chopper had become all-important to the rescue services and the races would not be run unless it was present. Single-engined helicopters as used at the TT and MGP had recently been banned from landing in built-up areas like those in which the Island's hospitals were situated. An exemption was gained for 1986 but twin-engined machines were required thereafter. Ferrying an average of about fifteen riders to hospital during each race fortnight, the rescue-helicopter is literally a lifesaver. Despite the length of the Mountain Course and the remoteness of some of its stretches, use of the helicopter can see an injured rider in hospital receiving expert medical help in a far shorter time than would be required to convey him to hospital from many short circuits in the UK by conventional ambulance.

*

Roger Burnett took his Honda two-stroke to victory in the Senior after several early leaders dropped out. Geoff Johnson (Honda) was second and Barry Woodland (Suzuki) third. Barry also won the Production race for Class D, the 'Proddie' event now having 4 classes. The increased emphasis on Production machines in the race programme was a

Honda's CBR1000 was a popular choice for riders in the Production race.

144

reflection of the manufacturers' continuing interest and of the fact that the organisers wanted to attract more motorcycle dealers as entrants. Road machines of the time were good enough to provide service as reliable racers and thus offered entrants the promise of reasonable TT success. As sports-minded road riders usually preferred to buy from sports/race-minded dealers, participation in the TT could be good for business. But worries were expressed about the handling of some of the big Production machines, for as one rider put it: *'up to 125 mph they're OK but above that they twist all over the place'* - and the fastest were hitting 155 mph.

Trevor Nation took the big Production race, setting the first under twenty minute lap on a Proddie when he muscled his Suzuki GSX-R1100 around to average 113.26 mph and win Class A. Phil Mellor took Class B on another Suzuki, a GSX-R750. He left Production race and lap records in tatters, averaging 110.69 mph for his 3 laps. A much closer battle was fought in Class C between Gary Padgett (Yamaha) and Malcolm Wheeler (Kawasaki), with the win going to Gary by 1 second. Unusually for a TT race, having started together they stayed that way for the 3 laps. Barry Woodland was victorious in

Class D, although Matt Oxley became the first to lap at over 100 mph on a 250 Proddie.

*

Joey Dunlop (Honda) achieved his fourth win in the TT Formula I race, and Brian Reid (Yamaha) won the TT Formula II with new race and lap records. Steve Cull gave Honda another victory in the Junior race which, in a rare occurrence, saw Joey Dunlop fall at Sulby Bridge and retire from the race. There were new names among the sidecar winners, with Lowry Burton (Yamaha) and Nigel Rollason (Phoenix) taking one win each.

*

Unfortunately the 1986 TT meeting was marred by four rider fatalities during the fortnight of practice and racing. Regular TT reporter for 'The Daily Telegraph', George Turnbull, was moved to write *'The TT Mountain Course plays more havoc with human emotions in one week of racing than any other circuit in the world. Joy, sorrow, exhilaration and fear - all are imposed on competitors and spectators by the unforgiving 37¾ miles of everyday road which for a short time each year become the most fearsome race arena ever devised for high speed sport'.*

Phil Mellor set new lap and race records during his winning ride in Class B of the 1986 Production TT. Here he cranks into Bedstead on his Suzuki GSX-R750.

145

'Radio TT'

In what was a good move for TT fans, Manx Radio created 'Radio TT' in 1987. It separated its TT coverage from its general programmes thus allowing more time to be devoted to all aspects of the 'TT Festival', and it was not long before Radio TT was calling itself *The Best Biking Station in the World*. Aware that many of its listeners on the Island were visitors from the Continent, summaries of information and results were also given in French and German.

*

Featuring in the top twelve in several races in 1987 were riders who would go on to TT wins. Amongst such solo runners were Nick Jefferies, Dave Leach, Brian Morrison, Carl Fogarty, Robert Dunlop, Ian Lougher, Iain Duffus, and among the 'chairs', Dave Molyneux. Most riders need to serve an 'apprenticeship' before challenging for a TT win and a young Steve Hislop showed that he had 'done his time' by bringing his Yamaha home first in the TT FII race at a record average race speed of 110.40 mph.

*

Mitsuo Itoh was the only Japanese rider to win a TT (1963, 50cc) and he had the honour of starting riders in the 1987 TT Formula I race. This had come to be regarded as Joey Dunlop's event, but his usual dominance was threatened by Phil Mellor. The signs were there in the duo's respective practice times, but Joey pulled out all the stops to set race and lap records and bring his Honda home first. 'Mez' Mellor couldn't quite match the speed he had shown in practice and finished second on his Suzuki, with Geoff Johnson bringing his Yamaha into third. In a wet and difficult Senior race Joey took victory on his Honda from Geoff Johnson (Yamaha) and Roger Marshall (Suzuki) third. With the race being shortened to 4 laps due to adverse weather, Joey averaged 'only' 99.85 mph in the appalling conditions.

*

In his book 'Japanese Riders in the Isle of Man', Ralph Crellin records how the unfortunately named (in Western minds) Satoshi Endo lived up to his name by coming last in the Senior and Classic races.

*

Anyone looking for results of the Production Class A and Class C races (usually run together) for the 1987 TT will not find any, the reason being that adverse weather caused them to be abandoned. With no time for them to be rearranged, they simply were not run. It was another 'first' at the TT, for the scheduled race programme had always been completed in previous

Honda mounted Joey Dunlop drops in to the dip at Governor's Bridge.

146

years, notwithstanding that there may have been delays, postponements and shortening of race distance.

*

Previous winners Lowry Burton and Mick Boddice each won a sidecar race, into which had been introduced a Formula Two (F2) class for up to 350cc two-stroke powered machines. Victory in both legs of F2 went to Dave Saville and his was a name that was to become familiar as winner of that class in future years.

*

In a move designed to add to the interest of spectators who were present during TT practice week, Classic races were run for the first time in 1988, over the Billown Circuit in the south of the Island.

*

Nineteen individual former winners entered the 1988 TT races. Heading the list was Joey Dunlop with ten wins to his name and he went on to take further wins in three solo races in 1988, they being the TT Formula I, Junior and Senior. As usual, he was Honda mounted in each race, using the production-derived RC30 in the Formula I and Senior.

Also on a Honda, Steve Cull set a new absolute lap record of 119.08 mph in the Senior. Looking a potential winner, Cull dropped back in the latter stages of the race with a holed expansion chamber on his three-cylinder RS500 two-stroke. Worse was to follow, and on the last lap the bike burst into flames near Creg ny Baa and was virtually burnt out.

Norton Returns

The level of 'works' support now provided to the TT by the large Japanese manufacturers varied, with Honda being the most committed. But spectator interest was caught by the return of 'works' Nortons to the Senior race in 1988. Ridden by Simon Buckmaster and Trevor Nation, the rotary-engined machines were fast but not yet reliable enough to meet the demands of the TT Course.

*

TT newcomer Robert Holden had a nasty moment in practice, but it wasn't on the TT Course. Like many other riders at TT time he went to Jurby airfield between official TT practice sessions to test some modifications made to his machine. Steaming up Jurby's main runway at 130+ mph on his GSX-R750 Suzuki, Robert lifted his head from under the screen to see a light aircraft coming in to land! Swerving to the edge of the runway, he watched over his shoulder as the plane passed. Seems that it had permission to make an emergency landing but there had not been enough warning to clear the runway.

*

Victory in the Production classes went to, Class A, Dave Leach (Yamaha), Class B, Steve Hislop (Honda), Class C, Brian Morrison (Honda) and Class D, Barry Woodland (Yamaha). Due to the heavy programme of racing in 1988 the first race (combined Production Classes C & D) took place on the Friday evening at the end of practice week.

*

Mick Boddice had turned into a consistent winner of the sidecar races, (there were still two races for the three-wheelers at each TT). With passenger Chas Birks he did the double with 700cc of Yamaha power that helped him lap at over 107 mph. Mick carried 16 gallons of petrol (equivalent to a second passenger) and this enabled him to run non-stop.

*

Some riders find out the dangers of the TT Course in their first appearance, whilst for others it takes a little longer. Seasoned sidecar competitor Roy Hanks was in his 22nd year of riding the TT when, in 1988, he crashed just beyond the 33rd Milestone at a point that he had raced past hundreds of times before. It was difficult to understand why such a mistake should be made (although there was a suspicion that the wind got under the fairing), but he is not the only experienced rider to do so. It was certainly a serious crash, with broken limbs for driver and passenger, and involving a difficult rescue operation by marshals and helicopter. However, as is the way of that tough breed known as TT riders, both Roy and passenger (his nephew Tom) returned to race again.

The rotary-engined machine that Norton brought to the Island for Trevor Nation to contest the 1988 TT.

Roy Hanks in the familiar orange and black racing colours that he used for many years.

In another sidecar crash at Kerromoar, the marshals who struggled to lift and carry Howard Langham away on a stretcher suggested that he might lose a bit of weight before next TT if he had thoughts about repeating the performance!

*

Making his Isle of Man race debut in the 250cc Newcomer's race of the 1988 MGP was a man who, with his all-out riding style, went on to thrill the TT crowds of the 1990s. With his dashing, elbows out, hunched over the tank riding, Phillip McCallen always looked as though he was on the limit - and usually was!

*

Riders were faced with a revamped programme of events in 1989 that recognised the growing popularity of racing roadster-based motorcycles. It also showed that the TT was prepared to move with the times, even if this occasionally meant bowing as much to what the supporting manufacturers wanted as to what spectators preferred. The race regulations for those production based machines were framed so that with relatively modest expenditure, the resulting performance allowed them to lap the Isle of Man at speeds that were not far short of those achieved by machines that were purpose-built for the job of racing.

*

The events listed for 1989 showed the creation of 'Supersports' races for 400cc and 600cc machines. Like the Production classes, Supersport machines raced on standard treaded tyres but modifications to engines and suspension were allowed. Two of the four Production races were dropped to make room for 'Supersport', and the two remaining were renamed Production 750 and Production 1300. The TT Formula II race was also dropped and a race for 125 cc machines was brought back (last run in 1974). The TT Formula I race remained, as did the Junior and Senior events. Sidecars still had two races, with each race incorporating a Formula Two class for up to 350cc machines.

*

Practice got off to a lively start and early passengers in the rescue-helicopter were 1988 Senior MGP winner Paul Hunt, regular leader-board finisher Malcolm Wheeler, and Robbie Boland. Although they may not have been aware of it, riders were now carried in a faster and roomier French 'Squirrel' helicopter which often carried the Chief Medical Officer Dr. David Stevens. Involved with the races since 1977 this was his second year in charge of medical services and he soon gained a bit of notoriety by carrying out unusual fitness checks on riders who had been injured earlier but wanted to race. Not for him a conventional surgery, his style was to summon riders to a room at the top of the Race Control tower at the Grandstand. If a rider with a suspect ankle could make it up the ninety steps of the tower he was well on the way to being passed fit to race.

*

Once again confirming that even the most seasoned race competitors can make mistakes and provide work for the rescue services, the vastly experienced Ray Knight had braking problems at the end of Sulby Straight and finished in the field. Although he escaped injury, Ray clouted tender parts on the tank as he went over the top. The next morning - by special request of the marshals at Sulby Bridge - Manx Radio dedicated to Ray their playing of 'The Nutcracker Suite'.

*

In contrast to all the experienced riders who had spent years learning the TT Course (and still managed to fall off) one rider at the 1989 TT was having his first ever view of the Island. American Chris Crew brought his GSXR Suzuki from San Francisco to contest the TT and he later described his experiences in 'The Northern California Motorcycle Guide'. Of early practice he wrote: *'You have to be willing to bet your life that you know where the next corner is going over the crest of the next hill'.* Of those crests he said: *'you go over wide open in top gear, 155 or 160 mph, whatever the bike will pull, with your elbows and toes tucked in, head under the fairing, just watching the white line, trying to see through the bugs'.* It was a stern baptism for the American newcomer who experienced inevitable problems in practice, was faced with the cost of an engine rebuild, coped with last-minute panics before the race, but was then rewarded with a race finish and an award for the fastest newcomer.

Whilst Chris Crew wrote his own words for 'The Northern California Motorcycle Guide', around 200 journalists, 200 photographers and 70 television personnel were accredited by the TT Press Office to spread the story of the 1989 TT across the world.

*

One rider who arrived but was not passed fit to race at the 1989 TT was Joey Dunlop. He suffered a bad injury in an early season meeting at Brands Hatch and so was a non-starter on the Island. With 'King Joey' out of the races there were plenty of aspirants to his throne and the one to take maximum advantage in 1989 was young Scotsman Steve Hislop.

Hislop's Hat-Trick
Steve Hislop was riding for Honda at the 1989 TT and he did not let them down, indeed his performances

dominated the week. With fine wins in the Supersport 600 and Senior races, Steve's star performance was in the TT Formula I event. In this he set a new outright lap record of an astonishing 121.34 mph on his 'works' 750 Honda, leaping over the 120 mph barrier, beating the old figure by over 2 mph, setting the first sub 19 minute lap and getting everyone talking about him. Was he at a mere 25 years of age about to take over from Joey Dunlop as 'King of the Roads'? In Joey's absence that question had to go unanswered, but everyone had an opinion on the topic.

Steve Hislop with the winners laurels and champagne after his record-breaking win in the 1989 TT Formula I race.

Steve was inevitably plied with questions about his riding and, in an observation that had overtones of some of the great road-racers of the past, he said: *'work at the bends to get the best out of the straights so that you can carry the speed with rhythm and flow, that's the key to TT success'.*

*

Yamaha showed signs of offering a real challenge in the Formula I class with Nick Jefferies bringing the new FZR750 OWO1 into third place and second place in the Senior, whilst in Sidecar Race A, local man Dave Molyneux used Yamaha power to gain his first TT victory, (with Colin Hardman occupying the chair).

Dave Molyneux (right) and Colin Hardman after their victory in the first Sidecar race in 1989.

Mick Boddice added a win in Sidecar Race B to his growing number of TT victories, accompanied by regular passenger Chas Birks. During the race Mick and Chas set a new lap record of 108.31 mph on their Yamaha, so beating the long-standing figure of 108.29 mph that had stood to Jock Taylor since 1982.

*

The Junior race of 1989 went to Johnny Rea and the re-introduced 125 event (limited to single-cylinder machines) to Robert Dunlop with Ian Lougher second. Those with reasonable memories could see that the podium finishers in the Junior Newcomers MGP of 1983 (1st Robert Dunlop, 2nd Steve Hislop, 3rd Ian Lougher) had come good at the TT, as so many MGP winners have done down the years. Another MGP Newcomers winner was Carl Fogarty (1985) and in 1989 Carl took his first TT win with victory in the Production 750 on a Honda, whilst Yamaha 1000 machines filled the first eight places in the Production 1300 race. Dave Leach was first man home in that event where concerns were expressed that performance of the big Proddies (on standard road tyres, brakes and suspension) was outstretching their handling.

*

With the Production 1300 race being won at an average speed of 115 mph there was a certain irony about the Club Team Award for the event going to members of the Bantam Racing Club, a feat they repeated in the Formula I race. However, their members were definitely riding big Yamahas and Suzukis rather than lowly BSA Bantams.

*

A young Carl Fogarty is pictured after his victory in the Production 750 class of the 1989 TT.

Whilst 1989 was undoubtedly Steve Hislop's year, he was fortunate to escape injury when he fell at high-speed at Quarry Bends during the Junior race. Regrettably, others were not so lucky, for there were five fatal accidents during practice and racing. It was a time when the Japanese manufacturers seemed obsessed with turning out ever more powerful road bikes that outstripped their tyres and handling, and the big Production machine race caused the deaths of experienced TT runners Phil Mellor at Doran's Bend and Steve Henshaw at Quarry Bends. Whilst the TT by then billed itself as *'The Greatest Festival of Motorcycling in the World'*, even the staunchest of supporters were forced to question the price that had to be paid - if not in public, then at least in their private thoughts.

Dave Leach tips his Yamaha into Sulby Bridge on his way to winning the Production 1000 class in 1989.

Chapter 12
TT MIXTURE

Ladies and the TT

Motorcycle-racing is usually looked on as a pursuit for men but women have had involvement in all facets of the sport, including the TT. Perhaps the two ladies with the longest and best-known TT associations are Sarah and Kate - indeed, they even have places on the Course that are named after them.

There really was a Sarah who lived at the side of the Course just a couple of hundred yards on from Glen Helen. That spot is now called Sarah's Cottage and it is a tricky, uphill, right-hand bend that has seen the downfall of many a rider, including such notables as Mike Hailwood and Giacomo Agostini. But Sarah was not on hand to see those two stars fall in 1965, for she was gone by the time that both MV Agusta stars threw their Italian 'fire-engines' up the road in the same race.

Whether there was a Kate (of Kate's Cottage) is doubtful. Evidence suggests that the cottage on the fast left-hander after Keppel Gate - a spot described by one rider as: *looking like a hole in the hedge'* when tackled at racing speed - was actually owned by a gentleman named Tate. Sometime in the 1930s, possibly on a radio broadcast, it was referred to as Kate's Cottage, and the name stuck amongst race-goers.

Frank Applebee negotiates Kate's Cottage in determined style on his way to winning the 1912 Senior TT on his Scott.

'Kate's' has a particular significance to many regular TT fans because it is the first point on the TT Course that can readily be identified from boats sailing into Douglas. A glimpse of Kate's always stirs the memories and lifts the spirits of returning race fans. From that exposed white cottage on the mountain-side they can trace the road down to Creg ny Baa, whilst above and to the left are the radio masts on Snaefell. Although the line of the Course as it rounds the far side of Snaefell cannot be seen from the boat, it is not difficult for those who know the Course to imagine riders sweeping round the four bends of the Verandah, over the railway lines at the Bungalow, up Hailwood Rise to the highest point at Brandywell, down through the left-handers of the 32nd to Windy Corner, on to the 33rd Milestone, Keppel Gate and then bursting into view at Kate's for the spectacular stepped drop that sees riders wheeling downhill to the Creg, giving them an awesome riding sensation at racing speeds.

*

A spot that is perhaps less well-known to spectators, but is quite famous to riders, is 'Gwen's'. Located on the right-hand side of the TT Course as it leaves Ballaugh, the detached Manx house is identified by a plaque on the wall as 'Gwen's' and is the home of long-serving TT marshal Gwen Crellin MBE. Known to countless riders as 'The Lady in White', she not only spent many years as a white-coated course marshal but was also heavily involved in behind-the-scenes activities that resulted in improvements to the marshalling of the Course as a whole and the founding of the TT Marshals Association.

The plaque at Gwen's of Ballaugh.

Ballaugh gets its fair share of rider retirements, and most of them finish up at Gwen's to partake of her famous hospitality. Even when she was busy marshalling she would tell riders to go into the house and help themselves, for she always left a table full of refreshments *'just in case'*. It wasn't just refreshments that were available at Gwen's, for riders have been known to borrow spanners, etc, to carry out repairs. One rider tells of stopping there with a loose exhaust system. When asked if he was going to continue, he replied *'Yes, if I can find some wire'*. He was soon distracted by the offer of tea and cakes, but when he came out ten minutes later, it was to find Gwen struggling with a pair of pliers as she cut lengths of ideal exhaust-binding wire from her garden fence.

In return for the assistance and friendship she has given them - for she operates an 'open-house' policy to riders and their families - grateful competitors have provided Gwen with countless framed racing photographs that now hang on her walls.

*

Although Gwen Crellin is probably the best known lady marshal on the TT Course, she was not the first. Among those with a claim to that title was Miss May Kneale who was a trained nurse. She marshalled from the late 1920s at the bleak 27th Milestone on the Mountain ascent.

*

Ladies have been in the background of the official side of TT and MGP organising, supporting and marshalling for many years and the work they do is immeasurable. There is also little doubt that where competitors are concerned, without the support of wives and partners many men would not get to race. Often unseen, and usually unsung, occasionally one achieves a higher profile by doing duty as Pit-Attendant. Indeed, there were two as far back as the Clubman's TT races in June of 1949, although the Manx MCC did not allow ladies in the Pits at their September races. Fanning the flames of any bid for equality of the sexes in those far-off days, 'The TT Special' reported of the 1948 MGP: *'Women who have been agitating for female riders in the TT will be interested to learn that no women Pit Attendants will be allowed'* (at the MGP). It was not until the mid-1970s that the Manx MCC changed their rule.

*

Maybe the Manx MCC's announcement at the 1948 MGP was made because of events that happened the previous year. Arthur Fenn's solitary MGP ride was in the 1947 Junior, and he claims that his wife served as his Pit-Attendant. Perhaps this caught the Manx MCC by surprise, for Arthur explains that his wife's presence was *'much to the consternation of the Chief Marshal'*.

*

In 1954 Inge Stoll-Laforge became the first lady to compete in a TT race when, amongst much publicity (not all favourable), she passengered Jacques Drion to fifth place in the Sidecar event. Some wondered what all the fuss was about, for Inge was a regular passenger at Continental events.

*

At the time of Inge's entry the TT regulations specified that a rider (or driver as they described them) had to be a 'male person' over 18 years of age, but the wording for sidecar passengers was that they had to be 'persons' over 18 years of age. Whether it was intended that females should be allowed to passenger or whether it was a slip in the drafting of the regulations is not known. Many ladies have occupied racing sidecars at the TT since Inge, with Rose Hanks and Julia Bingham both gaining second places and sharing the glory of standing on the podium. But the cruel side of such racing has been shown by two female passenger fatalities at the TT (and Inge was later killed whilst racing on the Continent).

*

As far back as 1936 'The Motor Cycle' poured scorn on the exclusion from TT entries of 'female persons', and they asked the ladies *'how long are you going to stand for this?'*. Each year in the TT issue of 'The Motor Cycle', Ixion, its long-standing columnist and TT reporter, wrote a fanciful and entertaining piece of fiction about the event. One year it might be about a mystery rider from behind the Iron Curtain who, against great odds, almost achieved a TT win. The next it might be about a mystery machine, never before seen (and never seen afterwards) whose practice performance had all the 'works' teams worried. The theme for 1950 was of an unknown rider who surprised everyone by going well enough to win a Replica. However, there was drama at the prize-giving when the rider came to the awards platform and announced that she was a lady and thus ineligible to receive the Replica, even though her riding had earned it. (She had conveniently been able to enlist the aid of her twin brother to avoid raising suspicions, but under the disguise of helmet and leathers it had always been a 'female person' doing the riding, in contravention of the race regulations.) It may have been a convenient piece of fiction, but it also allowed 'Ixion' to continue his propaganda campaign to allow lady riders to compete in the TT.

*

At the 1962 TT Beryl Swain became the first lady solo competitor in the 55 year history of the races.

Mounted on her Itom in the newly introduced 50cc class, Beryl finished 22nd and was said to have

Beryl Swain on her Itom in 1962. She was the first lady solo competitor in the TT races.

received more publicity that year than Mike Hailwood!

*

Beryl Swain's appearance in 1962 did not result in a flood of similar entries, for soon after her ride the FIM banned women from International events. Although the rule was later rescinded, there has been no more than a trickle of ladies in the TT and MGP during the intervening years. Among them have been Hilary and Gail Musson, Margaret Lingham, Kate Parkinson, Pam Cannell, fastest lady at the MGP Maria Costello and - fastest lady of all - Sandra Barnett who has lapped during the TT at almost 115 mph.

*

Wendy Davis made a little piece of history in 1997 when she became the first lady driver to contest a Sidecar TT. With Martyn Roberts in the chair, they finished both races. Another potential first was the

all-lady sidecar crew of Wendy Epstein and Dawna Holloway from America. They entered the 2000 TT, were given riding number 55 for their TT debut, but did not take up their entry.

What's in a name?
Most locations on the Mountain Course carry long-established Manx names, but since the TT races started using its 37 ¾ miles there are places that, for varied reasons, have become known after the names of TT riders. Taking a quick trip around the course, it is just past the bottom of Bray Hill that we reach Ago's Leap. The hump in the road that used to cause Giacomo Agostini's front wheel to reach for the sky in such spectacular fashion has been much flattened, but it is still an exciting spot.

*

About 8 miles from the Start is the sweeping left-

Middle of the road no.83, Harry Reynolds (Matchless Metisse), is in for a shattering surprise. In this photograph the front wheel of Giacomo Agostini's MV Agusta has only just started rising, but it gets higher and goes on to pass Harry's left shoulder at 140 mph. No wonder the spot is now called Ago's Leap.

hand bend after Ballig Bridge that is today called Doran's Bend. This is named after top rider of his day Bill Doran, who spilled and broke a leg there in 1950. Some 3 miles on from Doran's is the relatively little known Drinkwater's Bridge located among the sweeping bends after the 11th Milestone and named in memory of the unfortunate Ben Drinkwater who lost his life there in the 1949 Junior. Ben was a good rider whose best result was third place in the 1947 Lightweight TT. Although he had indicated his intention to retire after the 1949 TT, he planned to stay involved with racing and had already spoken to one or two young riders about sponsoring them in future races. Sadly, it was not to be.

*

Soon after the 11th Milestone comes Handley's Corner where first double-TT winner (in a week), Wal Handley, took a heavy fall in the 1932 Senior race but lived to ride another day. Less fortunate was Archie Birkin, and it was recorded earlier how, in 1927, he met his end in a traffic accident just outside Kirk Michael when the roads were still open to ordinary traffic as the racers practised. That spot is now called Birkin's Bend and, with the adjoining Rhencullen it makes a combination of bends where an experienced (and fearless) rider can gain time over more conservative rivals.

*

Not until after Ramsey do we come to the next rider-named place on the Course. That is the bend named Joey's which is located in the early stages of the Mountain ascent near the 26th Milestone. It is an

appropriate spot to commemorate the 26 TT wins career of Joey Dunlop who lost his life whilst racing in Estonia in 2000.

'Joey's', the bend at the 26th Milestone named in honour of Joey Dunlop and his 26 TT victories.

Another famous rider to lose his life away from the TT Course was six times TT winner Jimmy Guthrie who was killed while racing in Germany in 1937. He is commemorated at the Guthrie Memorial, a stone cairn located in a tricky sequence of uphill bends

The stone cairn that comprises the Guthrie Memorial on the TT Course, located between the 26th and 27th Milestones.

between the 26th and 27th Milestones at the spot where he retired in his last Senior TT. The location used to be known as The Cutting.

*

Nearly 30 miles round the Course is the Black Hut and, although not overly well known, the right-hand bend just before it is called George's Folly by some TT fans. It commemorates the spot where TT winner Alex George put his Trident into the ditch. There is the potential for the name 'Folly' to be applied to quite a few other spots on the Course!

*

After completing most of the Mountain climb the Course levels out for the spectacular run around the Verandah, and it is just after the Verandah that the Graham Memorial is located on the right-hand side of the Course. Erected in memory of World Champion and TT winner Les Graham, it is a tribute to a man who would surely have gone on to more TT wins had he not had a fatal crash on the 500cc MV Agusta, just after the bottom of Bray Hill during the Senior TT of 1953.

*

Although most of the 1400 feet of Mountain ascent is complete by the Verandah, there is another gradient shortly after. Running from the Bungalow to the highest point on the Course at Brandywell, it is known as Hailwood Rise and leads to Hailwood Heights (or Hailwoods Height as the nameboard says - take your pick!). It is named in memory of 14 times TT winner the great Mike Hailwood, who lost his life in a UK car accident in the early 1980s.

*

Several other points on the Mountain were known by riders' names for a few years, usually after those involved parted company with their machines in the vicinity, but the names didn't endure. Amongst them were Rice's Corner (the left-hander that followed the East Snaefell Gate in 1920), and Clark's Corner (the right-hander before Keppel Gate).

*

Running downhill from Brandywell to the Finish, the last point on the Course to carry the identity of a rider was, in fact, the first to be named. Located between Creg ny Baa and Hillberry, the fast left-hand sweep of Brandish Corner leaves little room for mistakes, being enclosed by banks on both sides. Walter Brandish did not get it quite right during practice in 1923, hit the outside bank on his Triumph, broke his leg, and is remembered more for that episode than for his fine riding performances, which included second place in the Senior TT of 1922.

Before being named Brandish, this bend was known as O'Donnell's Corner, though who O'Donnell was is lost in the mists of time.

Triumph mounted Walter Brandish raises the dust at Creg ny Baa on his way to second place in the 1922 Senior TT.

Nearing the finish of the lap, the left-hander of Bedstead was originally called Rectory Corner, although for a short while it was known to the TT fraternity as Bennett's Corner.

*

Probably the most respected TT riders within the memory of most current fans are Mike Hailwood and Joey Dunlop. Older ones would no doubt add names like Geoff Duke and Stanley Woods, although neither of those have places on the Course named after them. (Stanley does have a clock named after him, it is the one opposite the Grandstand.)

*

Mike Hailwood and Joey Dunlop not only have stretches of the Course named after them, they are also both the subject of commemorative plaques sited opposite the Start-line.

Mike Hailwood and Joey Dunlop commemorative plaques at the Start line on the Glencrutchery Road.

In addition to their plaques, etc., behind the Pits is a building known as 'The Mike Hailwood Riders Centre', (this is used for most of the year as a Rugby Clubhouse, although that is a fact that would not have troubled Mike one jot), and efforts are being made to raise funds for a Joey Dunlop Injured Riders Centre to be located nearby. Joey is also remembered by a life-size statue located adjacent to Murray's Motorcycle Museum at The Bungalow. It is exactly the same as one that occupies a place in a memorial garden to Joey in his home town of Ballymoney in Northern Ireland and, fittingly, shows him Honda mounted.

*

Proudly, and in many cases sadly, there are other less well known spots on the Course that carry memorials to former riders. Some are simple memorial plaques at the roadside.

This memorial at Ballaugh is to Karl Gall who was killed during practice for the 1939 TT.

There are also rather bigger memorials that take the form of marshals shelters and first-aid posts.

Other Place Names on the Mountain Course
There are names which occur on a lap of the 37 ³/₄ mile Mountain Course that are famous amongst motorcyclists the world over, even though many may never have visited the races. In years gone by those in far away countries learnt the names by listening to crackly, static-filled radio broadcasts and reading detailed accounts of the races in motorcycle magazines. The world may seem a smaller place today with major advances in air travel, but there are still enthusiasts for the races who will never get to Mona's Isle to see the daunting Bray Hill section of the Course, view the sweeping bends of the 11th Milestone, or enjoy the utterly unique experience of the lonely stretch over the Mountain. Although the BBC no longer transmits its static-filled broadcasts, TT fans world-wide can now listen to the whole-race commentaries of Manx Radio via the Internet and can often watch televised highlights the same day. But although such sources can deliver some of the unique race atmosphere, there is no substitute for actually being there!

*

Whilst many marshals and spectators have a thorough knowledge of place names on the Course, it is sometimes found that riders can be a little vague as to the precise whereabouts of some of the named spots. Even the vastly experienced Joey Dunlop was known to have difficulty in putting a name to Kirk Michael, and usually referred to it as *'that wee village'*. Many names are far less well known and having to locate places like Brough Jairg, Sky Hill and Ice-Man's would have many riders and spectators scratching their heads.

*

In addition to the problems experienced in describing the exact location of named spots on the Course, there are many small bends and curves that have no name. The length and complexity of the Course can be totally daunting on first acquaintance to anyone who arrives with thoughts of serious racing. A rider with experience of over 80 races on the Mountain Course is Ray Knight, and he estimates that there are 264 bends in its 37 ³/₄ miles. He describes most of them in his book 'TT Rider's Guide'.

*.

The derivation of several place-names on the TT Course may not be obvious to today's TT fans because of changes that have occurred since they acquired their names. It was explained earlier that Ago's leap, soon after the bottom of Bray Hill, is no longer quite the leap it was, and a couple of miles later there is little to be seen of the Union Mills that were on the edge of the course in the village of that name.

*

There is no nameboard to identify it, but the straight uphill stretch that follows Union Mills is known as (The) Ballahutchin. It goes up in a series of steps and riders travel with the throttle hard against the stop and with the front-wheel going very light. They gain extra speed as they swoop into the dip at Glen Lough, then have another short rise where the front again goes light before they heave the bike on its side to tackle the frightening, wall-bound, right-hand sweep of Ballagarey. It is a corner that encapsulates everything that is good and bad about the TT Course.

Getting it right gives another adrenaline boost and the best possible run through the top-speed section of Glen Vine and Crosby that follows. Getting it wrong just does not bear thinking about. It is no wonder that some riders know the bend as 'Ballascarey'!

*

Appledene just after Greeba Castle was named from the cottage that used to jut out into the road at that point. It has long gone in the cause of highway improvements.

*

At both the 11th Milestone and the 13th Milestone it is the bends some way after the Milestones that most riders know as 'The Eleventh' and 'The Thirteenth'. Amongst the bends at 'The Eleventh' is the previously mentioned Drinkwater's (Bridge), whilst amongst those at 'The Thirteenth' is the wonderful sweeping left-hander at Westwood.

*

Experienced MGP runner Keith Trubshaw thought he knew the Course pretty well when he was appointed to serve as a Travelling Marshal in 1986. However, while stationed at Ballacraine during his first year of duty he received a call to attend an incident at Westwood. It was with some embarrassment that Keith turned to another marshal at Ballacraine and asked him for directions to Westwood! The course-side marshal knew that it was the left-hander after the Thirteenth but Keith, like many riders, knew the whole stretch as the Thirteenth and had never heard the name Westwood.

*

Spectators will look in vain for a little dwelling at Alpine Cottage, but they will find the more imposing Alpine House.

*

The Whitegates on the outskirts of Ramsey from which this part of the Course received its name. They no longer exist.

A touch more confusion can be found when leaving Ramsey, where Cruickshanks, May Hill and Whitegates are met in sequence before riders leave the town at Stella Maris and head for Ramsey Hairpin.

*

On the Mountain stretch the names of the Mountain Gate and Keppel Gate live on as identifiable spots on the Course, although the sheep-confining gates were removed 70 years ago. Roughly half-way between where those gates stood is the site of the former Bungalow Hotel.

The Bungalow Hotel during a spectator-thronged TT of the early 1950s.

The Bungalow Hotel (usually now known as The Bungalow) used to be hugely popular on race-days. It was demolished many years ago and now exists as a tram-stop on the Laxey to Snaefell Summit tramway, with Peter Murray's fascinating Motorcycle Museum nearby. For riders it is quite a daunting spot, for they are faced with a tricky approach incorporating a right and left-hand bend, before having to cross the tram-lines whilst straightening-up as, at the same time, they seek to wind-on maximum power for the climb of Hailwood Rise.

*

What is now known as the Creg ny Baa Hotel (and you can take your choice of the various spellings that have been used down the years), used to be called The Keppel Hotel, although most people associate the name Keppel with the bends before Kate's Cottage, some half a mile or more back up the Course.

*

Photographs taken at Signpost Corner can serve to confuse. For many years this was true Manx countryside with a high stone field-wall on the inside of the bend. That was replaced with iron-railings.

Bob McIntyre rounds Governor's Bridge on his way to winning the 1957 Senior TT.

Today there is a mini-roundabout, houses and a distinctly urban feel to the area, not only of Signpost Corner but also down to Bedstead and the Nook.

*

The tight right-hand hairpin at Governor's Bridge is amongst the most famous of TT landmarks, but today's corner is not quite what it was.

The circular stone pier beloved of so many spectators down the years was demolished by an errant lorry in the mid-1990s and was rebuilt a little further back. Although bales, etc., are erected to keep riders on the original line, some of the originality has gone. The stonework of the original pier must have absorbed the sound of every racing motorcycle that rounded it during the previous 80 years, but all its visible and invisible heritage was lost in a moment's careless driving.

*

From their snails-pace progress round Governor's Bridge, riders still negotiate the infamous dip that follows (now no longer used by ordinary traffic), before bursting out on to the Glencrutchery Road, stretching the throttle-wire to the limit and thundering past the Pits at speeds of up to 170 mph.

The Pits

The TT Mountain Course offers a wide variety of vantage points for spectators to watch the racing over its 37 ¾ mile lap. Some choose a high-speed location where a bike's handling and its rider's bravery are tested to the limit. Others find that a bit too exciting and prefer a series of smooth sweeping bends where everything looks more under control. A surprisingly large number opt for quite slow spots like Ramsey Hairpin or Governor's Bridge. There are plenty of factors involved when seeking a viewing point. Those who choose to watch on their own often pick a heather-clad bank somewhere on the Mountain stretch. They know they will be there for the day so they take their own food, drink, radio, etc., and settle to watch the racing. The more gregarious and fidgety types pick popular vantage points where refreshments are available, and possibly the facility to move to another spectating point for the second race of the day.

A spectating spot that offers its own specialised form of TT drama and excitement is a seat in the Grandstand overlooking the Start and Finish area. Riders are usually only seen here briefly as they flash past at speed, but when the time comes for them to refuel (usually every second lap), much excitement can be generated by the overhead view of 'gasoline-alley' offered by a Grandstand seat.

*

Activity in the Pits became more easily seen by those in the Grandstand when in 1979 a new pit-

This 1922 photograph shows Geoff Davison having his Levis refuelled at his Pit on the Glencrutchery Road. While Geoff holds a funnel, his mechanic adds fuel to his Levis from a can. The job of the two boy scouts was to clean each riders number plates. Geoff went on to win this Lightweight race at an average speed of 49.89 mph.

Adrian Archibald keeps his hands out of the way as his Honda is refuelled in the Pits in 2002. To the right a Scrutineer does a quick tyre check, whilst in the background someone is timing the stop.

lane was created and thereafter riders came in to refuel on the Grandstand side of the Pits rather than the Scoreboard side as they had done for nearly seventy years. It was a move that also improved safety, although riders leaving the new Pit-lane and re-joining the Glencrutchery Road created some exciting moments for passing riders, despite the experienced Bill Boddice operating a set of warning lights.

*

It is something of a cliché (but also a proven fact), that races have been won and lost in the Pits. This may have been by way of bungled refuelling, by the requirement to carry out hasty mid-race repairs, or by any of the myriad of other unpredicted causes that have forced riders to call at the Pits during a race.

*

Refuelling during races has always been an important factor at the TT and one that has frequently influenced results. A pit-stop is a particularly high-pressure moment and, despite the fact that the rider and pit-crew will have rehearsed their procedures, mistakes are sometimes made. Most common is the failure to fill a bike's petrol-tank to the brim, thus causing the rider to run out before the end of the race.

Another common mistake during refuelling is for the tank to be over-filled causing a flood of petrol and with it the risk of fire. Sometimes the rider holds the filler nozzle while refilling and his pit-attendants do other jobs. If he lets the tank overflow there is a chance that he will compound the problem by getting petrol (often petroil) on his gloves, leathers and boots, with slippery results.

*

Thankfully, there have been very few fires during refuelling and those that have occurred have quickly been extinguished by the professional fire-fighters on duty in the Pits area. Recognising that there is a fire risk to the many personnel in the area, the organisers brought in a ruling at the 2002 TT that everyone in Pit Lane has to wear fire-retardant overalls.

*

The timing of a pit-stop can be crucial, for it takes longer to fill an empty tank than a still partially full one (assuming that the bike does not need two complete tankfuls of petrol to complete the race). Another factor on timing is that the Pits can get very crowded when a large number of riders stop together. In consequence, a rider can find himself hemmed in at his Pit and so lose time in getting out again.

*

Engines have to be cut during a pit-stop and it is always a worrying moment for a rider when he comes to restart. Most of today's riders enjoy the benefit of an electric start button, but the majority of TT riders down the years have had to push-start their machines. Engines are rarely at their most co-operative after a pit-stop and if carefully rehearsed starting techniques get forgotten in the heat of the moment, then precious seconds gained by skilful riding out on the Course can easily be lost. The ultimate blow in such situations - and it has happened - is that the engine refuses all attempts to restart it, forcing the rider to retire.

*

Riders have always been required to refuel at a point nominated by the race-organisers. During the first few years of racing on the Mountain Course the refuelling stations were located at Braddan and Ramsey, but thereafter the nominated spot has been

the Pits. Taking on fuel at any other point on the Course has always been grounds for exclusion from the race.

*

In the first TT races of 1907 & 1908 when riders were restricted as to the amount of fuel they could use in the race, they refuelled from sealed cans containing their race allocation. From 1909, when restrictions on the amount of fuel that could be used were lifted, riders initially provided their own refuelling containers. Race winner in 1912, Frank Applebee (Scott), was refuelled at Ramsey by previous year's winner Oliver Godfrey. As soon as Applebee stopped and opened his petrol cap, Godfrey inserted a funnel, inverted a two-gallon can of petrol over it and immediately pierced the bottom of the can with a file to allow air in and speed the transfer process. Whilst this was happening he topped up the water and oil and, so it was reported, got Applebee away in 15 seconds.

*

In the same race Hugh Mason had just completed refuelling of his Matchless when it burst into flames. It was extinguished by everyone around throwing sand on it from a nearby heap. The sand put out the fire but was not the best of lubricants for the bike's exposed valve gear.

*

In the mid-1920s the race organisers arranged for the provision of identical gravity-fed fuel fillers for all competitors. These were post-mounted adjacent to each pit, as they are today. Although all the refuelling rigs were supposedly the same, the Velocette camp got a sight of the fillers intended for the Norton pits at the 1938 TT and noticed *that the normally rough brass castings of the nozzles had been smoothed and internally streamlined to hasten the flow of liquid through them*.

*

Every TT rider used to be contracted to use a particular petrol company's product. For many years this was a relatively straightforward business, because after the use of alcohol fuels was banned from 1925 the majority of competitors used similar petrol-benzole mixtures, with only the occasional demand from a two-stroke such as DKW to complicate matters. With the growth in use in post-war years of highly-tuned racing two-strokes, the provision of fuel became something of a nightmare for the petrol companies. Most two-strokes required pre-mixed petrol and oil, and each maker wanted it supplied to their exact specification. Lew Ellis, for many years competition manager of Shell, claimed that he provided up to 50 different two-stroke mixes to satisfy rider and manufacturer demands.

*

In the 1953 Clubman's races, late-number rider Joe Finch had his worst dreams come true when he stopped to refuel and found his 'quick-filler' to be empty. He had to make-do with what was left in the filler at the adjoining Pit. Unfortunately this was insufficient and he ran out of petrol at Creg ny Baa on the last lap and pushed in for a belated finish.

*

To confirm how important a good pit-stop is to a rider's race strategy, there have been instances of very close races where a well-organised pit-stop has gained a rider sufficient time to win him the race over an opponent who was marginally faster on the track. (Maybe the pit-attendants should get the credit for the win!) As well as the actual time that can be lost by a poorly organised pit-stop, it can also be a considerable psychological blow to a rider to lose track position whilst stationary.

*

As a result of lobbying from some of the big Japanese manufacturers, the requirement to use standard gravity fillers was temporarily lifted in the 1970s. This allowed the use of pressurised dump-cans that transferred fuel at a far faster rate (32 litres in 9 seconds) and thus saved valuable time. At the 1975 Senior TT, Mick Grant was in second place some 15 seconds behind John Williams when they came in to refuel. Grant used a quick-filler for the job whilst Williams used the standard set up which took well over half a minute. This allowed Grant to leave the Pits with a clear lead, and he went on to win the race - his first TT victory. The rule on everyone using standard gravity fillers was reinstated in about 1985 and exists to this day.

*

Although most competitors rehearse their pit-stops with their Pit crews, few go as far as Roland Pike who built a dummy Pit in his home garage before his first MGP visit in 1937. Mind you, he later claimed in an article on his 250 racing Rudge in 'Motor Cycling' that it did 95-100 mpg, so with a decent sized petrol tank he would hardly have needed a stop!

*

Today's TT races for solos are generally over 4 or 6 laps, although Production races are sometimes 3. This usually means one pit-stop for a 3 lapper (which can be at the end of the first or second lap), one for a 4-lapper (at the end of the second lap) and

2 stops during 6-lap events. One side-effect of this is that riders only get one flying-lap during the race. The other laps are all subject to the extra time involved in a standing-start or in slowing to come into the Pits.

*

Many attempts have been made to increase machines' petrol carrying capacities down the years, but these have always had to be considered against the detrimental effect that the substantial increase in weight had on the handling and general performance. The Golden Jubilee Senior TT of 1957 was made an eight-lap race and several single-cylinder runners devised pannier tanks to allow them to run the entire 302 mile distance non-stop. It was an extreme test of stamina for bikes and riders.

*

Although the 'professional' TT riders of 1957 were permitted to race non-stop for 302 miles, the organisers of the MGP decided in 1954 that their 'amateur' riders would not be allowed to run their full 6 laps and 226 1/2 miles race distance without a pit-stop. However, the MGP requirement for each rider to call at the Pits was as much about taking away the advantage gained by runners who could afford to have big-tanks made (for a non-stop run), as it was about giving the riders a mid-race rest, for although the MGP required each rider to call at the Pits, stop his engine and dismount, there was no obligation for him to take on fuel.

*

A man who nearly pulled off a shock result in the Senior race at the 1998 TT was Bob Jackson. Bob was a top-flight TT runner but he and his Kawasaki could not quite match the pace of the 'works' Hondas during practice. Everyone planned to make two refuelling stops during the 6 lap race - except Bob! Fitting an enlarged petrol tank to his Kawasaki, he shocked the opposition by going straight past the Pits at the end of the second lap whilst the remaining top runners pitted for fuel. This hoisted Bob from fourth to first position and he made his single stop for fuel at the end of the third lap. Unfortunately, after his petrol tank was topped-up its cap refused to refit. During the struggle to get it back into place, a frustrated Bob sat on the Kawasaki and saw precious time slip away. He eventually re-started, but the lost time (and a defective exhaust) saw him slip from first place to second by just 3.7 seconds at the finish - it was a race that was lost in the Pits rather than on the track.

*

Out of Petrol

Running out of petrol has been one of the commonest causes of race retirement since the earliest days of TT history. Sometimes it occurs because of a mistake in the Pits where the tank is not properly filled or, occasionally, because of a plain miscalculation of the amount of fuel required. No one wants to carry more fuel than necessary because excess fuel means excess weight that can affect performance. It is difficult to get the balance right, particularly as the amount of fuel needed for a race can be affected by factors that are difficult to predict. For example, a rider may employ different riding tactics during a race to the ones he used in practice, particularly if he is riding in close company with others, and this can easily result in him holding on to lower gears for longer, using more revs and thus more fuel. Even a change of gearing can effect fuel consumption, as can a change of wind direction, for they will both affect the engine revs used and the amount of fuel consumed. Leaking fuel tanks - less of a problem nowadays than they used to be - are another obvious problem.

*

Many potential wins and podium places have been lost throughout the TT's history by riders running out of petrol. In the first year on the Mountain Course (1911), Charlie Collier was disqualified from his second place finish for refuelling outside the authorised refuelling points located at Braddan and Ramsey. In 1934 Stanley Woods looked set for second place in the Senior on one of the new Husqvarna twins, but he ran out on the last lap while on the Mountain section. George Brown admitted to being so carried away by the crowds waving him to victory on the last lap of the 1948 Clubman's TT that he gave his big Vincent everything that it would take (despite knowing he had a big lead). Afterwards, George wished that he had gone a bit easier as he pushed his empty bike up the long drag of the Glencrutchery Road and staggered over the line in sixth place for, although he did not know it, his pit attendant had not completely filled the tank at his pit-stop.

*

What looked like a certain win turned into 6th place for George Brown (Vincent HRD) in the 1948 Clubman's TT after his pit-attendant failed to completely fill his tank with petrol during his pit-stop. George had to push in to the finish after setting the fastest lap of the race.

It seems almost understandable when a privateer misjudges the amount of fuel required, but John Surtees must have questioned the efficiency of the MV Agusta organisation as he lost an almost certain win in the Junior TT of 1956, when his tank ran dry on the Mountain.

*

The ten lap Production race introduced in 1975 was bound to cause problems on the petrol front and so it proved. Clear leaders of the 500cc Class at the end of the fifth lap were Roger Sutcliffe and Bill Rae on their Suzuki. However, Bill was forced to push in from Governor's Bridge at the end of the next lap with an empty tank. After refilling it at the Pits, Roger set off in pursuit of the new leaders, but too much time had been lost and they did not make the top six.

*

In the 1976 Senior TT John Williams smashed the lap record by nearly 3 mph as he surged into a 3 minute lead over second man Tom Herron. But did his extra speed consume more fuel than his team expected? Whatever the reason, John's tank was empty by Signpost Corner on the last lap and he was forced to push in to a frustrating seventh place.

*

Dick Greasley was involved in a close struggle with Mick Boddice for victory in the first leg of the 1979 Sidecar race until his engine mis-fired and slowed through lack of fuel towards the end of the race. Mick also had difficulties when his chain come off at Creg ny Baa, and the problems experienced by the two leaders let Trevor Ireson through for the win. Greasley eventually came in second and Boddice was third.

*

In the 1981 Classic TT, Joey Dunlop raised the absolute lap record to 115.40 mph on his Honda, before running out of fuel on the third lap. There was a similar situation in 1983 in what had been renamed the Senior Classic. There the talented Norman Brown pushed the absolute lap record up to 116.19 mph before a dry tank put paid to his race chances. Joey was at it again in the 1984 Senior. Increasing the absolute lap record to 118.47 mph, he lost the lead and the race when his three-cylinder Honda two-stroke was reported to have run dry on the last lap, (although some said it was a mechanical problem that Honda did not want to admit). Brian Reid also ran dry at Hillberry in the 250 race in 1985 after breaking the lap record, as did Trevor Nation at the 32nd Milestone in the 1986 Senior, a feat he repeated in the 1987 Production B race, just three miles from the chequered flag and victory.

*

Running out of petrol near the end of a lap (or race) is just about understandable, but it is difficult to understand how someone manages to run out half-way round a lap, say at Ballaugh or Ramsey. Such an occurrence points to a complete miscalculation.

*

A serious mistake with regard to refuelling occurred in the 1993 Junior event where Honda works rider Phillip McCallen was due to bring his 250 Honda into his pit to take on more fuel at the end of the second lap. However, to the consternation of the Honda team, he screamed past the Pits flat on the tank at 145 mph having confused his laps whilst in a close dice with another rider. Holding a good position at the time, his bike inevitably came to a halt part of the way round the third lap at Quarry Bends. It happened right in front of a film crew who, seizing the opportunity for an interview, opened with the embarrassing question: 'What's the problem Phillip?'. Come the next race of the week and Honda arranged for a particularly large reminder board to be displayed to McCallen at Governor's Bridge on the lap that he was scheduled to stop for fuel.

On the first lap of the 1960 Senior MGP, newcomer Tony Wright arrived at Quarter Bridge with a brim-full tank of petrol and a little too much enthusiasm. In the resulting spill his immaculate BSA Gold Star caught fire and was badly damaged.

In 1994 McCallen lost what looked like certain victory in the Junior race when his Honda coughed to a standstill just five miles from the chequered flag. Once again lack of fuel cost him victory in a Junior race that (on a 250) he was destined never to win.

*

In complete contrast to those who run out of fuel, some people are caught out by having too much!

Many other riders have had their 'moments' at the tricky Quarter Bridge, although few have been as dramatic as the above.

163

Until 1934 a rider's single pit-attendant was there for the sole purpose of helping with refuelling. From 1935 he was also allowed to assist with work on the machine. Nowadays, two pit-attendants and a Team Manager are permitted for each rider. As well as refuelling, they will clean the rider's helmet visor, (some riders have the visor changed, some even change helmets), hand him a drink, wipe the screen, jack-up and change the rear wheel, tell him his race position, and cast an eye over the whole machine. All that is done in little longer than it takes to read about it.

*

The Pits have always been the scene of 'in-race' maintenance activity. Some of it is planned, such as the current vogue of changing the rear wheel (to provide a new tyre), but much is emergency work brought about by the punishment inflicted on the bikes by the Mountain Course. There is also a trend to change helmet visors and even helmets. One such visor-change went wrong for Phillip McCallen in 1993 and he claimed that the time lost cost him victory in the close-fought Formula I race.

*

Those who pay to sit in the main Grandstand at Douglas get a wonderful view of the Pits and associated activity. They also get a view of the massive 'double' scoreboard that records the leading riders in the race, every riders' completed lap times, and the moment that they pass several prescribed points on the Course. There is also a light over each riders' name that shows when he passes Cronk ny Mona. In earlier years the light came on when a rider reached Governor's Bridge, but as speeds increased the point was moved back up the Course to Signpost Corner in 1956, and then even further back to Cronk ny Mona.

The main scoreboard that keeps pit-attendants and spectators in the Grandstand informed of the progress of every rider.

Maintaining the information on the Scoreboard is a manual operation in every way. In these days of electronic wizardry it appears archaic - but it is highly informative and accurate. Other methods have been tried. Way back in 1927 'The Motor Cycle' reported: *'As usual the organisation of the races was excellent, but, unfortunately, the new electrically-operated scoreboard proved a failure and caused considerable confusion to those on the Grandstand'.* However informative it is, one feels that the long-standing Scoreboard's days are numbered, if only for the sake of the TT's 'image' in the wider world of racing.

*

Before the advent of race commentaries the Scoreboard was the principal source of information for the riders representatives in the Pits. Stuck in their small cubicles, they would attempt to interpret the Scoreboard information relating to their rider and his nearest rivals. As long as the pointer on their rider's positional clock continued to move, then they could breathe relatively easily. It was when a rider's pointer stuck in one position that his Pit-Attendant began to hold his breath. The danger of the Island races is apparent to everyone, but during a race the rider has little time to worry. That burden falls on his supporters.

*

The need to provide a Pit for up to 100 riders means that they stretch for a couple of hundred yards and, understandably, the last thing a rider making a Pit-stop at the far end of the line wants to do is to shut the throttle until the very last moment. This was not quite so bad when riders stopped on the outside (i.e. the track-side) of the Pits, but when the refuelling arrangements were changed to create an inner Pit Lane, riders travelled through the crowded Lane at very high speeds. To reduce those speeds the organisers introduced a 'Stop Box'. Riders peeled off the Course as usual into the Pit slip road and then had to brake to a standstill (to the satisfaction of the Stop Box marshal) before accelerating away to their Pit. Whilst this has certainly reduced speeds they are still high, and Pit Lane is not a place for the faint-hearted or slow-witted. At busy times it seems that speeding bikes are everywhere, and as soon as a bike stops, pumped-up mechanics go into action in their own restricted areas. The safest place to watch all that action is from a seat in the Grandstand.

Marshalling the Course

What the marshalling arrangements were on the original St John's Course in 1907 are lost in the mists of time. What we do know is that - compared to today's races - the number of competitors was small, speeds were slow, spectators were few and the only control was by use of a single flag, and that was a red one. A report of the time said: *'when this was displayed competitors either stopped or proceeded slowly, according to the vehemence of the waving'.*

*

With the move of the races to the longer and more testing Mountain Course in 1911, riders were faced with many more corners and long empty stretches of road, so the need for marshals increased. However, those early marshals were still very thin on the ground compared to the multitude of orange-jacketed helpers seen at today's races. This was particularly so on the remote stretches, for not only were these often barren and uninviting but they were also inaccessible, except to the very few people of the time who possessed personal transport.

*

No one could doubt the enthusiasm of those early marshals and another report from those far-off days said: *'hats off to the Bray Hill flagman, an ex-policeman, who cycles to duty from Foxdale, and was on the job at 4.00am'.* Drawn from all walks of life, marshals were mostly Island residents who were supported by local policemen, doctors and members of the first-aid organisations.

*

One man who marshalled in the very early days and became a truly venerable figure in TT & MGP history was Canon EH Stenning. He was a Master at King William's College at Castletown and spent some ten years marshalling at Ballacraine, before taking on duties at the Start area. His marshalling experiences went back to the earliest events on the Mountain Course, about which he wrote: *'In the days before the First War this was a very pleasant duty, and the responsibilities were not too grievous'.* He would make an early morning start from Castletown with his wife in the sidecar of their AJS combination, to take up post ten miles away at Ballacraine. This right-angled corner located 7 1/2 miles from the Start, where the Course changes direction from west to north, has always been an important marshalling point and was provided with a telephone for communication with the Start area. But Canon Stenning told: *'there were no organised (marshals) posts between Douglas and Ballacraine, so anything that happened between these points had to pass unnoticed'!* Such vagueness about what was going on must have been an organiser's nightmare but was the inevitable result of having

thinly spaced and static marshals. It was a feature repeated on other parts of the Course.

*

Although boarding pupils of King William's College were not permitted to possess bicycles, the occasional one sneaked out on a borrowed machine for the long uphill pedal to watch the racers at Ballacraine. If Canon Stenning came up behind one he would slow and as the outfit passed the cyclist, Mrs Stenning would hand out the end of a piece of rope that was attached to the sidecar. The lucky cyclist then got a steady tow to Ballacraine. The AJS could manage to tow up to three cyclists at a time!

*

Canon Stenning's AJS combination that he used to get to Ballacraine to carry out marshalling duties.

From Ballacraine, a couple of marshals would usually be sent to nearby Ballig Bridge. They were probably reluctant to do so as it was quite a social gathering at Ballacraine, with Mrs Stenning bringing copious supplies of sandwiches, meat-pies and hot drinks in the sidecar. Riders soon became aware of this and it was not unknown for an occasional one to stop for a warming cup of coffee during the chilly early morning practice sessions.

*

Although Canon Stenning found marshalling *'a pleasant duty'*, it was a job that extended over two weeks of early morning practice sessions (no evening practices). Those sessions went ahead whatever the weather and, although he attended alternate mornings, those early duties must have been wearing on all concerned. Part of the Mountain section was marshalled by men from Douglas. Such was their enthusiasm that some of them would set off from Douglas the previous evening, camp overnight on the Mountain, and thus be in place for morning practice.

*

There were very few telephones around the Course in the early days and they were only operated by trained telephonists. Ordinary traffic went about its business as the racers practised and a report of the time said: *'Every morning there was a considerable procession of horse-drawn fish-floats carrying fish from Peel to Douglas Market or to the morning boat to Liverpool.*

*

Although the races were organised by the ACU from London, they relied on the Manx Motor Cycle Club to co-ordinate the appointment and allocation of Course marshals. As an incentive to the locals to turn out at the 1921 TT, the ACU offered to present a silver cigarette case to each club member who marshalled at all practice and racedays.

*

The general instructions to marshals were quite basic. In the case of an accident in practice they were told: *'the nearest Police Constable (all of whom are qualified first-aid men) should be sent for, he will decide whether a telephone message should be sent to the Starting Point asking for a doctor'.* The organisation moved up a gear for race-days and if an accident occurred during a race: *'marshals should either telephone or dispatch a Boy Scout or other messenger, to the nearest first-aid or medical station, and should also telephone the Clerk of the Course at the Starting Point giving full particulars. Although full provision has been made for medical attention, marshals will realise that only in necessitous cases should the Clerk of the Course be asked to send a doctor'.*

*

Scouts have long been a part of the TT organisation and in the early 1920s a Boy Scout was stationed at 300 yard intervals throughout the length of the Course. A note from 1927 emphasises the extent of their involvement: *'During the practising period eight Scouts under a Scoutmaster, will be on duty each morning at the starting point. On each of the Race Days as many Scouts as can be mustered will be stationed round the course, Their duty is to watch for and endeavour to prevent accidents, to capture and detain any stray dogs, to pass messages, to call for medical assistance or, if able, to render first aid, and to assist in keeping the course clear. In addition to those stationed around the course, 20 scouts will be required on Race Days at the starting point for operating the scoring boards, as messengers, etc, etc'.*

*

As speeds increased, flag marshals were introduced in their white-coated form in 1920 to give riders warning of hazards ahead. Their coats were supplied by Dunlop (they also wore sashes with the

company's name thereon) and they were often referred to by the nickname of 'Dunlops'. It was the time when roads were still used by ordinary traffic whilst the riders practised for the races.

A white-coated 'Dunlop' flag marshal watches Harry Harris negotiate Ramsey Hairpin in the 1925 Senior TT.

Today, every flag-marshal has four different coloured flags with which to warn riders of danger on the Course, (Yellow, Yellow and Red stripes, White, Red) and some have Sun and Fog flags to warn of visibility problems. In the early 1920s they had just two flags and competitors were told that the red flag meant stop and the white one required caution. By the mid-1930s they were still using two flags but they were:

Blue   When waved, 'danger'.
           When motionless, 'keep close to
           your left side of the course'.
Yellow 'Complete and immediate stop'.

*

All riders passing major marshalling points like Ballacraine were recorded and the information telephoned to the officials at the Start via an indicator circuit. This basic recording of riders passing strategic points was essential in keeping a check on their whereabouts and safety, particularly as stretches of the Course were not visible to marshals and overall communications were extremely basic. If Race Control (based at the Start) became concerned at a rider's whereabouts, they would telephone to the point at which he was last recorded and a search would be instigated. Telephones were supplemented by systems of signalling-flags, whistles and the use of Scouts as runners, and a Scout or Marshal would sometimes be sent along the Course or across the fields to search for a missing rider. Unfortunately, it could be a somewhat 'hit and miss' business.

*

George Rowley, a TT competitor from 1925 to 1939, told a tale from the 1929 Senior TT in which he was forced to retire at a remote spot on the Mountain with clutch trouble. The nearest 'civilisation' was the Bungalow Hotel and he set out to walk there. After about half an hour he still had not reached it but he came across several ambulance-men, carrying a stretcher and looking for a 'lost' rider. Somewhat against his wishes, George allowed himself to be persuaded to start walking back the way that he had come, as the ambulance-men thought that his expert knowledge of where a rider might have fallen off would be useful to them. After another half an hour of trudging in heavy boots and leathers, they arrived at George's abandoned machine. One of the ambulance-men spotted that the number on the stricken machine was the same as the number of the rider that they had been sent to search for. With a silent curse, George realised that he had earlier removed the numbered waistcoat that every rider wore while racing, and was carrying it in his helmet!

*

To avoid 'losing' riders, various methods were tried to cope with recording those who retired from a race or practice. At one stage they were required to sign a marshal's form to confirm they were no longer racing, and in another scheme each rider was provided with a card before joining the circuit and this was to be passed to the nearest marshal upon retirement or on leaving the Course. But, although riders were supposed to make the effort to communicate their retirement, the frustrations caused by forced retirements meant that they did not always do so and occasionally one would leave the Course and return to his lodgings or garage, leaving the organisers to worry as to his whereabouts.

*

Although the organisers were extremely conscientious about keeping track of rider retirements, once logged as retired their official responsibilities towards them were at an end. They could do nothing, for example, about the rider who went missing after reporting his retirement to marshals at Ballacraine. Last observed talking to a friendly young lady from Peel, he was not seen again until three days later.

*

The number of riders involved in the Races in those far-off days (and thus to be kept a check on) was far fewer than today. During the pre-Second World war period, practice sessions would rarely see more than 60 riders out at any one time. Total entry for the three race classes was usually just over 100, with some riders contesting 2 or 3 races. However, it was the sheer length of the Course to be marshalled rather than the number of riders involved, that meant one could still quite easily be 'lost', and the organiser's really hadn't come up with a reliable system to cope with such situations.

Even by the mid-1930s, the Course coverage by marshals was still quite low, particularly during the practice sessions (all held early in the morning until 1937). A reporter from 'The TT Special' watched practice from Creg ny Baa in 1934 and wrote that one rider stopped to report another rider was off at the Keppel and that marshals left (from the Creg) to investigate. As they were faced with an uphill walk of half a mile, the fallen rider certainly did not receive instant attention.

*

It was another incident at the 1934 TT that brought home to everyone just how important it was to have adequate marshals so as to be able to keep track of all riders on the Course. Weather conditions were poor on the morning of the 1934 Lightweight event but riders, officials and spectators confidently went about their preparations for the start of the event. Today the possibility of a delayed start or a postponement might cross peoples' minds but, as for every event since 1907, back in 1934 people expected the race to get away on time - and it did. Among the competitors was popular campaigner Syd Crabtree from Warrington. Syd rode his first TT back in 1922 and had been a regular ever since, taking a victory in the 1929 Lightweight race on an Excelsior. He was a seasoned competitor and if anyone knew their way around the 37 ¾ mile Mountain circuit, he did.

What precisely happened to Syd Crabtree on the Mountain on the first lap of the Lightweight race will

The unfortunate Syd Crabtree on his Excelsior.

never be known, although several versions of the event are told. What is known is that after telling Excelsior Team Manager, Alan Bruce, that he intended to go flat-out for the lead from the moment he was flagged away, Crabtree crashed between the Stonebreaker's Hut (often called the Black Hut) and the Bungalow and was killed. With fog restricting visibility to 20 yards, what few marshals there were on that lonely stretch of the Course were forced to operate more by sound than sight of the machines. Unfortunately, no one heard or saw Crabtree's crash, and other riders continued to pass the spot in ignorance of the tragedy that had occurred.

It was the race organiser's system of recording all riders past strategic points that led them to detect that Crabtree was missing. On the instructions of the Clerk of the Course, marshals were despatched on foot from the Bungalow and the Stonebreaker's Hut to search the Course; it was an inevitably slow

business. A spectator, who had been enlisted to help, found the body some 400 yards on from the Stonebreaker's Hut. The published report of the inquest told that Crabtree hit the bank, struck a gate-post and died instantly. His death was a shock to his multitude of friends and to TT followers. What made it worse for them was to know that he passed the Stonebreaker's Hut at about 10.40am but that he was not found until 11.15am. Some reports say the interval was longer but those were the times quoted at the inquest. That a crashed rider could lie undetected was clearly an unacceptable state of affairs and the Sid Crabtree incident caused the ACU to take a detailed look at its organisation for 1935, particularly in respect of racing in bad weather and with regard to 'lost' riders. One of their responses was to appoint two motorcycle-mounted Travelling Marshals to patrol the Course on race-days.

*

TRAVELLING MARSHALS

Appointed for the 1935 TT with the primary duty of searching for missing riders, a report of the time said: *'These Travelling Marshals relieve much anxiety when a man breaks down far from a telephone point'.* Quickly proving their worth, it was not long before the new mobile marshals were providing feedback to the Clerk of the Course on many other matters.

*

The first two Travelling Marshals were Arthur Simcock and Vic Brittain, both of who were former TT riders. The numbers used gradually increased in post-war years and they began to be based at recognised 'stations' like Ballacraine, Douglas Road Corner at Kirk Michael, Parliament Square in Ramsey, The Bungalow and at the Grandstand - all places that were in telephone contact with the Race Control office. When a Travelling Marshal was despatched to an incident, the others would move ahead to the next 'station', so that the Course remained properly covered.

*

When he arrives at an incident a Travelling Marshal takes charge, for course-side marshals know that he represents the chief official of the race, the Clerk of the Course. Indeed, several men who have held the position of Clerk of the Course have described Travelling Marshals as their *'eyes and ears'* around the Course.

*

It has always been regarded as an honour to be appointed as a Travelling Marshal at the TT or MGP and during the 1940s and 1950s no less than five World Champions did the job. They were Bob Foster, Freddie

Jimmy Linskey shows off one of the Triumphs used by Travelling Marshals at the 1956 TT. For the first time, they were fitted with experimental radio equipment to improve communications, but it was to be more than 20 years before radios became a standard fitting on each Travelling Marshal's bike.

Frith, Les Graham, Cecil Sandford and Geoff Duke. On occasions some of them probably stood to gain from doing so. At the 1949 MGP Bob Foster brought his 'works' 500 Velocette along to ride whilst he did Travelling Marshal duty and freely admitted to experimenting with different exhausts, jetting, etc, at the Velocette factory's request. Les Graham was mounted on an AJS 7R when he did the job and Geoff Duke fitted 'M' plates to a Manx Norton when, short of competitive riding time due to a ban in 1956, he put in some useful high speed laps while on Travelling Marshal duty at that year's MGP.

*

Although initially those appointed were only required to ride like a racer, think like a racer, and have a sound head that permitted them to act coolly under pressure, the qualifications for a Travelling Marshals' job developed down the years and included the need for each of them to be more aware of aspects of general Course safety and to be trained in first-aid. Whilst their duties increased, improvements to communications (telephones and radios) meant that the amount of time they spent riding the Course decreased.

From the outset, manufacturers were happy to loan bikes for the high-profile duties of Travelling Marshals at the TT although even into the early 1950s those doing duty at the MGP sometimes had to provide their own machines. Triumph publicised their bikes use with: *'For the complete dependability and high performance which their duties demand, the TT Travelling Marshals again chose Triumph'*. The bikes used were almost exclusively British until 1977 when, against a background of supply difficulties with British machines, Honda stepped in with the offer of seven of their four-cylinder 750cc F2 models. Their offer was gratefully accepted and Hondas have been used ever since.

*

The team of Travelling Marshals escort the last rider home after a Parade of vintage bikes.

To ordinary racegoers it must seem like a dream job to be one of the eight Travelling Marshals at the TT and MGP. After all, they are handed the latest Honda sports motorcycle and permitted to ride them on the closed roads of the 37 ³/₄ mile Mountain Course in the company of racers - surely the ultimate road-test. But although those appointed each year as Travelling Marshals may agree that it is a dream job, they know that it brings considerable responsibility and that it is one for which dreamers need not apply.

In the late 1930s there was a change to the organisation of the course-side marshals. Instead of them all being controlled from Douglas, four sectors (North, South, East and West) were created and each controlled the marshals over their allotted section. The total number of marshals on duty on race-days was about 350. That number gradually grew in post-war years to about 800 in 1964 and later the Course was split into twelve Sectors under the control of Chief Sector Marshals, each of whom appointed Deputies to help in allocating

duties and controlling what nowadays amounts to 1,200 marshals on duty on race-days. Chief Marshal for the races is the Isle of Man's Chief Constable and the huge administrative task of dealing with all the voluntary marshals, arranging their training, their appointment, 'swearing-in', etc., is done by The TT Marshals' Association that was founded in 1962.

*

It was not only the number of marshals around the Course that increased down the years. As telephones came into general use, more were installed to cover recognised marshalling points, Travelling Marshals bikes were fitted with radios, the local Civil Defence established a radio network and some marshals employed hand-held radios. All these contributed to improving communications with the Race Control office located at the top of the Grandstand Tower.

*

In efforts to provide the best possible control of the event and support to the riders, the 1200 course-marshals are supplemented by doctors, paramedics, nurses, Red Cross and St John's personnel, plus first-aid trained policemen. Everyone knows that accidents will happen in motorcycle racing, so extensive medical support, plus the use of the rescue helicopters, is aimed at giving riders qualified attention at the scene of an accident, before flying them to hospital.

*

Steve Hazlett goes past the point of no return at Quarter Bridge.

Braddan Bridge gets the occasional faller, as do locations like Sarah's Cottage, Mayhill and Cruickshanks at Ramsey, The Bungalow and Windy Corner on the Mountain, plus the tricky Nook a short way above Governor's Bridge.

*

Recognition that accidents will happen means that some 6,500 conventional straw bales, 250 large round bales and increasing amounts of air-fencing are used around the Course. Thirty years ago 1,300 bales were considered enough to do the job.

*

Under the protection of yellow flags, marshals clear the scene of a TT Course incident whilst riders pass at reduced speed. Note the tyre-marks left by the racers on the road - there is obviously more than one line around this bend!

The organisers are aware of which locations cause riders the most trouble and endeavour to see that such spots are well supplied with marshals. Well ahead in numbers is the ultra-slow Governor's Bridge, where riders rarely get hurt - it is more a case of falling over than falling off. In second place is the slightly quicker Quarter Bridge.

Most marshals are trained in incident management and each can put in well over 50 hours of duty during a TT fortnight. Throughout that time they must remain alert and expect the unexpected. Such a need was illustrated by a rider who entered Parliament Square at Ramsey too fast, on the wrong line, and with both wheels locked. He described a marshal trying to get out of the way as *'having his legs moving faster than my con-rods'.*

*

There is a vast reservoir of TT experience among the marshalling force, that includes many people who have done the job for 20 or 30 years. Whole families get involved and some visiting fans devote their holidays to the job. The voluntary support provided by marshals is essential to the running of the event, indeed, the last words on the subject of marshalling the Mountain Course come from the race organisers who, on more than one occasion have indicated that: *'without marshals there would be no TT races'.*

Chapter 13
THE 1990s

The TT welcomed the 1990s with buoyant entry lists, a host of top riders and varying degrees of support from the major manufacturers. Safety was very much on the organisers' minds after the tragedies of 1989 and although the emphasis was still on the racing of production-derived machines, the big 750 and 1300cc pure Production events were dropped (but the related Supersport 400 and 600cc classes were retained). Maximum capacity for the Senior race became 750cc (having been upped to 1000cc in 1985 and 1300cc in 1987). Worries over the speed and stability of the main Sidecar Class (up to 1000cc) saw a reduction in maximum engine size and all sidecars ran to F2 regulations from 1990. An F2 class had run with the 1000cc outfits from 1984 and their specification of up to 350cc two-stroke or up to 600cc four-stroke engines now applied to everyone on three-wheels. Dave Saville and his two-stroke Yamaha had seven previous F2 class wins and he took the little 350 to a double success in the sidecar races in 1990 with Nick Roache in the chair. Although Dave averaged 100.72 mph in winning the first race, the days of the TZ 'Yam' ruling the roost in F2 were nearing their end and the four-cylinder, 600cc four-strokes took command after 1990.

Dave Saville and Nick Roache after winning both Sidecar races in 1990, the first year that all competitors ran to F2 specification.

*

In other safety-orientated moves the starting system was changed from riders leaving in pairs at ten-second intervals to riders being despatched singly at ten-second intervals. And in an attempt to reduce high speeds in the Pit-lane, each rider was required to brake to a halt in a 'Stop-Box' at the entrance to Pit-lane before accelerating away to his Pit. The allocation of individual Pits was by ballot.

*

Complaints were heard from riders about the growth in use of white lines on the Mountain Course but, after tactfully pointing out that the roads were there for use as every day highways by the Manx motoring public, former racer, scrutineer and local Highway Engineer Steve Woodward was also able to tell them that the special paint used for the white lines gave better skid-resistance than the normal road surface. That must have been reassuring for a racer required to crank his bike into a 135 mph sweeping bend whilst running over a cross-hatched area of white road paint.

*

The TT Formula I series (with rounds run at several circuits) no longer had its own World Championship, there not being enough events to justify such status. It was downgraded to the Formula One Cup (FIM TT Coupe).

*

The Isle of Man's Department of Tourism announced efforts to increase the TT's attraction to foreign riders (and thus they hoped to foreign spectators) and also that *'the festival nature of the event which has been increasing in recent years will be strengthened further'*. In a strange way, their attempts to increase the number of foreign riders was made easier by the downgrading of the Formula I race from World Championship status. This was because some national motorcycling authorities were hostile towards the TT because of its perceived safety record and refused their members applications to compete on the Island. With riders no longer 'obliged' to race for championship points, their national governing bodies were expected to take a more relaxed attitude and allow more freedom of choice.

*

The organisers had always tried to keep the TT meeting associated with some form of championship in the belief that it would protect the TT's dates in what was becoming a very crowded racing calendar. However, although date clashes were to be avoided if possible, there was a growing belief that the TT could stand alone as an International race meeting.

A Busy Fortnight

For TT competitors their fortnight on the Island was divided into practice week and race week. There were three morning, four evening and one afternoon practice sessions. A typical evening practice session was divided into three segments of about 50 minutes each, being:

18.15-19.05	Senior/Formula I, Junior, Production classes.
19.10-20.00	Newcomers, Ultra-Lightweight, Single-cylinder, Lightweight classes.
20.05-20.50	Sidecars.

Riders queue on the Glencrutchery Road waiting for their turn to practice.

Races were programmed over their customary four days: Saturday, Monday, Wednesday and Friday.

*

Practice for the 1990 TT was badly affected by weather - a factor beyond the organisers' control. They always try their utmost to make an accurate assessment of conditions by maintaining a hot-line to the local weather office and obtaining round-the-course reports from Travelling Marshals. When conditions are border-line they sometimes send an official car on an inspection lap and ask a couple of riders' representatives to go as passengers. The riders can then give their first-hand opinions to the organisers and communicate the true conditions to their fellow competitors.

Scrutineering

Before a bike is allowed out for a practice session or race, it has to be scrutineered to ensure that it is safe to be used and that it conforms to the race-regulations.

Experienced riders and mechanics know the extra demands that the Mountain Course puts on a bike and of the need to take special care in preparation. Chief Scrutineer of the early-1990s Alan Verity, who had seen thousands of bikes before and after racing, explained: *'The circuit is so demanding that bikes get an incredible pounding and even the best prepared machines can find things shaking loose or even disappearing'*. The need for scrutineers is well illustrated by another of Alan's comments in which he said: *'I have scrutineered bikes which I wouldn't pass fit for a trip to the shops, let alone the TT course'*. Nowadays scrutineers are also in attendance at pit-stops, where they do a quick visual inspection of machines as they are refuelled.

*

Racebikes undergoing scrutineering at the rear of the Grandstand.

Carl Fogarty was the star of the 1990 meeting with wins in the Formula I and Senior races. Unfortunately, the Senior race was run in mixed weather that produced conditions for racing described by one rider as: *'survival of the maddest'*. Steve Hislop retired himself from the race after two laps saying: *'that's not for me'*, and victory went to Carl who, in his autobiography: 'Foggy', claimed that to achieve the win he forced himself to new limits of bravery and skill. Despite the conditions his race average speed was 110.95 mph.

*

The other races in 1990 were run in better conditions, and solo wins went to Robert Dunlop, Ian Lougher, Brian Reid and Dave Leach, all young men with bright TT futures ahead of them. The Junior was a particularly quick race with young-guns Steve Hislop and Ian Lougher pushing each other every inch of the way. Steve lost a few seconds to Ian at his first pit stop when his mechanic had to retrieve a dropped filler cap from inside the fairing. At the end of the race Ian was just 1.8 seconds ahead of Steve - what if the cap had not been dropped? Ian's record breaking last lap of 117.80 mph on his 250 was to stand for many years.

*

Norton had developed their 588cc rotary-engined racer into an all-conquering device on UK short circuits and in 1990 it showed that it was beginning to be a threat at the TT, with Robert Dunlop taking third place in the Formula I and Trevor Nation second in the Senior. There could hardly be two dissimilar riders of the same type of machine. Robert was 5ft 4ins in height and weighed 9 stone, whilst Trevor was 6ft 1in and weighed over 13 stone.

*

Steve Hislop was Honda mounted in 1990 and in one of the few dry practice sessions he lapped at over120 mph with a camera fitted to his bike. Copies of the video showing that lap were available in the paddock at the Austrian Grand Prix a few days later and it was reported that it: *'had the GP stars wide-eyed'*. Top GP runner Wayne Rainey could not grasp the fact that Hislop was still on the same lap for over eighteen minutes. (The 500cc class of that Austrian round of the World Championships had a mere thirteen starters.)

*

At the 1991 TT race fans showed their forgiving nature and gave Giacomo Agostini a warm welcome when he did a solo demonstration lap on a three-cylinder MV Agusta between races on the Monday. This was despite his damaging anti-TT attitude and actions of earlier years. The Manx police also showed their forgiving nature when they caught Ago firing-up the MV for a blast on open roads at Ballaugh.

Classic Parades
In addition to the occasional solo lap of honour by the likes of Agostini, TT race-week traditionally incorporated a Classic parade lap for former racing

Getting a chance to relive former memories, a rider sets off on his Parade lap. Some Parades have up to 200 riders on machines of yesteryear.

machines and riders. Usually organised by Allan Robinson, in 1990 it was run after the Senior race.

*

A combination of the TT Festival's increasing popularity and a reduction in the amount of holiday accommodation available in hotels and guest-houses, meant that there was a shortfall of places to stay on the Island at TT time. In an attempt to ease accommodation problems a tented village was created in Nobles Park to house 600 TT race fans. There are almost 2,000 tent pitches available on some 18 sites around the Island at TT time.

*

The race programme for 1991 was:

Saturday	TT Formula I, Sidecar 'A'
Monday	Ultra-Lightweight
	and Supersport 400, Sidecar 'B'
Wednesday	Junior, Supersport 600
Friday	Senior

*

Every TT race has a 180 minute count-down sequence when essential aspects of the pre-race organisation click into place at appointed times. It starts with the opening of scrutineering and finishes with what everyone has been waiting for - the drop of the starting-flag that sends the first rider away to create a 37 ³/₄ mile adrenaline surge for riders, pit-crews, race officials, commentators, marshals and spectators.

*

Yamaha celebrated thirty years (and almost one hundred victories) at the TT in 1991. Everyone knew of their race-winning solo performances but not so many were aware that they had won every race (except one) in the 1,000cc Sidecar Class from 1976-1989 (when it was dropped). Wanting more race wins, they provided Brian Morrison with a full 'works' 750 for the Formula I and Senior events, but he could not stop Steve Hislop taking victory for Honda on their very special RVF750. Dave Leach brought his Yamaha FZR400 home first in the Supersport 400 race, and Steve earned himself a hat-trick of wins by taking the Supersport 600 race on his CBR600 Honda. Robert Dunlop gave Honda and Yamaha an additional win each when he was victorious in the Lightweight 125 and Junior races. Mick Boddice (with Dave Wells in the chair) won both sidecar races using a 600cc four-cylinder Honda engine. It was Honda's first victory in the class.

*

Although Joey Dunlop was back racing at the TT, it was taking time for him to recover the winning form

Regular speed check figures were no longer published, but everyone knew that the top bikes were mind-blowingly fast. At the 1991 TT the names of Hislop and Fogarty were on everyone's lips as they pushed each other to ever faster laps in practice. After taking Senior and FI victories with a new lap record of 123.48mph, Steve commented: *'That's scary – it's frightenly fast – at the speeds we're doing you just head for the gaps between the green bits'*. He was clocked at 192mph by police radar on Sulby Straight during the race. When, in 1992, he returned a practice lap speed of 124.36 mph, he became the first rider to achieve a metric 'double ton' (200.13 kph) over the Mountain Course. Steve went on to officially break the outright lap record during the Formula I race at 123.48 mph.

that he had shown before his Brands Hatch accident in 1989 and he had to be content with two second places. Getting the use of Carl Fogarty's RVF helped him to runner-up spot in the Senior behind Steve Hislop, and with RC30-mounted Phillip McCallen coming third, Honda achieved an impressive 1-2-3.

*

The growth in race speeds caused Manx Radio to adjust their 'around the course' commentary points. Out went Ballacraine, Ballaugh and the Bungalow. In came Glen Helen and Ramsey Hairpin, thus giving commentators Peter Kneale, Fred Clarke and Maurice Mawdsley (with Geoff Cannell on the roving-mike) a little longer to gather race times, positions, etc, before delivering them over the air to information-hungry spectators and race teams.

*

During the 1991 TT period riders completed 4,615 laps. Racing accounted for 1,283 of the laps, practice the remainder.

*

The post-TT Steam Packet races were introduced on the Billown circuit in 1991. They were held on the day after the Senior and served as additional entertainment for those who stayed on. They also increased the earnings of riders like the brothers Dunlop and others who, despite having spent two hard weeks racing over the Mountain Course, were still keen for a day's scrapping over Billown's testing 4½ mile lap.

*

In the late-1980s radial tyres had become generally available on the race scene. Claimed to be: *'simpler in design, lighter yet stronger and essentially cooler running'*, they also allowed greater use of different 'compounds' to vary the tyres performance. But the demands of the TT required the use of tried and tested compounds and makers like Michelin typically brought just two front and rear slicks, plus one front and one rear wet tyre and two or three road-legal production tyres. 'Intermediate' tyres for

damp and uncertain conditions were created by the hand-cutting of rain grooves into slicks.

*

A man who literally brought a bit of colour to the TT on his debut in 1992 was American Wade Boyd. His very long purple hair guaranteed that he could not be missed. The colourful Wade returned to the Island on several occasions (sometimes with hair of a different hue) and extended his TT-time activities to ride in moto-cross and as a sidecar passenger.

*

Back to full fitness in 1992, Joey Dunlop entered all five solo classes. He was looking for at least two wins to lift his total number of TT victories from 13 to 15 and thus overtake Mike Hailwood's record of 14. Joey had a full factory RC30 from Honda for the big races, which was the racer version of the VFR750 V-four roadster, although it also owed much to the RVF750 factory racers. With its 360 degree crankshaft the RC30 had a standard output of 112 bhp.

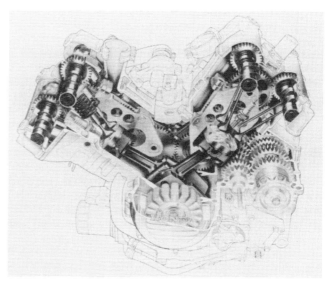

The V-four Honda RC30 engine that delivered 112 bhp @ 11,000 rpm and was used in both road and racing machines.

It was an ultra-busy TT fortnight for Joey in 1992, but at its end he had to be satisfied with a single victory in the Ultra-Lightweight class on his McMenemy Motors RS Honda (all 46 starters were on Hondas). There was little doubting his pleasure at having equalled Mike Hailwood's record and of breaking his personal drought (last win the Senior in 1988) but, at the age of forty, there was a question mark over the issue of whether he would be back to try for win number 15, because Joey's racing career by now operated on a one-year-at-a-time basis. However, his many fans were pleased to hear him say in 1992 that he might well return the following year. It sounded as though a record-equalling 14 wins was not enough for the publican from Ballymoney and that he considered there was some unfinished business to deal with.

*

Many Irish riders were reared and did the majority of their racing on road circuits and they were 'naturals' at the TT. They almost monopolised the solo events in 1992, for as well as Joey's win in the Ultra-Lightweight, Phillip McCallen (Honda) proved after a very successful North West 200 meeting that he had really 'arrived' with a resounding first TT win in the Formula I, followed by victory in the Supersport 600. Brian Reid had a double on Yamahas in the Supersport 400 and Junior classes and it was only Scotsman Steve Hislop who prevented a clean-sweep by the Irish boys of the solo classes.

Norton Win
Although it is vital for a top rider to have first-class machinery at the TT if he is to achieve success, he also needs the best of support services. Steve Hislop chose the rotary Norton for his Formula I and Senior rides, and although a complicated funding arrangement saw his bike being leased, he enjoyed back-up from the Norton factory, as did the other Norton rider, Robert Dunlop. In charge of the Norton set-up was the highly experienced Barry Symmons. Previously with Honda, he had the myriad of contacts necessary to iron-out the inevitable TT related problems regarding accommodation, transport, workshop provision (Norton even brought their own special bulbs for the workshop lighting), fuel, spares, practice, race-timetabling, pit-organisation, public relations, etc. A competitor simply cannot do all that on his own, and do justice to his riding.

*

Steve Hislop spent the practice period getting used to riding the 150 bhp rotary-engined Norton for, with

Norton team boss Barry Symmons talks to Robert Dunlop about his practice times at the 1992 TT.

its almost total lack of engine-braking, its riding characteristics were very different to what he was used to. Fortunately, the Norton's use of a twin alloy spar frame, telescopic forks, single-shock rear suspension and radial tyres was fairly conventional for the class. Second place in the week-opening Formula I race behind Phillip McCallen (after early leader Carl Fogarty on his Yamaha struck gearbox problems) showed that Steve learnt quickly, particularly as he lost time at his first pit-stop. This was because, for all Barry Symmons thorough preparation, as he pulled in for his first refuelling session, Steve confused the black and gold overalls worn by Johnny Rea's pit-crew with those of the similarly coloured Norton team and stopped at the wrong pit. Then, as a result of Robert Dunlop's early retirement at Kirk Michael with over-heating, he lost more time as his mechanics stripped off his front mudguard to get more cooling air to the motor.

*

The Senior TT had recovered much of its former prestige and was run as the last race of the week. Senior race-day of 1992 dawned fine and with riders like Hislop, Fogarty, McCallen, Joey and Robert Dunlop all in with the chance of a win after their scorching practice times, fans knew they were in for a treat. They were not disappointed, for it turned into one of those races that would be talked about for years to come. Four seconds covered the first three (Fogarty, Hislop, Robert Dunlop) at the end of the first lap. Four seconds then covered the first two for the remaining five laps (apart from a bit of ebb and flow at pit-stops), and the lead changed five times between Fogarty (Yamaha) and Hislop (Norton). Manx Radio kept everyone right up to date throughout the 226 mile battle in which the top two did not see each other, for the interval start kept them 2½ minutes apart (Fogarty rode at number 4, Hislop at 19). Informed only by signals from their support crews, it was down to each rider to ride his own race in a typical against the clock TT battle, whilst his opponent did the same elsewhere on the course. Pushing to the limit, Steve Hislop eventually triumphed over Carl Fogarty and his Yamaha, giving Norton their first Senior TT win since 1961. The evenly matched duo both entered the record books with Steve setting a new race record average speed of 121.28 mph whilst Carl grabbed the outright lap record in his all or nothing last lap attempt to catch Steve, leaving it at 123.61 mph.

Too Fast?

After reflecting on their Senior performances, Steve and Carl called for an upper engine-capacity limit of 600cc to be introduced at the TT. Both felt the big bikes were too fast, with Steve saying: *'it would limit the mind-numbing spots like Sulby Straight and Glen Duff, where the 750s are going so quick on the bumps you can't focus properly'*. It was a bold call that some other top runners didn't agree with, but Steve tactfully pointed out that there was a lot of difference between a 123 mph lap (his) and 120 mph laps (theirs). He also knew that faster 750 machinery was on the horizon, something that he did not relish. Indeed, he left the TT in 1992 indicating that he would not be back.

*

Although the pace of the sidecars had been slowed by the move to F2 specifications, they still lapped at over 100 mph. Geoff Bell and passenger Keith Cornbill took a double win in 1992 and, in an amazing display of consistency, averaged 101.50 mph over the three laps of Sidecar Race 'A' and 101.49 mph over exactly the same distance in Race 'B'. That represented a difference of 0.6 seconds over 113 miles.

*

A front-wheel landing for Steve Hislop (Norton) at Ballaugh Bridge in 1992.

Manufacturers were still keen to associate their products with the prestige that accompanied TT winners, making extensive use of advertising and machine stickers.

TT HISTORY MADE ON MICHELIN

Norton men re-write 31 years of Isle of Man TT history. Honda men dominate the Formula One and Supersport 600 races. And all these men are Michelin men. Technically there has never been an alternative if you want to be a winner.
TT history in 1992 went like this :

SENIOR TT
1st Steve Hislop, Norton
3rd Robert Dunlop, Hymac Norton
4th Nick Jefferies, Castrol Honda

SUPERSPORT 600
1ST Phillip McCallen, Castrol Honda
(on standard TX Hi-Sport Radials)

JUNIOR TT
2nd Steve Hislop, Padgett Yamaha
4th Ian Lougher, TCR

SUPERSPORT 400
2nd Phillip McCallen, Castrol Honda
(on standard TX Hi-Sport Radials)

FORMULA ONE TT
1st Phillip McCallen, Castrol Honda
2nd Steve Hislop, Norton
3rd Joey Dunlop, Castrol Honda
4th Nick Jefferies, Castrol Honda

Will TT history repeat itself?

Whatever bike you ride, Michelin have the range and performance to make a Michelin man out of you. See your tyre dealer now and fit a pair of Michelins.

MAKE SURE IT'S A MICHELIN
TECHNICALLY THERE'S NO ALTERNATIVE

Michelin advertised the TT successes gained on their tyres.

Race fans probably assumed that the rash of product stickers plastered on the fairings of the top runners in 1992 indicated that they were making use of the products named on those stickers. But Ferodo were left feeling a little aggrieved, for they claimed that the first three riders in each race used Ferodo discs and brake pads but that the fairings of some of the top runners suggested the use of products from other manufacturers.

*

Regular leaderboard finisher and highly enthusiastic TT runner Nick Jefferies recorded four 4th places in 1992, a TT period in which he celebrated his fortieth birthday. Untroubled by the fact that he had yet to record a TT win (he had managed four 2nd places), Nick was also seemingly unfazed by provocative former multi-TT winner Phil Read telling him: *'If you*

are still enjoying it as much as you say you are, then you're probably not going fast enough'.

*

Armed with Castrol Honda machinery at the 1993 TT, perhaps Phil Read's words had hit the mark, for Nick Jefferies found that extra little bit of aggression and got himself into the TT record books with a win in the opening Formula I race.

These spectators are feeling a little too close to the action as Nick Jefferies (Castrol Honda) powers away from a corner on the back-wheel.

All-rounder Nick would have been pleased to take the generous prize money - worth £6,000 to a rider who led from start to finish - and to have achieved a second record, that of being the only man to have won a TT race, the MGP and the Manx Two-Day Trial. The Senior event was the richest race of the week paying £6,250 (going to Phillip McCallen), and the poorest was the Lightweight 125 (Joey Dunlop) and Supersport 400 race (Jim Moodie) - the two classes ran together - with £1,600 to each winner. The Junior winner (Brian Reid) took £3,000 and Supersport 600 (Jim Moodie) £3,000. Locals Dave Molyneux and Karl Harrison took victory in both sidecar races (£3,600 for each race), and every race starter, up to a maximum of 80, was guaranteed a payment of £250 *'subject to the competitor making a bonafide attempt to compete in the race'.* In addition to the chance to win prize-money, top runners received substantial start money.

Rising Stars

Amongst the top six finishers in the solo classes in 1993 were men who were well on the way to completing their TT apprenticeships and would go on to wins or podium places; among them being Steve Ward, Jason Griffiths, Iain Duffus, Dave Morris, Mark Baldwin, Bob Jackson, Simon Beck, Ian Simpson and Colin Gable. In the sidecar races newcomers Rob Fisher and Vince Butler showed promise of things to come with sixth place.

*

Joey Dunlop's Ultra-Lightweight win was his fifteenth TT victory and it took him to the top of the all-time winners list. Official prize presentation ceremonies follow each TT. (These are in addition to the post-race garlanding ceremonies.) Usually held in the evening, they are where the winner and other award winners receive their trophies and the congratulations of fans for their race efforts. The cheering that greeted Joey when he walked on to the stage at the presentation ceremony for the Ultra-Lightweight race went on for several minutes. There have been many popular TT winners down the years but, surely, Joey was the most popular of all.

*

As with many TT wins, Joey's Ultra-Lightweight victory was achieved after a week of problems with the bike. Indeed, the engine with which he won was borrowed from James Courtney's sponsors just hours before the race. It was reminiscent of the experiences of the man whose record he had broken, for Mike Hailwood's 14th win was achieved after his Suzuki engine was rebuilt in the early hours of race morning.

Britten

A team that was new to the TT in 1993 was that of Britten from New Zealand. It brought an unconventional machine that had been designed from scratch by owner John Britten and it shook the established teams with its speed. It also grabbed the attention of spectators with its individual engine note and striking red and blue colour scheme. Bristling with John Britten's innovative ideas, the chassis was of kevlar and carbon-fibre and used the engine as a stressed member. Unconventional suspension and relatively light weight plus its liquid-cooled, eight-valve, fuel-injected, V-twin engine with belt-driven dohc, meant that the 150 bhp unit offered plenty of

speed for the power-hungry TT Course. Unfortunately, the Britten team and rider Shaun Harris were robbed of a good finish by an oil-line failure.

Shaun Harris on the Britten at the 1993 TT.

The Britten was back at the 1994 TT with three riders, Nick Jefferies, Mark Farmer and the dashing New Zealander Robert Holden. It was a bold challenge that was buoyed by a win at Daytona earlier in the year. Nevertheless, there could be no greater contrast to what 'Motorcycle News' described as *'a backyard special'* and the might of the Honda organisation with its latest RC45 V-four that the Britten was challenging, even though the RC45 was far from 'sorted' in 1994 and the factory parts to make it go really well were in short supply.

*

Kiwis were present in large numbers in 1994, with Chester dealer and former TT winner Bill Smith supplying a fleet of standard 600 Yamahas for some ten aspiring TT riders from New Zealand. All performed creditably, finished the race, and were later awarded The Maudes Trophy by the ACU for their outstanding achievements.

*

At 32 years of age Steve Hislop was back at the TT to ride one of the Castrol Honda sponsored RC 45s and he was joined by Joey Dunlop and Phillip McCallen. After saying in 1992 that he would not return to the TT, Steve was quite open about the fact that his come-back was all about money. He hoped to earn enough from his start money (which he said was £7,000) and his race winnings to finance a large part of his World Superbike campaign. The money aspect gave the media a topic to latch onto and it all helped heighten the interest in Steve's return.

*

There was much else to interest race fans at the 1994 TT, including a race for single-cylinder four-stroke machines run concurrently with the 125s that received

46 entries on a wide variety of machinery. Although single-cylinder machines had dominated the TT races from 1920 into the early 1950s, thereafter they faded and the top positions were taken by twins and multis. The exception was in the 125cc class where Joey Dunlop held the record for the fastest ever TT lap by a single-cylinder machine of any capacity, at 108.55 mph.

*

TT fans who could not get to the Island were served by ever increasing televised broadcasts of the event on both satellite and terrestrial channels. There was also a choice of TT videos available for armchair viewing over the winter months.

*

The Britten team effort was struck by tragedy when Mark Farmer was killed in a practice accident on one of their machines. The whole Britten project received another huge blow a few years later when John Britten died young.

*

Racing opened with the Formula I event in 1994 and victory went to the returning Steve Hislop (who by then lived on the Island), from Phillip McCallen and Joey Dunlop. Apart from the riders' performances the race was notable for the fact that at its first running, on Saturday, the weather deteriorated and the race was stopped after two laps, much to the disgust of Nigel 'Cap' Davies who held the lead. The race was re-run on Sunday in perfect conditions that gave Honda their 1-2-3, but brought disaster to top runner Robert Dunlop when the back wheel of his machine collapsed as he left Ballaugh. Sustaining injuries that would have taken a lesser man out of racing for good, Robert had a long struggle to get back to race fitness and, in a move whose consequences for the sport have not yet been fully evaluated, he sued his sponsor. Some seven years later he was awarded damages of £700,000.

Doubles
1994 turned into a year of double wins. Steve Hislop added the Senior to his FI victory, Joey Dunlop took the Ultra-Lightweight and Junior, Jim Moodie the Supersport 400 and Singles. In only his second year at the TT, Rob Fisher (passengered by newcomer Mike Wynn) joined the double winners with victories in both sidecar classes and Ian Duffus completed the list of winners by taking the Supersport 600 class for his first TT win. Duffus had spent rather longer than Fisher on his TT apprenticeship, having first ridden the event in 1985.

*

There were yet more changes to the Race Programme in 1995, some being a little difficult to follow! The Junior TT had been a race for 201-350cc twin-cylinder two-stoke machines for several years but had been dominated by 250s. The new schedule saw the Junior race title taken over by machines of 600cc (that were to Supersport regulations), and the Supersport 600 race was dropped. The title of Lightweight race came back into the Programme and was for 250 twin-cylinder two-strokes. Within the Lightweight race was a class for 371-400cc four-cylinder four-strokes (the Supersport 400 class also being dropped).

*

Whatever the race title, Joey Dunlop showed that he was top-man on a 250 at the 1995 TT on his Castrol Honda. Rating it as one of his finest TT victories, Joey put aside the disappointment of retirement from the 125 race earlier in the day and led James Courtney (Honda) home by 25.5 seconds at a new race record average speed of 115.68 mph. Talking to reporter Norrie Whyte at the finish, he said: *'The bike went 100 per cent, the conditions were 100 per cent - dull and cool - and once I got going I was 100 per cent'*. Although Joey could always be looked upon to deliver a good result at the TT, it was acknowledged that he was not always able to ride at 100 per cent. He readily admitted the fact and explained that it was not until he plunged down Bray Hill on the opening lap of a race that he knew if he was going to be really on the pace. It was veteran TT commentator Peter Kneale who, if the Ulsterman was going well, would say that *'Joey's got his race face on'*.

*

Joey may have been among the quickest of men around the TT Course on two-wheels but he was not a happy man after being picked up at The Hawthorn by the Course Inspection car following his retirement in the 125 race. As its name suggests, the Course Inspection car is used to allow a couple of officials to do a lap between races. Describing his ultra-rapid 31 mile ride back to the start as *'a frightening experience'*, Joey was obviously a man who liked to be in control of his own destiny. The vastly experienced driver of the car, David Mylchreest, rated it as one of his slower laps for, after all, he was out there to inspect the Course, and it fell well short of the 90+ mph laps he put in when in a hurry to get the roads open at the end of racing.

*

After several tries, ace rally driver of the time Tony Pond had achieved a 100 mph lap of the TT Course on four-wheels a few years earlier, and he did it using a Rover Vitesse on closed roads. It was a flying lap and he had a co-driver reading him pace notes. Bet Joey would have loved that job!

Rob Fisher took another sidecar double win in 1995 and revealed that, prior to his TT debut in 1993, he watched a video of the Tony Pond 100 mph lap every day as the time for the TT approached. Through no fault of his own, Rob had a third different passenger (Boyd Hutchinson) in his third year of racing at the TT.

A Close Race

The Ultra-Lightweight race for 125s produced an incredible ride from 33 year old Mark Baldwin. Coming to the TT with virtually no warm-up race rides in 1995 and riding a rented Honda, he snatched victory from Mick Lofthouse by 0.6 of a second after a storming ride over the last half lap of the race in which he broke Joey Dunlop's lap record.

Mark Baldwin snatched victory from Mick Lofthouse by just 0.6 of a second in the 1995 Ultra-Lightweight TT.

Second-place man Lofthouse's disappointment was compounded by the fact that he had been greeted as the winner when he arrived at the finish, only to be told a couple of minutes later that he was runner-up. In the Singles race run at the same time as the 125s, Robert Holden brought a Ducati Supermono into first place ahead of Dave Morris (BMW).

*

Riding a controlled race, Iain Duffus took the Junior event on his 600cc V&M Honda, setting new race and lap speeds on the way. Concerned when Phillip McCallen passed him on the third lap he held his own pace, saying *'McCallen was riding so hard - much harder than I wanted to - he was hairy'.* On the last lap, Iain rounded Waterworks above Ramsey to find bits of McCallen's Honda all over the road and Phillip crawling off the track. Phillip had been trying to make up time on a bike that had run poorly until it received fresh fuel at the mid-race pit-stop. Thereafter, on his own admission: *'I was right up on the banks, using the verges everywhere and couldn't have pushed the thing any harder . . . I was sliding it into every corner . . . real manic short circuit stuff'.* It could not last, and a false neutral fetched him off at Waterworks, whilst Duffus rode on to victory. Nick Jefferies was second, Colin Gable third and, with Duffus, they took the Manufacturer's Team Award for Honda.

*

As an experienced TT rider, Iain Duffus knew how to control his pace. He found the section from Ramsey to the Finish to be the easiest part of the Course, saying: *'It's the time to get your breath back after the Ginger Hall to Ramsey section which I rate as the hardest and toughest part of a lap. It can be pretty scary through there especially if you have to get round other riders. If you are not bang on line all the time you lose out all the way through the section'.* Having been "one of the lads" when he first came to the TT, Ian explained in an interview with seasoned journalist John Brown: *'In the early days I used to be up late and having a few drinks, but I wasn't fit and used to sweat a lot during the races.I remember the first time I raced the TT I was nervous and not so fit and forgot to breathe properly. My body overheated, I started to sweat and my visor misted up. It was then I decided you simply had to be physically and mentally fit to do the job properly. When you get them both together you can start to let the bike do some of the work. It cuts down the effort and you start to go quick'.* To watch a TT master like Duffus at speed is to see as close a union between man and machine as can be reached. It is no wonder that ordinary spectators have held the top TT men in awe down the years.

*

Amongst the sounds of the four-cylinder 750cc Japanese machines that dominated the entries for the Formula I race there could be heard the occasional booming exhaust of a twin-cylinder Ducati, for the race had been opened up to 1000cc twin-cylinder bikes. The Senior race had similar provision, and also allowed 250 two-stoke twins and 600 fours. Prize-money was increased to £8,000 for each of those races and it was Phillip McCallen and Joey Dunlop who shared the top winnings, with Phillip taking the Formula I and Joey the Senior. Both were on Castrol Hondas.

*

The 'Road Racing Capital of the World' welcomed competitors and spectators in 1996 with the claim that *'Not only is the TT the pinnacle of pure road racing at a world level but it is the lynchpin of a major festival of bikesport and motorcycling'*. Racers were attracted by another substantial increase in prize-money and thousands of fans flocked across the Irish Sea to be part of the festival.

*

Surprising as it may seem, the majority of TT visitors do not come by bike. With total visitor numbers over the TT period being in excess of 40,000, figures from the Steam Packet Company show that they ship about 12,000 motorcycles, plus 3,500 cars and vans. However, many of those vans carry motorcycles, some being exotica that only comes out for special occasions like the TT to rub handlebars with everyday machinery. Such is the variety of bikes to be seen that some motorcycle fanatics could get everything they wanted out of a week on the Island by walking up and down Douglas Promenade for the whole of their stay.

A walk along Douglas Promenade always yields a wide variety of bikes.

The range of people on view at the TT is almost as interesting as the bikes, for the past-time of motorcycling has many sub-specialisations. They range from Barbour-clad vintagents who rub shoulders with those in the latest coloured leathers (complete with knee-sliders and back protectors), whilst chopper riders, 'middle-of the-roaders' and those who look as though they have just completed an enduro, all go about attired in their chosen gear. The TT Festival takes a hold on people in many different ways, but once they are hooked, most stay hooked and return year after year, renewing acquaintances on the boat crossings, at their digs and at the many events they get to during their time on Mona's Isle.

Another 'Proddie' Return

Production bikes were back with their own race in 1996. With everyone now confident that their handling on road tyres was up to the demands of the TT Course, the Production TT for four-stroke machines of 701-1010cc ran over three laps on the morning of Friday's Senior race-day. With over seventy entries on models such as the Honda CBR900R Fireblade, Suzuki GSX-R750, Yamaha Thunderace, Kawasaki ZX-9, Ducati 916SP, and Triumph Speed Triple, spectators looked on with real interest as these same models that many of them were riding on the road were pushed to their limits by the top racers.

*

Few would dispute that TT week of 1996 belonged to 32 year old Phillip McCallen. Despite the fact that TT greats like Mike Hailwood, Steve Hislop and Joey Dunlop had made the record books by taking three wins in a week, McCallen became the first man to take four TT victories in one year, all on Hondas. Setting the pace in practice, come race-week he started with a win in the opening Formula I race, and used the same RC45 to take the last race of the week, the 'Blue Riband' Senior event. Wins on his 900 Fireblade in the Production race and CBR600 in the Junior made up his quartet of victories and earned him £35,000 in prize-money. Phillip's only defeat of the week came in the Lightweight where he lost out to Joey Dunlop. Mind you, he was leading that race until he holed his exhaust and dropped to fourth place. With Joey also taking the Ultra-Lightweight, Honda all but swept the board in the solo classes with record-breaking performances from the two Ulster stars. The only other make to get a look-in was Yamaha, when Jim Moodie took one of their big bangers to victory in the Singles race.

*

Phillip McCallen gave the impression of riding in an all-or-nothing style and managed to hole his exhaust in the Lightweight race when his suspension compressed to its maximum going through the bottom of Barregarrow, (after limited practice time on the 250 he'd softened the suspension just before the race). Joey Dunlop, who won the race, was riding a similar Honda but did not hole his exhaust. Had Joey perhaps done a similar thing in his young and fiery days? It will never be known, but a competitor must ride with his head as well as with his right-hand at the TT. There are some who maintain that Phillip's problem in that Lightweight race was rider induced, but perhaps they didn't have as many bikes to prepare as he did. He rode in black and red leathers that matched the colours of his Honda in the Formula I and Senior, but in the Production and Junior races his leathers and machines were in the livery of dealers Motorcycle City who provided major support to his race programme.

Phillip McCallen on his Motorcycle City sponsored Honda prepares to go out for a damp practice session.

This changing of leathers to suit sponsors was a growing trend amongst top riders that fans had to be aware of when trying to identify competitors in the various classes. They could, of course, fall back on helmet colours - Joey Dunlop's yellow and black Arai was a constant down the years - but many riders also changed their helmet colours each year. It was a strange tactic in a publicity orientated sport, for it initially made them anonymous to all except the most dedicated fans (and sometimes to the race commentators).

*

There was speculation before the reintroduced Production race as to what lap speeds the road-going machines would achieve. The fastest lap went to McCallen at 118.93 mph and he believed that he could have gone round at 120 on the Fireblade if pushed. For comparison, his fastest lap in the Senior was 122.14 mph. There were no major handling problems with the 'Proddies' although fuel consumption was a concern for some, with several of the top runners having to back off on the last lap in order to get to the finish of the three-lap race. There were an impressive 47 finishers from the 53 race starters, showing that the Production bikes had reliability as well as speed.

*

Dave Molyneux and Peter Hill won both sidecar races on their 600 Yamaha and left the lap record at 111.02 mph. It was only six years earlier that the sidecar races were limited to F2 machines that just managed to lap at 100 mph. Now machines to that formula were going much faster than the 'too fast' 1000cc machines that they replaced. 'Moly's' practice times were so fast that there were whispers of illegal fuels and/or oversize engines. Seriously offended by such rumours and determined to scotch them, he had his fuel tested in practice - result, all in order- and his engine was stripped and measured after the first race - result, well within the limit at 598cc.

*

Making his debut and showing promise of things to come was third generation member of the Jefferies family - David. He finished 10th in the Production race and 16th in the Senior and Junior, taking the award for the best Newcomer.

*

The TT showed its traditional side when, as part of their 75th anniversary celebrations, Moto-Guzzi were represented in the Classic Parade by sixteen of their former race machines. The Parade was headed by an original V-eight (ridden by original rider Bill Lomas) and a replica V-eight ridden by its builder Giuseppe Todero. Veteran Bill rode the full lap whilst young Giuseppe threw his £500,000 machine down the road at Braddan Bridge less than two miles from the Start. Fortunately only the bike's fairing and Giuseppe's pride were damaged.

*

Unfortunately, the darker side of the TT was shown by the death of four fine riders during the fortnight, amongst them being potential race winners Robert Holden and Mick Lofthouse. Both had been going extremely fast in practice, but, as others before them had shown, trying to ride the fine line between running at race winning speed whilst continuing to show respect and make allowances for the unforgiving Mountain Course was a task that left riders with so little margin for error.

*

After his four wins in a week, Phillip McCallen left the Island in 1996 with some people suggesting that he had earned the title 'King of the Mountain' - it was one held at the time by 'King Joey'. Not everyone agreed on Phillip's elevation to the title, but he did his claim no harm by taking another three TT wins in 1997 - all on Hondas - bringing his total number of wins to 11, (half the number of Joey Dunlop's TT victories at the time). Finishing as fastest man in practice, McCallen went on to take victories in Formula I from Michael Rutter and Bob Jackson, in the Production race (shortened to two laps) and in the Senior, with fastest laps in each. However, he lost his chance of a fourth win when he came off his 250 Honda in the Lightweight race at 140 mph at Quarry Bends. By an incredible coincidence, Steve Hislop was robbed of four-in-a-week TT victories back in 1989 when he also came off his 250 Honda at Quarry Bends at high speed.

*

Further comparisons can be made between McCallen and Hislop with regard to the 250 Lightweight class. Both particularly wanted to win on a 250, mainly because they had won the other classes they had entered but also because the quarter-litre Hondas were pure racing bikes with no Production machine ancestry. However, McCallen also thought quite highly of the Production bikes, saying: 'Street bikes are real race bred machines these days'. He was a rider who did not favour any particular part of the Course, considering: 'it's all part of a package' and saying 'you can't start treating parts of the course differently . . . start to like or dislike sections and you start slowing down here, going faster there and you're soon in trouble, particularly at a place like the TT'.

*

Joey Dunlop was the man who took the Lightweight win on his 250 Honda from Ian Lougher, with John McGuinness third. Ian Lougher's Lightweight lap record of 117.80 mph set in 1990 was still proving tough to beat and the fastest lap in 1997 was by John McGuinness at 116.83 mph.

*

The Junior race turned into a first TT win for Ian Simpson, from Phillip McCallen and Michael Rutter. The race took place only two days after McCallen's high-speed fall from his 250 at Quarry Bends and he was particularly cautious through there.

Understandable really, as he could still see the tyre and scrape marks on the road from his earlier spill!

*

90th Anniversary

It was the TT's 90th anniversary in 1997 and Geoff Duke unveiled a plaque opposite Tynwald Hill at St John's to commemorate the occasion.

*

On the occasion of the 90th anniversary of the TT in 1997, Geoff Duke unveiled this memorial plaque opposite the original starting line at St John's.

Fast Lady

Sandra Barnett proved that she was far and away the fastest woman around the TT Course with a lap of 114.63 mph and 15th place in the Junior race in 1997.

*

Veteran Roy Hanks won the first sidecar race and Rob Fisher took the second. Tom Hanks (Roy's nephew and former passenger) was the overall winner with 4th and 2nd places.

*

The 1997 Senior race broke with tradition because instead of riders submitting their entries in advance, entry was now by invitation of the organisers, and consisted of the fastest 80 riders in practice over the Formula I, Junior, Production and Lightweight classes. Starting numbers were also allocated in accordance with the earlier speeds achieved and whilst it was no surprise to see Phillip McCallen at number 1, it meant that Joey Dunlop appeared as an unfamiliar number 5. It was three Honda mounted riders, number 1 McCallen (RC45), 2 Michael Rutter (RC45) and 3 Jim Moodie (NSR500) who contested the lead in the early stages. Rutter dropped out just before the end of the first lap, Moodie was troubled by a race-long mis-fire, whilst McCallen changed his rear-tyre at both of his pit-stops, where he also lost time when the refuelling rig was not turned on. Overcoming his problems and the opposition, Phillip

McCallen won by just eight seconds from Jim Moodie, with Ian Simpson (Honda) third.

*

A closely fought Ultra-Lightweight race saw Ian Lougher home in first place just two seconds ahead of Derek McCullough, with Robert Dunlop third. This was Robert's first TT race since his major accident in 1994. The Singles race ran with the Ultra-Lightweights and resulted in victory for Dave Morris on his BMW.

Bushy's

Many fans departed the 1997 TT with a touch of sadness, for they knew that one of their favourite haunts - Bushy's - was due to close before they returned in 1998. Conveniently located on the sea-front, Bushy's Brew Pub and its immediate environment developed its own sub-culture of whacky evening entertainment with wheelies, stoppies, burn-outs, mini-motor racing, streakers-on-wheels, and a constant parade of passing bikes for those who liked a bit of two-wheel entertainment with their drinking.

Providing their share of off-beat entertainment at official and unofficial functions were the Purple Helmets, a bunch of mainly Manx motorcyclists riding much modified Honda step-thrus. Their act is difficult to describe but once seen it is never forgotten!

*

Shock news at the 1998 TT was that after an accident at Thruxton, Phillip McCallen would not be riding. Even worse was the fact that he was unlikely to return to racing in the future as doctors had warned him that further damage to his back could result in him being paralysed. Phillip was present at the TT to provide assistance and advice to the Honda runners, but he could only look on in envy as they set out to lap the Mountain Course. Iain Duffus was another top Honda runner to miss the 1998 races. In a freak, non-racing incident, Iain fell over in the Paddock and broke his leg. Also in the wars was yet another of Honda's riders, Joey Dunlop. After an early season crash at Tandragee in which he suffered hand and shoulder injuries, Joey felt unable to wrestle the big bikes around the Mountain and so limited himself to riding his 125 and 250 Hondas. All three riders had

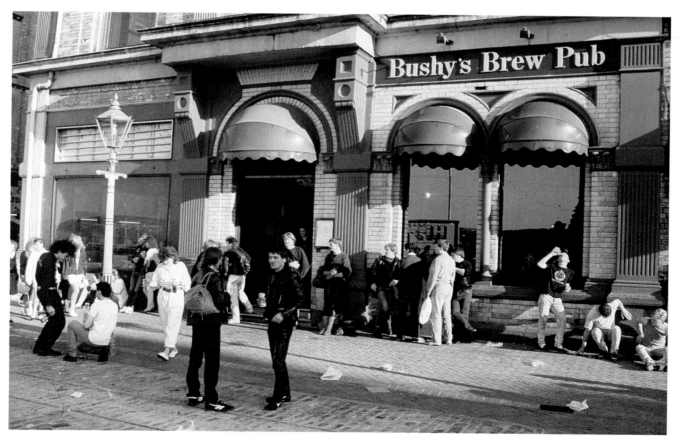

Bushy's Brew Pub in Douglas pictured at a fairly quiet moment.

been due to ride for Honda Britain who desperately wanted a successful TT to coincide with Honda's 50th birthday celebrations. Out to spoil Honda's party were long-time rivals Yamaha, and riders of their machines topped the practice leader-boards in the Lightweight and Production classes. As if that was not worrying enough for Honda, Simon Beck put his Kawasaki at the head of the Formula I and Senior qualifiers.

*

The 1998 race programme got off to a bad start when the opening Saturday's races were washed out. The organisers abandoned the first sidecar race (throwing the prize-money into the pot for the second race) and ran the Formula I race the following day over a reduced four-lap distance.

*

The TT is always preceded by the North West 200 races that take place a couple of weeks earlier on an ultra-fast road circuit in Northern Ireland, and the results from the North West usually serve as a pointer as to who will do well at the TT. Ian Simpson and Michael Rutter starred in the big classes at the Irish races and they carried that form through to the Formula I and Senior TT races. Both were sons of former TT winners and in both races it was Michael Rutter who set the pace in the early stages with Simpson tracking him. Unfortunately, in each race Rutter lost the race win to Simpson. Both were riding 'works' Honda RC45s and in the Formula I Rutter led for three laps before losing a contact lens. This enabled Simpson to pull back in drying road conditions, take the lead on the last lap, set the fastest lap speed at 123.28 mph and win the race from Rutter by 17 seconds. It was a similar story in the six-lap Senior where Rutter led for two laps only to get a puncture and retire. Simpson was only a couple of seconds behind and he inherited the lead and went on to win. However, the big story in the Senior was Bob Jackson's ride to second place (a mere 3.7 seconds in arrears) on a Kawasaki fitted with an enlarged petrol tank that meant he only stopped once to refuel. Everyone else stopped twice and the advantage gained would have been sufficient to earn victory for Bob had he not been delayed during his single stop by a filler-cap that was reluctant to screw back in place. After many years of trying and leader-board places, a margin of just 3.7 seconds was the closest Bob got to a TT win.

*

Bob had already made news of a different sort earlier in the week when he scratched his entry in the delayed-to-Sunday Formula I race. This was to meet the wishes of his sponsor Winston McAdoo who would not allow his bikes to be raced on a Sunday.

*

The Formula I race had been run in damp/drying conditions that restricted speeds until the closing stages. The Senior was run in good conditions and saw riders like Jim Moodie, Simon Beck, Ian Lougher, James Courtney and Jason Griffiths all recording 120+mph laps. (A certain David Jefferies showed that he was learning fast by lapping just a fraction short of 120.) Although Steve Hislop had not competed in the TT since 1994, he still topped the list of riders who had achieved 120+ mph laps with a figure of 31, Phillip McCallen was second on 29 and Joey Dunlop third on 17.

*

Despite his bad luck in the two big races, Michael Rutter gained some consolation when he brought his Honda home first in the Junior event ahead of Ian Simpson and local-man Paul Dedman. A new electronic speed-trap with a huge digital display showed crowds in the Grandstand that Rutter's Honda 600 was hitting 147 mph as it passed them on the Glencrutchery Road.

*

Having lost their first race on Saturday, sidecar crews were up in arms when their second race was also delayed and rescheduled for Tuesday morning, meaning that some crews would have left the Island. When the three-wheelers eventually got their race, it turned into a £10,000 pay-day for Manxman Dave Molyneux and passenger Doug Jewell when they brought their Honda 600 home in first place.

Canny Joey

The injured Joey Dunlop barely scraped on to the top-twelve leaderboard during practice and had thoughts of scratching from the 125 and 250 races. However, he was on the line for the Lightweight (250) race in what were deplorable wet and misty racing conditions. Gaining advantage from the wet (reduced speeds meant less high-speed wrestling with the bike), Joey also used his many years of experience of the TT to second-guess the organisers. Due to stop for fuel after just one lap of the already shortened to three-lap race, Joey went straight through, gambling that with the weather deteriorating the race would be stopped after two laps. It was, he was at the head of the field and he took what was perhaps the least expected of what now amounted to 23 TT victories.

*

Despite all the work that goes on during practice, there are often final decisions to be made before a race as to suspension settings, tyres to be used, etc. Perhaps the hardest of those is what tyres to use under mixed weather conditions where the Course can alternate between wet, dry and damp. Joey Dunlop took what seemed to be a reasonable decision to use cut slicks in the Ultra-Lightweight (125) race while brother Robert gambled on slicks. Barely recovered from injuries sustained in the NW 200 a couple of weeks before, Robert made the right choice and took his little Honda to victory, whilst the injured Joey finished an unaccustomed ninth. Dave Morris was again top-man in the Singles race run at the same time as the Ultra-Lightweights. Riding the Rotax-engined BMW 650 that he largely prepared himself, Dave relegated the full-blown 'works' Honda single of Jim Moodie to second place and so prevented Honda from achieving their sought after clean-sweep of the 1998 TT races.

*

Asked about Honda's high-level of support for the TT over many years, General Manager of Honda UK, Bob McMillan, replied: *'Our TT aims and objectives at Honda UK are to prove beyond doubt the engineering capability of our motorcycles in a testing environment and way above the capabilities of normal motorcyclists. There is no greater test of a machine or rider than the TT Course'.*

*

Bob McMillan of Honda responds to a few probing questions from the man with the 'roving-mike', Geoff Cannell.

Yamaha hoped that their new R1 model would steal some of Honda's TT glory in Friday morning's Production race. All the pre-TT magazine assessments rated the R1 as a giant leap forward for road-use, several describing it as *'the ultimate sports*

bike', and Allan Benallick seemingly confirmed their words by putting his on top of the practice leaderboard. Designed from scratch by a team led by Kunihiko Miwa, the R1 had the appearance and weight of a small 600 allied to an output of 140bhp. But how would it rate at the TT? Race fans on other sports bikes like Honda Fireblades and VTRs, Suzuki GSX-Rs, etc., were as keen to find out as the manufacturers, for a good Production TT result could influence their buying and thus future sales. In the event, Jim Moodie and his Fireblade vanquished the opposition and gave Honda their 100th TT victory, setting race and lap records on the way. Jim's second lap was run at a staggering 120.70 mph. Nigel Davies (Kawasaki) was second and Michael Rutter (Honda) third. The new Yamaha R1s filled 4th to 6th places.

*

Racing a tried and tested Suzuki GSX-R750 to 41st place in the Production race was Peter Small. Showing that it was genuinely fit for the road as well as the track, Peter rode the Suzuki from his home in Idaho to Vancouver where it was air-freighted to Gatwick, and he then rode it to the Island. After a busy TT fortnight, Peter set off on the Suzuki to tour Germany, Italy and Slovenia. It just shows what can be done with a bit of imagination (and determination)!

*

The last TT of the 20th century ran over the period 31st May to 11th June 1999. The organisers accepted 558 entries from 20 different countries to contest what was now a ten race programme. Joey Dunlop had entries in five races, riding, not at number 3, but at number 12 in each race. Not overly keen on racing Production bikes, Joey gave that race a miss.

*

Ian Simpson, double winner in 1998, was forced to spectate in 1999 as he recovered from a leg injury sustained at Snetterton. Steve Hislop was back at the TT, but only to do a demonstration lap on his British Superbike Championship Kawasaki (at 113 mph!). Also missing was Manxman Paul Dedman. After his third place in the 1998 Junior event, local race fans were looking to cheer one of their own to greater things. Unfortunately, a crash in the NW 200 left Paul with severe injuries and, although he recovered to race again on local short circuits, his TT career seemed to be over. Perhaps the biggest surprise was to see Phillip McCallen entered in four races - on Yamahas. His TT career had seemingly come to an end when he did not enter in 1998 on medical grounds, but he was back. Proving that it was a serious racing return, he set fastest practice lap in the Production class and second fastest

Joey Dunlop rode his Honda at number 12 at the 1999 TT. Ron Clarke's photo shows him on the approach to Quarter Bridge in the Formula I race where he finished in second place.

behind Adrian Archibald in the Junior, even though the effects of past race injuries caused him serious discomfort. There were other familiar names near the head of the practice leaderboards that included Jim Moodie, Iain Duffus, David Jefferies, Jason Griffiths, John McGuinness. Ian Lougher, Dave Morris, and on three-wheels, Dave Molyneux and Rob Fisher.

*

Simon Beck was a rider who had worked his way through the ranks at the TT, improving year on year. In 1999 he received reward for his sterling privateer efforts with support from Honda on an RC45. But tragedy struck during Tuesday evening's practice when he crashed at the 33rd Milestone and was killed. A past Senior MGP winner, Simon had just set the fastest lap in practice before his accident.

*

By the end of a practice week, where much track-time time was lost due to bad weather, the busy scrutineering team had examined a total of 1,316 solos (most several times) and 333 sidecars.

*

The first race in 1999, the Formula I, was now open to 1000cc machines and 500cc Grand Prix type two-strokes. It saw the young David Jefferies bring his NW 200 winning form to the Isle of Man and take his first TT win. In doing so he also gave a first Island success to the Yamaha R1, prepared for him by V&M Racing in their striking red and yellow colours. Joey Dunlop took his 'works' Honda RC45 into second place after leading for the first two laps, and Iain Duffus was third on another V&M R1. It was a giant-killing performance by young David Jefferies and 'Motorcycle News' headlined his achievement with: *'A £20,000 Proddie Bike Shouldn't Humble £500,000 Honda RC45s. Someone Forgot To Tell David Jefferies'.* The Yamahas also vanquished two exotic Honda NSR500 V-twins ridden by John McGuinness and Ian Lougher, and brought to an end Honda's long run of victories in the Formula I TT. It was the same story in the Senior race with Jefferies taking his second win and this time Duffus finished as runner-up. Jim Moodie proved that the RC45 was still quick when he set a new absolute lap record of 124.45 mph.

Unfortunately he shredded his rear tyre in the process and was forced to retire.

*

To complete a hat-trick of wins for himself and Yamaha, David Jefferies led home Jason Griffiths and Phillip McCallen (both on R1s) in the Production race. All David's wins were achieved on Pirelli tyres. Another hat-trick, this time for wins over three consecutive years, went to Dave Morris and his BMW in the Singles race, where he averaged 110.56 mph. The Singles ran in the same race as the Ultra-Lightweights where Ian Lougher brought his Honda home first at an average of 107.43 mph.

A TT First

In a first at the TT, the Formula I race was red-flagged on the first lap after Paul Orrit fell from his machine going down Bray Hill. It was a truly heart-stopping incident that was captured on video for the whole world to see. Races had previously been stopped due to deterioration in the weather, but never for a rider coming off. Marshals at the scene felt that they could have handled the incident and that the race should have continued. After a delay to get all riders back to the Start, the race was re-run but reduced from six to four laps.

*

Honda had been staunch supporters of the TT since they first entered in 1959. In 1999 they were celebrating the 40th anniversary of that event with much publicity and several parades of their historic race machinery. It really was unfortunate for them that both David Jefferies and the Yamaha R1 chose 1999 to come good and snatch race victories in the prestigious Formula I, Production and Senior events.

*

John McGuinness was a young Honda-mounted rider who achieved his first TT victory in 1999 and it came in the Lightweight 250 race. Breaking Ian

Lougher's long-standing 1990 lap record and ending Joey Dunlop's five consecutive wins, McGuinness controlled the race throughout to win from Jason Griffiths and Gavin Lee and finish with a new lap record of 118.29 mph.

Third finisher in the Lightweight 250cc race in 1999 was Gavin Lee (Yamaha).

The Lightweight 400 race ran with the 250s and victory went to New Zealander Paul Williams for the second year, with Nigel Piercy second. Unusually, there was a tie for third place between Nick Jefferies and Geoff McMullan. After 4 laps and 151 miles of racing, they could not be separated on time.

*

Sidecar man Dave Molyneux was in record-breaking form in the first three-wheeler race but, unfortunately, he was in bike-breaking form in the second where victory went to Rob Fisher. 'Moly' left the lap record at an incredible 112.76 mph.

*

For the first time since 1991 Joey Dunlop failed to win a TT. Up against it with an RC45 that he could not get

---

SPEEDS

The electronic speed check near the Start and Finish line indicated to those in the Grandstand just how fast the bikes were going. Showing remarkable consistency between the top runners, Jim Moodie's Honda RC45 was fastest at 164.9 mph, followed by Iain Duffus (Yamaha R1) and Joey Dunlop (Honda RC45) at 163.8 mph, plus David Jefferies (Yamaha R1) and Ian Lougher (Honda NSR500) at 163.5 mph. Ducatis were about 5 mph slower. The above speeds were certainly not the maximum achieved on the Course, indeed, some of those big-bike riders were still accelerating in 5th gear as they passed the Grandstand.

In the Production race, David Jefferies and Iain Duffus (Yamaha R1s) were quickest at 153.2 mph, followed by three more R1s. Fastest Honda was Michael Rutter (Fireblade) at 146.3 mph. In the Junior race Phillip McCallen (Yamaha R6) and Joey Dunlop (Honda CBR600) were joint fastest at 148.9 mph.

to handle, Joey showed that he still had what it took to challenge at the highest level by recording his fastest ever lap at 123.06 mph in the Formula I race. But he called for Honda to give him something better to combat the new breed of Yamahas that also threatened in the Junior class, where they took second and third places behind Jim Moodie's Honda CBR600.

*

Another past winner who did not have a very good TT in 1999 was Phillip McCallen. At 35 years of age, suffering from injuries and under pressure from wife, employer and doctor to stop racing, it turned out to be the last year of competition on the Island for the eleven-times previous TT winner. Phillip was a rider who gave his all, saying: *'People talk about riding the TT at ninety or ninety-five per cent, but those riders don't win, it's a hundred per cent or nothing and that's the only way I know how to ride'*.

*

Of concern to spectators was the growing number of non-starters, particularly in the Formula I and Senior races. The Formula I race had 20 non-starters from an entry of 77 and the Senior 23 from an entry (perhaps more fairly described as a qualifying total) of 80. This seriously diminished the spectacle and must have been an embarrassment to announcer Peter Kneale when he read out the huge list of riders not honouring their entries. However, if the number of non-starters was increasing, the number of retirements was decreasing. Showing the reliability of modern race machinery, retirements were 10 from 57 starters in the Formula I event, 6 from 57 in the Production class, a mere 4 from 66 in the Junior and, perhaps understandable at the end of a fortnight's racing, 23 out of 57 in the Senior. In the sidecar races the figures were 20 from 71 and 21 from 70.

Chapter 14
THE TT TODAY

It falls to the Isle of Man Government through its Department of Tourism and Leisure to promote the TT Festival, with the TT races being organised by the ACU. The Minister for Tourism and Leisure in year 2000 was former MGP rider and 100 mph lap man David Cretney and with spectator and rider interest running at a high level, he welcomed everyone to the first TT Festival of the new Millennium. Determined to maintain the TT's attraction to the top riders, the event paid £13,000 to a start-to-finish winner of the Formula I race, £10,000 for the Senior, £6,000 for the Junior and £5,000 for each sidecar race.

*

The entries for 2000 contained all the top specialist road-racers of the day like Joey and Robert Dunlop, Jason Griffiths, James Courtney, Adrian Archibald, Ian Lougher, Richard Britton, Gary Dynes, etc.

Joining them were David Jefferies, Michael Rutter, Iain Duffus, Jim Moodie and John McGuiness, they being star riders who competed at high-level in both road and short circuit racing.

*

Practice for the 2000 meeting started on Saturday evening and there were only two early morning sessions during the week. That was good news for those riders, mechanics, marshals and spectators who did not enjoy stumbling out of bed at 4.00 a.m. into the chilly Manx morning air. However, it probably disappointed a few others. They were the ones who actually looked forward to early morning practice, knowing that being out round the Course and listening intently as the distant sound of a racing motorcycle grew gradually louder before it burst into view, provided a wake-up call that was unique to the TT.

Hard on the throttle exiting the Gooseneck, former TT podium place-man Shaun Harris chases former MGP winner Gary Carswell up the Mountain.

Second Helicopter

The helicopter rescue service has supported the TT races since 1963 and, as is the way of things, everyone had come to expect an immediate response to calls for assistance from the 'chopper' and its on-board medical support team. But the twin-engined Aero-Spatiale 'Squirrel' could only be in one place at one time and if there was a flurry of calls, then someone had to wait. Due to the relatively heavy load that it carried (pilot, doctor, paramedic, up to two injured riders, spare medical equipment, fire-extinguishers, etc,) it carried a limited amount of fuel. Although it could refuel at two locations around the Course, that was a relatively time-consuming manual operation and so to improve the rescue service the organisers brought a second helicopter into use in 2000.

*

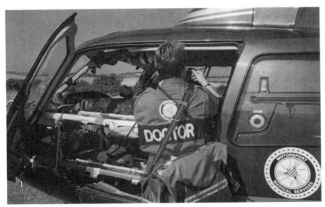

A Doctor attends to an injured rider before the rescue-helicopter flies him to hospital.

Early practice sessions for the first TT of the new millennium showed the best and worst sides of this glamorous but dangerous meeting. Riders, officials, marshals and spectators were thrilled by the immediate high speeds achieved by the top runners in the near perfect dry and sunny conditions that prevailed. David Jefferies was immediately on the pace and threatened the outright lap record on two occasions with speeds of over 124mph on his Yamaha, while Honda-mounted Adrian Archibald showed that he was a growing threat to the established stars when he became the first man to lap at over 120mph on a 600cc machine. That, of course, was the best side of the TT, but the worst side was shown by the deaths of three riders in separate practice incidents. As if to match the mood this created, the weather changed on Wednesday evening causing the long Thursday afternoon and the Friday

morning practice sessions to be lost to dismal rain and lowering cloud. This meant that by the time of the last practice scheduled for Friday evening, many riders were desperately short of track-time to get their bikes set-up properly, and some still needed to complete more laps in order to qualify to race. Travelling Marshals' reports of low cloud and generally wet conditions had the organisers in a quandary on that Friday evening, for while they wanted to run the session, the safety of competitors and the problems associated with using the rescue-helicopter in poor visibility had them in two minds. Travelling Marshals were in almost constant motion on the Course seeking information for Race Control, and eventually it was decided to allow the solos to run in an untimed session, with the sidecars to follow. However, when it came to the sidecar's turn, even lower cloud from the Gooseneck to Kate's Cottage put their session in jeopardy. In a compromise move – for the first Sidecar race was due to run the following day and competitors wanted to bed-in new tyres, chains, brake-pads, etc., - the chairs were allowed to run at racing speed on the twenty-three miles from the Start to Ramsey where they were red-flagged. The forty or so outfits that had taken advantage of the restricted session were then escorted in convoy by Travelling Marshals, across the misty Mountain and down to the finish at Douglas.

Suzuki's 40th

Suzuki were celebrating the 40th anniversary of their first TT race, and although Japanese bikes had swept to several hundred victories over the TT Course, Mitsuo Itoh's victory in the 1963 TT on a 50cc Suzuki was still the only win to be taken by the combination of Japanese rider on Japanese machine. Suzuki were proud of their contribution to TT history even though they had given little open support to the event in the 1990s. But in 2000 they were present with a tented 'Suzuki Village' near the Grandstand, a parade of their historic race machines, and sponsorship of a fearsome hill-climb event at Sulby. It was a clear indication that, even if not totally involved with providing machines for the races a motorcycle manufacturer could still find publicity opportunities at the TT, for images from the event went around the world and generated promotional statements like *'500 million will tune in to watch the TT'.*

*

In addition to Suzuki's parade-lap, the traditional Lap of Honour saw almost 200 machines and riders of yesterday piloting TT-related machines from

Gilera, Norton, Triumph, MV Agusta, Bultaco, Moto Guzzi, Honda, Velocette, Itom, Mondial, Maico, Cotton, Ducati, BSA, Aermacchi, BMW, AJS, Matchless, Ossa and Yamaha, in a nostalgic lap of the Course. It also included a concentration of Benelli machinery ranging from their early racers to the Tornado 900 Triple with which the company was hoping to revive its fortunes and maybe make a racing come-back.

Record Breakers

In their pre-race reviews most pundits felt that wins in 2000 would go to up and coming riders and that the older generation had had their day. Well, Joey Dunlop was entered in six races and he was not on the Island just to make up the numbers, as he proved by taking his Hondas to wins in the Formula I, Ultra-Lightweight and Lightweight 250 races. With those three wins he boosted his total number of TT victories to 26. It was a staggering performance by man of 48 years of age, particularly as in the Senior race he posted his fastest ever lap of the Mountain Course at 123.87 mph. Honda had brought a 'works' SP-1 model for Joey to fight off the threat from Yamaha and various young guns in the big-capacity races, but the twin-cylinder machine could not be made to handle at first and in Joey's words; *'It won't stop shaking its head'.* What had been good enough handling for Superbike racing was not up to the standard required at the TT. It took the combined might of Honda and all of Joey's TT race and course knowledge to get the SP-1 fit for the ultra-demanding Mountain Course.

*

Younger rival David Jefferies also had a hat-trick of wins in 2000, his being in the Junior, Senior and Production events on Yamahas. That left just two solo race wins to be shared by all the other riders, and they went to John McGuiness and Brett Richmond. John took the Singles race on the AMDM bike run by the sons of former Singles TT winner the late Dave Morris. Brett thought that he would have to be satisfied with second place on his Honda in the 400cc class of the Lightweight race but then found himself elevated to first when original winner Geoff McMullan was disqualified for using an oversize engine. Geoff protested that he was not aware that he was using an oversize motor but few believed him, for it was not just a couple of extra cc that the engine-measurers found, it was a full 200 of them. Geoff had used a 600cc motor in a 400cc race, a fact that must have been obvious the moment he turned the twist-grip.

*

Nick Jefferies took a virtually standard Triumph Daytona to a lap speed of 116.21 mph in the Production TT. It was the fastest ever lap by a Triumph. Not fast enough to win but, when compared to Triumph's lap speeds of about 40 mph in the first TT of 1907, it showed that they had come on a bit!

*

David Jefferies' win in what was a shortened Production race was achieved in extremely wet weather, yielding an average speed of only 98.58 mph. He was followed home by double-MGP winner Manxman Richard 'Milky' Quayle. Conditions worsened after the Production race, and the Senior race, due to be held the same day, was postponed until Saturday. However, the delayed race was worth waiting for, because on the last lap of the week (his only flying lap of the race) Jefferies smashed the outright lap record when he stormed around on his Yamaha at 125.69 mph, becoming the first man to lap at over 125 mph.

*

It is difficult for the ordinary road rider to imagine what it must be like to lap the TT Course at an average speed of over 125 mph, but that figure conceals the fact that the average varies over different stretches of the Course. From the Start to Ballacraine top riders are estimated to average 133 mph, from Ballacraine to Kirk Michael 126 mph, Kirk Michael to Sulby Crossroads 136 mph, Sulby Crossroads to

Another winning-race is over for multi-TT winner and 125cc lap-record holder Ian Lougher and the interviews start before he can get his helmet off.

Ramsey 123 mph, Ramsey to Bungalow 120 mph and Bungalow to Finish 115 mph.

*

When talking of speeds and TT lap records there is a tendency to concentrate on the absolute record set by the 180 bhp large-capacity racers and pay little attention to the smaller classes, but the 125s are well worth a look. Their current lap record stands to Ian Lougher at 110.21 mph, and that was achieved from a single-cylinder two-stroke engine developing, at best, 46 bhp. Remember, that 110.21 is an average speed and it is a phenomenal one for such a small motor on the power-hungry Mountain Course. The secret of such high average speeds lies in the 125 riders using every single scrap of engine power for every moment of the race. To protect that precious power a 125 rider spends the maximum time crouched beneath the perspex bubble of the fairing with arms, legs and feet tucked in to minimise drag. The high cornering speeds they generate have to be seen to be believed and, as sometimes happens when the various capacity classes get a bit mixed-up in practice, some of the less committed big bike riders are none too happy with the way the 125s ride under and around them through the bends.

*

So, with Joey Dunlop adding three more wins to his list of TT victories at the 2000 TT, the same questions were asked at the end of the TT Fortnight as had been asked for many years before - would he back and, if so, just how long could he continue his winning ways? What was not known during the post-victory euphoria of the 2000 TT was that the cruel hand of fate would intervene and make those questions meaningless.

JOEY DUNLOP

In many peoples' eyes Joey Dunlop was the greatest rider in the history of the TT. Making his Island debut in 1976, he started in a total of 98 TT races, won 26 of them and took 80 replicas. Joey raced all sizes of bikes between 125 and 1000cc, two-strokes and four-strokes, single and multi-cylinder. Often riding in all the solo classes, practice periods were intensely busy times for him as he jumped off one bike at the end of a lap and took out another. Not only did he then have to make an instant adaptation to the different power, braking and controls characteristics of the new machine, but he promptly had to assess its speed, handling, carburation, etc., and check them against changes made since the last session to judge if they had been effective. It must have seemed a never-ending quest to bring his bikes up to race trim, and whilst other riders stayed in bed on wet and misty practice mornings, claiming that they would not learn anything, Joey knew that there was always something to be learnt and he rarely missed a practice session. Although it was undoubtedly hard work for him, in an interview with 'Motorcycle News' Joey revealed that even when the bike was fully race-worthy there was another reason why he was out in every session. In his words: *'Many's the time that the bike is all set up ready to race. But I can't resist taking it for another lap. I just love riding round the Island that much'.*

*

Someone, somewhere, is probably aware of just how many laps Joey rode of the TT Course. It is no doubt a staggering number, for he is known to have done 256 laps at an average speed of more than 110 mph and 32 at over 120 mph - incredible!

*

The level of 'works' support he received at the TT seemed to vary from year to year and from class to class. But that did not worry Joey, for he was always ready to wield the spanners himself, either in full-scale race preparation, or if a last minute adjustment or change of wheels was necessary - even on the start-line.

*

Usually riding under number 3 at the TT, he occasionally made a tactical decision to ask for a change of number. He rode several makes of machine but was best known for his long association with Honda. They allowed him to do as much of his machine preparation as he chose to do and to operate mostly without a formal contract.

A serious accident at Brands Hatch in 1989 saw Joey concentrate on racing 125s for a while after his return to the sport. As his strength returned he went back to bigger bikes and became the man to beat in all solo classes at the TT although, on his own admission, he did not always get on well with the 600cc machines.

Joey Dunlop acknowledges the cheers of the crowds after his victory in the 1988 Senior TT.

At the 1980 TT Joey uses a ladder to climb from his Douglas garage to return to his boarding-house - most people would have used the footpath!

His smooth riding style over the TT Course was honed by years of experience. Subtle adjustment of speed and line allowed him to use the smallest of straights to pass slower riders and this gained him ground over those who lacked his experience and finesse. Joey's favourite section of the Course was Glen Helen to Ramsey. In his words: *'it's proper road-racing along there, plenty of bends and very quick'*. He found the Mountain section less interesting, preferring to ride between the hedges.

*

Joey was an unconventional racer and this trait extended to other aspects of his life - there often seemed to be an unusual twist to his activities.

Foregoing conventional ferries and travelling to the Island by fishing-boat brought about the shipwreck prior to the 1985 TT that is recounted earlier in this book, but Joey is the subject of many other stories. Looking for a lift home after the 1978 Southern 100 races, he was glad to accept the offer of a flight in a small private plane. However, there was no seat available for him and he was put in the luggage compartment amongst sundry race spares and baggage.

*

During the 1980 Classic TT the tank strap of his TZ750 Yamaha broke on the first lap and for the rest of the race Joey held the huge eight-gallon tank on with his arms and knees, whilst also holding on to first place. Losing time at places like Ballaugh Bridge where he could not jump, he lost more time and the lead to Mick Grant at his pit-stop (Mick used a quick-filler for a 12 second stop, Joey's was a gravity type and took 53 seconds). Undaunted, he gradually pulled back lost time, took the lead on the last lap, set a new outright lap record of 115.22 mph, and won the race. Although a victorious one, Joey's 1980 TT was filled with thoughts of retirement from racing, for his brother-in-law Mervyn Robinson had been killed a few weeks earlier in the North West 200.

*

At the 1984 TT Joey won the opening Formula I race and was all set for a good week. However, after setting a new absolute lap record of 118.48 mph in the Senior race he retired on the Mountain when out of fuel. After his retirement he took the Manx Electric Railway down from the Bungalow to Laxey where he was jokingly presented with a free train pass. Come the 250cc race and Joey had cause to use his new pass for, once again, he ran out of fuel on the Mountain.

*

Joey walks to the Bungalow in 1984 with Travelling Marshal Des Evans, following his second retirement in a week through lack of fuel.

Leading the 1988 Junior race, the filler-cap from his Honda was dropped into the fairing during a pit-stop. Only after a frantic search was it found, extricated and refitted. Although this lost him much time, he hung on to win the race from Eddie Laycock.

*

Another filler-cap incident arose in 1995. Joey retired in the morning's Ultra-Lightweight race at The Hawthorn and hitched a lift back to the Start in the Course Inspection car. It was only later, when his Castrol Honda was being fuelled-up for the afternoon's Lightweight race, he remembered that, incredible as it may seem, he used the same filler-cap on the 250 as he did on the 125. It was too late to recover the one from his stranded 125 at The Hawthorn, so a cap was 'bodged' for the 250 and, being very careful at his pit-stop, Joey went on to win the race.

*

He made an unscheduled pit-stop in 1996 to change to a slick rear tyre in drying track conditions. The crew were not ready, no tyre was available and he had to go straight out again. Joey gave no sign of being troubled by such events and although his apparent outward casualness at times of stress showed a man in control of his emotions, he was also one who possessed a strong inner will to win.

*

Notorious for arriving on the TT start-line at the very last moment, when he did arrive Joey would have already gone through his own pre-race ritual (taking account of a few personal superstitions in the process). He would then get on the bike, deal with the job of racing and disappear as soon as decently possible.

*

Although thorough in his machine preparation, he had a streak of forgetfulness. Former Honda team manager Barry Symmons tells of how Joey turned up in Japan with two left racing boots - on two different occasions!

*

Joey's total of TT wins would have been greater if he had not lost a couple of races by running out of fuel on the last lap. He ran out again at the 2000 TT, but fortunately it was during practice that his 250 Honda spluttered to a halt at the Bungalow rather than during a race. As ever, busy Joey had another bike waiting in the Pits that he wanted to take out for practice that morning, but how was he to get back to the Paddock? Finding a plastic cup at the side of the road, he used it to transfer petrol from Travelling Marshal Dick Cassidy's Honda. But as the 250 was a two-stroke, he needed oil to mix with the petrol. Borrowing a screwdriver, he removed the sealing plug from a fork leg, drained-off some oil, added the oil to the borrowed petrol in the tank and thus had an acceptable 'petroil' mixture that allowed him to ride back to the Paddock .

*

Joey Dunlop and his Honda - this commemorative statue is located outside Murray's Motorcycle Museum near the former Bungalow Hotel on the Mountain section of the TT Course. It is identical to one in his home town of Ballymoney.

By the time of the 2000 TT Joey (who described himself as full-time publican and part-time racer) was 48 years old and was a veteran of 25 years of TT racing. But instead of slowing with age, he actually set his fastest ever TT lap that year when he took three TT victories to bring his total number of TT wins up to 26. The motorcycling world was stunned to hear of his death three weeks later in a rain-soaked 125cc race in far-off Estonia. At his funeral, 50,000 people turned out to pay their respects to the family man who cared about others and who was known to everyone simply as 'Joey'.

*

It was inevitable that Joey's death brought a flood of memorabilia onto the market ranging from books, stamps, prints, photographs, T-shirts, badges etc. Whilst this might ordinarily have been expected to get a bit 'tacky', in this instance it did not, for it seemed that so many of his fans genuinely wanted to have something to help them hold on to the memory of the great road-racer from Ballymoney.

*

For much of his racing career Joey avoided the press as far as he could politely do so, and he showed little sign of enjoying the adulation of race fans. In later years his attitude to the media mellowed, he gave them more time, and he also seemed a little more willing to accept the attentions of race-goers.

Commemorative stamps issued by the Isle of Man Post Office.

Having become more comfortable with his fame, Joey would have made a fantastic ambassador for his sport after retirement from active competition. His name alone would have opened many doors and on a wider scale the honours he had received of MBE and OBE would have opened even more. Whilst his loss to motorcycling and the TT races is self-evident, we shall never truly know just what he might have achieved in the wider world. He had already shown that he cared for his fellow-men with his humanitarian trips to Eastern Europe and it is difficult to believe that he would not have extended such activities when he stopped racing. His death was not just a loss to motorcycle-racing.

*

The 2000 MGP took place some six weeks after Joey's death and in an unforgettable tribute, 5,000 motorcycle-mounted fans did a lap of the closed roads of the Mountain Course in his honour. Bikes of every size and description travelled the same 37 3/4 miles that Joey had done so many hundreds of times, and it took the cavalcade well over twenty-minutes to pass.

No Racing

Everyone knew that the 2001 TT period was going to be different without Joey Dunlop's presence. What was not evident until the Spring of the year was just how different, because for the first time since 1907 (apart from the effects of war), no TT or MGP race meetings were held. The need to prevent a foot and mouth epidemic that raged among farm animals in the UK from spreading to the Isle of Man brought about the cancellation of the races. Their non-running brought home to Island businesses and to TT fans just how much the races meant to them both financially and 'emotionally'.

*

Despite there being no racing in 2001, people were still free to visit the Island although there were some restrictions as to where they could go once they were there. Showing how much they enjoy their annual visits to Mona's Isle, some 12,000 TT fans still visited in what would normally have been TT Fortnight and enjoyed the Island's many other attractions. They probably got to see places that they would never see in the normal hustle of a TT period. Perhaps some used the opportunity to weigh up new spectating positions, to be tried when the racing returned.

The selection of the right point to spectate is all important to the enjoyment of the races, but the task of getting to a chosen spot to watch can be very time consuming. This is a fact that first-time spectators often find to their cost, for with thousands of cars and bikes seeking to leave Douglas at the same time on race-days, delays are inevitable. Road closing times are strictly enforced and - although, say, a bunch of race-fans may have intended to watch from the civilised surroundings of the pub forecourt at Ballaugh - if they had only reached the wilds of the Cronk y Voddy crossroads at the official road closing time, they would find themselves directed off the Course and left to make the best of it.

*

After the lack of racing in 2001, all the pre-event talk in 2002 was that the TT was going to be a bigger and better event, even though no one really knew what effect the lack of a year's racing would have on rider and visitor numbers. The many Island businesses that are underpinned by their trading at TT time heaved a collective sigh of relief as it became apparent that the event had been badly missed by riders and fans in 2001, and that bookings for accommodation and travel in 2002 were up to the levels of earlier years. The race organisers certainly did their bit, upping the total prize-money to £430,000. This meant that with a once-off special welcome-back bonus of £5,000 available for each race, the start to finish winner of the Formula I event could net an impressive £25,000 with the same figure for the Senior. Each Sidecar race offered £11,000 to the winner and similar levels of riches were available to those who came home first in other classes. The organisers were rewarded with 625 entries from 22 different nations for the 8 races that comprised the 2002 TT meeting. Showing that the MGP still served as a training ground for future TT racers, there were 22 former MGP winners amongst the successful TT entries.

*

Most people would consider that getting to ride in the TT was a big enough mountain to climb, but not Manxman John Crellin. He had entries in the Formula I, Lightweight 400 and Junior races at the 2002 TT and was also on target to climb the highest mountain on each of the world's seven continents. So far it's five down and two to go for John - including the small matter of Everest.

*

New for 2002 was the introduction of random breathalyser tests for riders and the experimental use of transponders for timing purposes in several classes. In the race programme the poorly supported Lightweight 250s were down to run with the Junior (600) runners and a new Production race for 600s was introduced in addition to the 1000cc Proddies. Several entries in the Production races were from talented MGP riders seeking to enhance their Mountain Course race experience. Riding the Production events does not preclude riders from competing in a subsequent MGP, although an entry in a full International TT race does.

*

As a tribute to the late Joey Dunlop, riding number 3 was not used in the solo races except for the Senior. In that race numbers are allocated strictly in accordance with the fastest times set in practice.

*

For the first time for some years the opening practice session of 2002 was on a Saturday morning (usually Saturday evening). The weather was generally poor during practice week and the organisers were forced to make use of the reserve practice session on Friday morning. So poor were the conditions on the Tuesday evening and Wednesday morning that, for the first time, sidecars were quicker than solos and set the fastest times in both sessions, albeit at 'only' 97.17 mph.

*

The poor weather was frustrating for all concerned, none more so than for six-times previous winner and lap record holder David Jefferies who, after a late change from Yamaha machinery, was Suzuki mounted for the first time at the TT and itching to see what his 1000cc 'Temple Auto Salvage' GSX-R would do on the Mountain Course. With team-mate Ian Lougher he did manage to give the big Suzuki its head in the last (Friday evening) practice and was well satisfied with the 125+ mph lap that resulted. Having broken Honda's monopoly of Formula I race wins with victory on a Yamaha in 1999, he was hoping to give Suzuki their first win in the event since Graeme Crosby's controversial success in the 1981 race.

*

David Jefferies is a rider who gets much satisfaction from the Mountain section of the Course saying: '*As I come out of Ramsey, it's tail up and head down. I just go for it and blast over the Mountain as one section*'. David may have his head down but, as those who have seen recent TT videos will know, that does not prevent him from giving the filming helicopter an occasional cheeky wave (and suggesting that they get a faster helicopter if they want to keep up with him). His attitude to the Mountain section is in contrast to Joey Dunlop who did not enthuse over it, and of 1995 winner Iain Duffus who used the stretch to take a breather. But despite the way he muscles his bikes around the Course, Jefferies does not seem to need a breather. He may be sweating a bit when he makes a pit-stop but mentally he is ice-cool. He will, unprompted, proffer a few calm words into Dave Moore's roving-microphone on how he feels, how the bike's going, what conditions are like, etc., before slamming down his visor and blasting off to put in more 125+ mph laps.

*

SPEEDS

The narrow ribbon of road on which top riders flash past the Grandstand at 170 mph.

The fastest ever publicly recorded speed on the TT Course was that of Steve Hislop when police radar showed him travelling at a frightening 192 mph on the Sulby Straight. Now Sulby Straight (which is far from 'straight' at 192 mph) is one of the fastest sections of the Course, but some think that the road from Creg ny Baa to Brandish is faster and Phillip McCallen considered the drop past The Highlander was fastest of all. It would be very interesting to know what speed current top-runner David Jefferies is hitting at those spots. It is known from the electronic timing device on the Glencrutchery Road that on his big bikes he regularly reaches 170 mph passing the Grandstand, with his 600 getting up to 150 mph at the same location.

There has been much written down the years about riders taking Bray Hill flat-out in top gear, but it comes as no surprise to hear the straight-talking David Jefferies say *'I was going back a gear on the R1 - it had too much power and I rolled it back'*. Acknowledging the danger involved in the event he said: *'The TT is dangerous there's no two ways about it, and anyone who says I shouldn't say that is wrong: you have to be able to sit down, talk about the risks, and understand them before you go there'*. He went on: *'All you need to do is leave a little more room for error at the IOM. The biggest thing at the IOM is knowing your limits, and knowing that if you're a little unsure - you shut off. You don't keep the throttle on until you know where you're going. If you ride it like that, you're fine'*.

*

Not much room for error here as David Jefferies blasts his Suzuki out of the Gooseneck during the Formula I race of 2002.

Jefferies rides with self-confidence but not over-confidence. With six laps to a major race, 264 bends each lap, a total distance of 226 miles. It is too much to expect to get the speed, line, revs, gear-changes, etc., right every single time and a rider must allow some margin for error. Like David Jefferies, all riders must have faith in their own abilities but occasionally that faith can be misplaced. For those tempted to ride up to their personal limits it is easy to get carried over the edge by the intoxicating sensations experienced in riding a TT race. Although David Jefferies is calm and collected at his pit-stops, others arrive in a stressed condition with hands shaking and an air of agitation. Tanked-up again and ready to go out and ride more laps of the formidable and unforgiving Mountain Course, their friends can but hope that such riders keep their undoubted bravery in check and prevent it from tipping them over the edge into disaster.

*

When riders reached their maximum speeds of 90 mph on the Sulby Straight in the early 1920s, they could never have imagined that riders of the 21st century would travel the same stretch of road 100 mph faster than they were doing and set 125 mph laps that were more than twice as fast as their 60 mph averages.

Under 18 Minutes

It was little surprise that David Jefferies turned out to be the man-of-the-meeting at the 2002 TT, but the manner in which he did it was quite awesome. Taking three wins, he annihilated lap records on the way. Lifting his outright lap record to 126.86 mph in the opening Formula I race, he also broke Steve Hislop's long-standing race record, even though he completed the last 13 miles of the race with his Suzuki stuck in third gear. In the 1000cc Production race he lapped at more than 124 mph to add nearly 3 mph to the lap record and in Friday's Senior race he again increased his outright lap record, this time to 127.29 mph. That equated to just 17 minutes 47 seconds to cover 37 ¾ twisting and undulating miles.

Perhaps slightly disappointed in not making it four wins in a week when his Suzuki let him down in

David Jefferies became the first winner of the The Joey Dunlop Trophy awarded to 'The Rider of The Week' at the 2002 TT.

the Junior race, Jefferies saw Suzuki team-mate Ian Lougher come in as runner-up to him in a couple of races, win the Production 600, and take a win and new lap record of 110.21 mph in the Ultra-Lightweight race on a Honda.

Ian Lougher (TAS Suzuki) attacks Ballaugh Bridge in the Senior TT of 2002.

Jim Moodie (Yamaha) won the Junior and Bruce Anstey (Yamaha) the Lightweight 250. 'Milky' Quayle (Honda) won the Lightweight 400 race and, with leaderboard placings in the Formula I, Junior and Production 1000 classes, this likeable young Manxman showed (despite jokingly riding on 'L' plates in the Formula I race) that he was a TT force to be reckoned with. Another Manxman, Dave Molyneux, was back at the TT after a tilt at the world championships, but his efforts in the sidecar races were curtailed by a road-bike accident to his passenger Colin Hardman that left Colin with less than full strength in his hands and arms. Already a multiple winner in the Sidecar TT, Rob Fisher added a fine double-win to his total in 2002.

*

Although David Jefferies left no one in doubt that he was the 'Number One' at the 2002 TT, there were other riders who recorded personal best performances including several who got over 125

mph, among them being John McGuinness. John was riding for Honda who were under more pressure from Suzuki and Yamaha than they were used to at the TT. Giving his Honda maximum revs to stay with the opposition in the Junior race, his 600 four failed in a massive cloud of oil-smoke at the end of the Cronk y Voddy straight. The resultant oil-slick created a few nasty moments for following riders and, asked what was the problem was as he parked his stricken bike at the 11th Milestone, the unguarded revelation from John that the bike had *'blown its guts'* confirmed that Honda were being pushed beyond the limit to stay with the opposition (the 600's rev-counter was red-lined at 15,500). Honda's lack of a big-bike race win at the 2002 TT brought early post-race talk of them bringing the ultra-special VTR 1000 SP2 machine of their World Superbike Champion Colin Edwards to the 2003 TT, and early 2003 information was that Ian Lougher was switching from Suzuki to ride it for them. Colin Edwards spent several days on the Island as a guest at the 2002 meeting and even rode a Parade lap waving to the crowds. It was good promotional stuff for Honda and went down well with TT fans, but everyone realised that it was only a holiday visit for Colin, there was absolutely no chance that he would return and compete, for by now road-racing and circuit-racing were poles apart.

*

Almost 100 years have passed since the first TT for motorcycles was run on the Isle of Man and the competitive spirit of the early races still exists as successive generations of riders take on the unique challenge of racing motorcycles over the Island's roads. Twenty-five years ago the TT lost its full World Championship status as the racing of motorcycles began to polarise between road and circuit events. Over those twenty-five years the TT has proved that it is still a top-class meeting for those that seek one of the greatest challenges in motorcycle racing. The Isle of Man Government as funders of the event, the ACU as organisers, and most importantly the riders and supporters, are all still enthused by the TT. The future of the event appears secure, and this was confirmed by the Isle of Man's Chief Minister, Richard Corkill, when he said in 2002: *'There has been a tremendous effort both by the Isle of Man and the ACU to develop the TT into a unique and sustainable force in world motorcycling. It is part of our history and heritage as well as very much a part of our modern Island and, we trust, our future'.*

INDEX